Exports to Jobs

SOUTH ASIA DEVELOPMENT FORUM

Exports to Jobs

Boosting the Gains from Trade in South Asia

BY ERHAN ARTUC, GLADYS LOPEZ-ACEVEDO,
RAYMOND ROBERTSON, AND DANIEL SAMAAN

A copublication of the International Labour Organization and the World Bank

World Bank
ISBN (paper): 978-1-4648-1248-4
ISBN (electronic): 978-1-4648-1249-1
DOI: 10.1596/978-1-4648-1248-4

International Labour Organization
ISBN (paper): 978-92-2-131576-6
ISBN (web pdf): 978-92-2-131577-3

Cover photo: © triloks / Getty Images. Used with the permission of Getty Images. Further permission
required for reuse.
Cover design: Alejandro Espinosa/Sonideas

Library of Congress Cataloging-in-Publication Data has been requested.

South Asia Development Forum

Home to a fifth of mankind, and to almost half of the people living in poverty, South Asia is also a region of marked contrasts: from conflict-affected areas to vibrant democracies, from demographic bulges to aging societies, from energy crises to global companies. This series explores the challenges faced by a region whose fate is critical to the success of global development in the early 21st century, and that can also make a difference for global peace. The volumes in it organize in an accessible way findings from recent research and lessons of experience, across a range of development topics. The series is intended to present new ideas and to stimulate debate among practitioners, researchers, and all those interested in public policies. In doing so, it exposes the options faced by decision makers in the region and highlights the enormous potential of this fast-changing part of the world.

Contents

Boxes

Figures

Tables

Foreword

South Asia's economy is growing faster than any other region in the world. But it remains a development paradox. The exceptionally high economic growth shrunk the number of poor and created modest job growth. But many South Asians still lack a regular job in the formal economy, and there are still huge differences in pay. Every month, almost one million additional jobs are needed.

Related to South Asia's jobs challenge, the region's trade as a share of the economy is much lower than in other regions and has been falling lately. These developments are not good. This is because trade, growth, and jobs typically go hand in hand. But could trade, and particularly more exports, bring higher wages and better jobs for South Asians? If so, then how big an impact could result from South Asia integrating more strongly into the world economy?

This book, *Exports to Jobs: Boosting the Gains from Trade in South Asia*, breaks new ground by examining the impact of turning to more exports on wages, jobs, and the creation of more regular jobs in South Asia. Traditionally, economic research on the relationship between globalization and labor markets has focused on the impact of falling tariffs or rising imports. There are few studies looking at the growth of labor market opportunities that follow from exports. This report uses a novel way to estimate the relationship between exports and their effect on labor markets. It combines household-level or worker-level surveys with trade data from India and Sri Lanka to construct a unique dataset. In doing so, this book contributes to our understanding of the impact of big changes in trade and bridges the gap between academic research and informed policy making by governments.

The findings provide key insights about the relationship between international trade and local labor markets. They show that increasing exports leads to higher wages and jobs, and also leads to more formal jobs for women.

The results also show that to expand and spread the benefits from higher exports widely, policies are needed to raise skills and get certain groups, such as women and youth, into more jobs. Other complementary measures include increasing the ability of workers to find alternative employment or sources of income when they lose their jobs, along with removing barriers that stop workers from becoming employed in higher-paying jobs. Together, these actions would help South Asian countries spread the gains that come from being more closely linked into the global economy through exporting.

Greater global integration thus provides an opportunity to address the South Asian paradox of remarkable growth with persistent labor market shortfalls and a stagnant or declining openness to trade.

Hartwig Schafer
Vice President, South Asia Region
The World Bank Group

Deborah Greenfield
Deputy Director-General for Policy
International Labour Organization

Acknowledgments

The preparation of this report was led by Erhan Artuc (Senior Economist, Development Research Group, Trade and International Integration World Bank), Gladys Lopez-Acevedo (Lead Economist, Poverty and Equity Global Practice, World Bank), Raymond Robertson (Helen and Roy Ryu Professor of Economics and Government, Texas A&M University), and Daniel Samaan (Senior Economist, Research Department, International Labour Organization [ILO]). Team members included the following consultants working with the Chief Economist's office for the South Asia Region (SARCE) of the World Bank: Diego Cardozo, Adam Elsheikhi, Muhammed Faisal Ali Baig, Deeksha Kokas, and Kyoung Yang Kim. The team is grateful to Laura Wallace for her skillful editing of the report, and to Michael Alwan for formatting and additional editing.

The peer reviewers for the report were Elizabeth Ruppert Bulmer (Lead Economist, Social Protection and Jobs Global Practice, World Bank), and Sanjay Kathuria (Lead Economist, South Asia Regional Integration, Macroeconomics, Trade and Investment Global Practice, World Bank). Background documents were prepared by Dr. Nazneen Ahmed (Senior Researcher, Bangladesh Institute of Development Studies), Nisha Arunatilake (Research Director, Institute of Policy Studies of Sri Lanka), Bilal Khan (Assistant Professor, University of International Business and Economics, Beijing), and Rubina Verma (Assistant Professor, Georgetown University).

The work greatly benefited from guidance and encouragement by Martin Rama (Chief Economist, South Asia Region, World Bank) and Ekkehard Ernst (Chief Macroeconomist, ILO). Funding by the World Bank's Multi-Donor Trust Fund for Trade and Development, the ILO–World Bank Group Research Program on Job Creation and Shared Prosperity, and the Strategic Partnership on Economic Development is gratefully acknowledged.

Administrative support came from Neelam Chowdhry (Program Assistant, SARCE). The publishing team was comprised of Deb Appel-Barker (printing and file conversion), Susan Graham (project manager), and Jewel McFadden (acquisitions).

About the Contributors

Erhan Artuc is a senior economist in the World Bank's Development Research Group (Trade and International Integration Team). Before joining the World Bank in 2011, he was a faculty member at Koc University in Istanbul, Turkey, where he taught international trade, microeconomics, and macroeconomics classes. He received a BA in 2001 from Bilkent University, Ankara, and a PhD in 2006 from the University of Virginia, both in economics. His research focuses on international trade policy and its effects on labor markets. He has studied the distributional effects of trade liberalization on workers from different age, education, and human capital groups; timing of trade policy; occupational and sectoral mobility of workers; unemployment; and changes in skill premium in response to trade shocks and discount window borrowing from central banks. His research papers have appeared in the *Journal of International Economics, American Economic Review,* and other academic or policy journals.

Gladys Lopez-Acevedo is a lead economist at the World Bank in the Poverty and Equity Global Practice for the South Asia and MENA regions, working in the areas of trade, welfare, gender, conflict, and jobs. Previously, she was a lead economist in the World Bank Chief Economist's Office for the South Asian region (SARCE), and senior economist in the World Bank Central Vice Presidency Poverty Reduction and Economic Management (PREM) unit and in the Latin America region at the World Bank. She is a research fellow of the Institute for Labor Economics and at the Mexican National Research System. Prior to joining the World Bank, she held high-level positions in the Government of Mexico and she was a professor at the Instituto Tecnológico Autónomo de México (ITAM). She holds a BA in economics from ITAM and a PhD in economics from the University of Virginia.

Raymond Robertson holds the Helen and Roy Ryu Chair in Economics and Government in the Department of International Affairs at the Bush School of Government and Public Service at Texas A&M University. Robertson is also a research fellow at the Institute for the Study of Labor in Bonn, and he currently chairs the U.S. Department of Labor's National Advisory Committee for Labor Provisions of the U.S. Free Trade Agreements. He is a member of the Center for Global Development's advisory board.

Daniel Samaan is a senior economist at the Research Department of the International Labour Organization (ILO) in Geneva. He has been working on the impacts of globalization and technology on international labor markets. Recent publications include analyses of the effectiveness of labor provisions in free trade agreements, and research for the ILO's Future of Work Initiative, which discusses the effects of artificial intelligence on the world of work. Daniel worked previously at the economic policy research center, SCEPA, in New York City. He holds a PhD in economics from the New School of Social Research in New York, as well as a master's degree in economics and business administration from the University of Passau in Germany.

Diego Cardozo Medeiros is a consultant at the World Bank's SARCE unit and has wide experience in conducting advanced econometric analysis using survey data. His current research covers trade, poverty, and jobs. He has been an economist at the Banco de México. He graduated from the Tecnológico de Monterrey in 2014.

Deeksha Kokas is a consultant at the World Bank's SARCE unit. Her current research covers trade, poverty, and jobs. Previously, she worked on finance and private sector issues as part of the World Bank's Development Research Group and Trade and Competitiveness practice. Outside the World Bank, she has experience in conducting impact evaluations as part of J-PAL, South Asia. She received a master's degree in economics from University College London in 2014.

Abbreviations

ADH	Autor, Dorn, and Hanson (2013)
BSIC	Bangladesh Standard Industrial Classification
FLFP	female labor force participation
GDP	gross domestic product
GVC	global value chain
HOS	Heckscher–Ohlin–Samuelson (model)
HPAE	high-performing Asian economy
ISI	import-substitution industrialization (paradigm)
ISIC	International Standard Industrial Classification
LFPR	labor force participation rate
LFS	Labor Force Survey
NAFTA	North American Free Trade Agreement
NSS	National Sample Survey
OECD	Organisation for Economic Co-operation and Development
RTE	Right to Education (Act of Indian Parliament)
UN	United Nations

Overview

Key Messages

- South Asia has grown rapidly with significant reductions in poverty, but the fast-growing working-age population feeds lingering concerns about jobless growth and poor job quality.

- Could export growth in South Asia result in better labor market outcomes? The answer is yes, according to our study, which uses a new methodology to rigorously estimate the potential impact from higher South Asian exports per worker on wages and informal employment over a 10-year period.

- Our study shows the positive side of trade. It finds that increasing exports per worker would result in higher wages for workers generally found in the formal sector and falling informality for many marginalized groups.

- Several policies could help spread these benefits more widely, including (1) boosting and connecting exports to people (for example, by removing trade barriers and investing in infrastructure); (2) eliminating distortions in production (for example, through more efficient allocation of inputs); and (3) protecting workers (for example, by investing in their education and skills). Scaling up exports in labor-intensive industries could significantly lower informality for groups like rural and less-educated workers. Other workers would also benefit from increasing skills and the participation of women and young workers in the labor force.

South Asian Paradox

In recent decades, a number of economic and social trends in South Asia do not seem to add up—so much so that there is now talk of a "South Asian Paradox," and possibly even "jobless growth."

- South Asia has grown at an unprecedented rate. In fact, forecasts predicted a pick up of 6.9 percent in 2018 and further strengthening to 7.1 percent on average in 2019–20, reflecting a broad-based improvement across most of the region (World Bank 2018). South Asia could, therefore, maintain its position as the fastest-growing region and even extend its lead over East Asia and Pacific.

- It has also been moderately successful at translating these high growth rates into positive job growth—with a modest increase in the share of wage and salaried workers as a total percentage of the population (rising from 21.6 percent in 2008 to 26 percent in 2016) and a slowly declining unemployment rate (falling from 4.1 percent in 2008 to 3.9 percent in 2017).

- Despite these advances in the labor market, millions of people still live in extreme poverty, although a lot of progress has been made on this front. The proportion of people living on less than US$1.90 a day was estimated at 12.4 percent, or about 216 million people, as of 2015—one-third of all the poor globally.

- Moreover, labor markets continue to grapple with serious issues, including (1) low-quality jobs (informal employment is widespread); (2) sizeable wage gaps between different demographic groups; and (3) significant population growth pressure. In fact, South Asia's population increased by almost 56 percent between 1990 and 2016 (World Bank 2017), and the growth of the working-age population is especially problematic—between 2005 and 2015, the number of South Asians aged 15 and above grew by 1.8 million per month, a trend that will moderate slowly in the next decade.

- Further complicating matters, South Asian trade as a fraction of total gross domestic product (GDP) is much lower than in other regions, and lately trade has been falling.

These developments are not only confusing but also of great concern. A key reason is that it is widely accepted that international trade contributes to economic growth and could play a significant role in creating jobs and improving labor market outcomes.

Why is the story in South Asia different from that in other regions—where trade, growth, and jobs typically go hand in hand—and what can be done about it? One potential solution has been globalization because of the observed positive relationship between trade and growth. But could a greater export orientation in the region result in better labor market outcomes? And, if so, what are the magnitudes that might be expected from different levels of increasing exports?

This report seeks to explore these questions by rigorously estimating the potential impact from increasing South Asian exports per worker on employment and earnings.

Chapter 1 sets the context by introducing the South Asian Paradox and providing a road map of the report. Chapter 2 takes an in-depth look into this paradox by reviewing labor market challenges, policy priorities, and trends in trade in South Asia. In chapter 3, the report breaks new ground, given that there have been few efforts to estimate the effects of exports on local labor market outcomes. The results, as discussed in chapter 4, suggest that this is a promising strategy—one that could result in higher wages and less casual work (a reduction of informality). But it will also require complementary policies to ensure that the benefits from exports are more widely shared, with possible options raised in chapter 5.

A New Approach

For advanced economies, a new literature has emerged that credibly assesses the response of employment and wages to a greater exposure to imports—the so-called "China Shock" (see appendix A). One of the seminal studies comes from Topalova (2010), who studies the effects of tariff changes on poverty rates across India's districts. The author measures the effective changes in tariff rates for districts (*zila*) by weighting industry-level changes with the number of workers in each district—and shows that poverty rates increased (or decreased more slowly) in districts that were more exposed to import competition from falling tariffs.

One of the author's key contributions is to implement an approach proposed by Bartik (1991). This approach takes advantage of a concentration of production and local labor markets to identify the relationship between globalization and local labor market outcomes. It has been used in other developing countries as well, with the results showing that local labor markets matter.

A methodology similar to Topalova (2010) and Bartik (1991) was later adopted by Autor, Dorn, and Hanson (2013) (henceforth ADH) to study the impact of the "China Shock" on local labor markets in the United States. ADH contributed to the research on trade and local labor markets in two important aspects. First, it is virtually impossible to argue against the exogeneity of their instrument because ADH use growth of China (measured by the change in exports of China to countries other than the United States) as the main instrument, rather than a potentially endogenous policy variable such as tariffs. Second, ADH identify one of the largest negative exogenous shocks to labor demand in recent history: China's rapid growth. This discovery has attracted a great deal of attention. ADH find that the U.S. regions with a high concentration of import-competing industries experienced a significant decline in employment levels but not much of a decrease in wages.

The ADH methodology relies on the fact that, because of labor market frictions and mobility costs, workers are not fully mobile across localities. As a result, import shocks differ depending on the structure of the local economy. If workers were fully mobile between locations or industries, the labor markets in all districts would be fully integrated into the national labor market. In other words, if workers were freely mobile, a trade shock would affect all workers similarly, independent of their location or region.

Which localities suffer most? It turns out that it is those where production is more specialized in goods that suddenly become cheaper to import. In measuring the effective changes in tariff rates, Topalova (2010) calculates the effective change in import protection for Indian districts after the 1991 trade reform. The variation in the author's sample comes from differences among districts in their industry and import compositions. The districts with a larger share of import-competing sectors and sectors with larger tariff reductions are exposed more severely to the trade liberalization shocks. Topalova assumes that tariff reductions are exogenous to the districts, because those reductions were planned by the central government through international agreements.

These papers typically exploit the variation in the trade exposure of districts on the basis of employment shares. For example, regions with high shares of import-competing industry employment are exposed to more-intensive trade shocks than districts with high shares of nontraded or export industry employment. Our approach differs from these studies by focusing on exports (box O.1).

We use a two-stage econometric analysis, as illustrated in figure O.1. In the first stage, we estimate the contribution of import demand by Organisation for Economic

---

BOX O.1 Our Approach

Our methodology follows the "Bartik" (1991) approach that has been applied to assess the effects of globalization on labor market outcomes. To illustrate, we can use the variable y to denote different labor market outcomes (employment, wages, and informality in our case). The outcomes are observed for different regions i at time t. Each of these regions at time t is associated with a change in exports, which we can denote using the variable x. Unfortunately, we do not observe the specific quantity of exports from any given region, but we do observe the share of employment in industry j in each region i. If we define the employment in region i in industry j at time t as L_{ijt} and the total employment of region i at time t as L_{it}, then we can define the employment share as

$$\lambda_{ijt} = \frac{L_{ijt}}{L_{it}}.$$

Thus, the estimated effect of exports is calculated as

$$y_{it} = \beta \lambda_{ijt} x_{jt}.$$

Our main interest is the coefficient β, which is what we estimate. Of course, our actual estimation is more complicated. Exports might be driven by workers in the exporting country, which means exports could be endogenous. Therefore, in the actual estimation, we add different controls and use the changes in labor market outcomes as a function of changes in exports, and then use instruments to control for the potential endogeneity of exports. Accordingly, the results should be interpreted as, for example, the change in average wages after a change in exports per worker. Hence, if the effect is negative, it means that there is a reduction in wages.

FIGURE O.1 Illustration of the Two-Stage Econometric Analysis

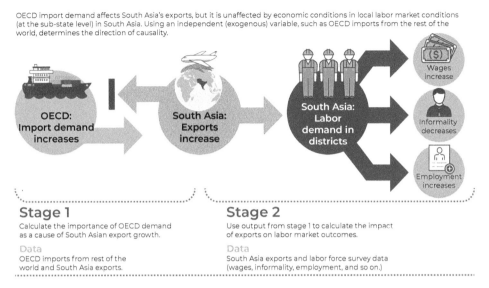

OECD import demand affects South Asia's exports, but it is unaffected by economic conditions in local labor market conditions (at the sub-state level) in South Asia. Using an independent (exogenous) variable, such as OECD imports from the rest of the world, determines the direction of causality.

Stage 1
Calculate the importance of OECD demand as a cause of South Asian export growth.

Data
OECD imports from rest of the world and South Asia exports.

Stage 2
Use output from stage 1 to calculate the impact of exports on labor market outcomes.

Data
South Asia exports and labor force survey data (wages, informality, employment, and so on.)

Note: OECD = Organisation for Economic Co-operation and Development.

Co-operation and Development (OECD) countries to the increase in South Asia's exports. Having an independent (exogenous) variable, such as OECD's imports from the rest of the world, ensures that the chain of causality is flowing in the right direction. Without the first stage, our estimates would show only correlation—not causation— and they would be biased. In the second stage, we estimate the effect of an increase in exports on local economic outcomes. These economic outcomes include informality rates, wages, employment, and wage variance for different worker types (male, female, rural, skilled, unskilled, young, and old).

In performing this two-stage econometric analysis, we emphasize two aspects. First, we allow for the endogeneity of exports by using OECD demand from non-South Asian countries as instruments. Second, we exploit the spatial variation to estimate the local labor market effects of exports.

We also apply other novel empirical approaches to Sri Lanka. For this country we combine household-level or worker-level surveys with trade data at the sectoral level to construct a unique, at least to our knowledge, dataset that allows us to estimate the local labor market effects of exports.

It should be noted that we can think of an increase in an economic outcome as an economy-wide general increase plus a region-specific increase. Our geography-based methodology can identify only the region-specific part of this increase and not the aggregate effect. Hence, if workers were perfectly mobile across districts, the positive impact would spread equally across districts, and we would not see any differential impact. Therefore, the sign of the aggregate impact should be the same as the differential impact, and the size of the aggregate impact should be negatively correlated to the moving costs.

The standard practice is probably to run the regressions with log of dependent and independent variables. Then the coefficients are easily identified as elasticities. Because the independent variable (trade exposure) is often zero in our regressions, we cannot take log of this variable, thus we cannot directly show elasticities using the coefficients. The trade exposure is much smaller in India than in the United States, so we chose to show the impact of change in exports in real currencies to the change in wages in real currencies and to the number and percentage of formal jobs. Accordingly, it is easier for the reader to judge the magnitude of the impact and see how much wages, employment, or formal jobs could increase if trade exposure (as increase in exports) was similar to other developing countries. In order to compare our results with other papers in the literature, we also present the results as percent change in labor market outcomes for both a US$100 and a US$1,000 change in trade per worker, which is the main format used in ADH. Overall, our results are consistent with ADH and other comparable studies.

Effect of an Increase in Exports on Local Labor Market Outcomes

Our results show that increases in exports per worker over a 10-year span can increase the wage bill for most worker types. Employment effects emerge as a change in the mix of formal and informal workers employed in local labor markets. In particular, informal workers seem to be drawn into the formal sector as exports increase.

RESULTS FOR INDIA

First, higher exports go hand in hand with higher wages. Our results show that rising exports per person in the sector exposed to higher exports are associated with rising wages per worker (figure O.2). If the value of India's exports increases by US$100 per worker, average annual wages would increase by Rs 572 per worker. The wage improvement is larger for college graduates and urban workers. Males benefit more than females, but only slightly; and there is significant variation across states. Notably, rural workers and less-educated workers do not benefit. Our results are consistent but larger in magnitude than those of ADH.

Second, higher exports seem to draw workers from the informal sector into the formal sector. Our results show that higher exports reduce the level of informality, especially for male and low-skilled workers (figure O.3). Increased exports can explain the conversion of about 800,000 jobs from informal to formal between 1999 and 2011, representing 0.8 percent of the labor force. Low-skilled workers seem to benefit from exports through an increase in formality rates. We do not further explore the economic mechanism behind this decrease in informality, but exports to high-income countries

FIGURE O.2 **Largest Wage Rewards Go to the Most-Educated and Experienced Workers**

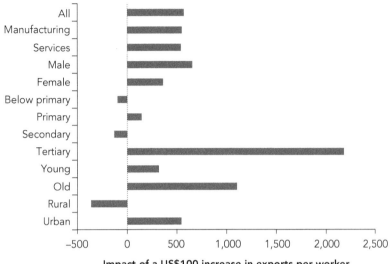

Impact of a US$100 increase in exports per worker on wages in India, 1999–2011 (Indian rupees)

Source: Calculations based on wage regressions.

FIGURE O.3 **Higher Exports Mean Less Informality**

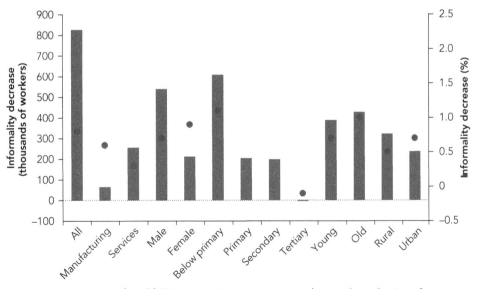

Impact of a US$100 increase in exports per worker on the reduction of informality levels for various worker types in India, 1999–2011 (thousands of workers and percentage)

■ Number of workers   ● Percentage (right axis)

Source: Calculations based on informality regressions.

FIGURE O.4 **Higher Exports Lead to Greater Wage Inequality, Especially for the Least Educated**

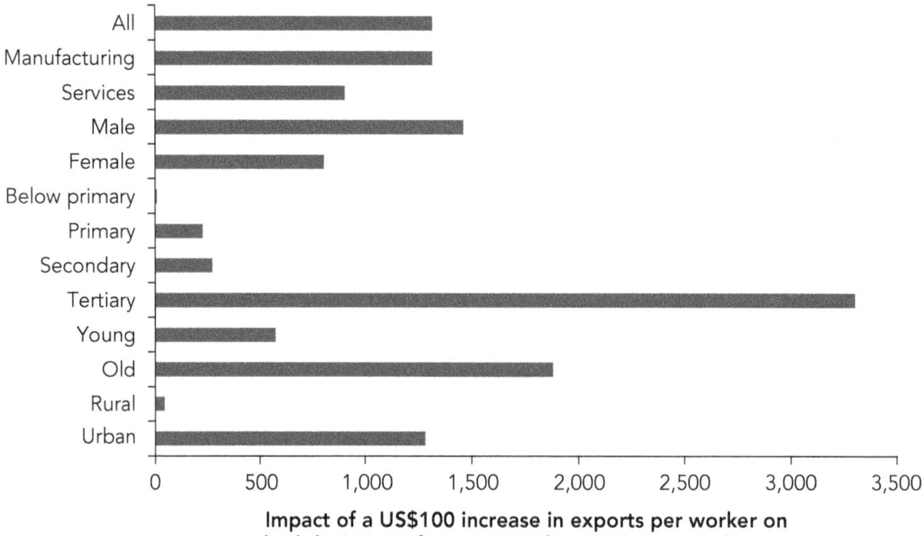

Impact of a US$100 increase in exports per worker on
standard deviation of wages in India, 1999–2011 (Indian rupees)

Source: Calculations based on standard deviation of wages regressions.

possibly come from formal firms that draw from the pool of informal workers. High-skilled workers, who are less likely to be informally employed, seem to experience wage increases as opposed to an increase in formality levels.

Third, higher wages and less informality will have differentiated effects across the population. Our results show that the impact of a US$100 increase in exports per worker is to increase wage inequality (see figure O.4). Those who experience the largest increases in the standard deviation of wages (our measure of inequality) are males, tertiary school graduates, urban workers, and experienced workers. Workers who saw the least are the least educated and rural workers. Because exporting usually requires more-skilled workers, rising exports increase the demand for the skilled workers who are at the top of the formal sector wage distribution. If workers are entangled geographically (that is, when they are unable to move between cities or towns easily or to acquire the newly demanded skills), the increase in demand translates into rising wages. If education is costly and access to education systems limited, low-skilled workers may not be able to apply for new and more lucrative job opportunities right away, resulting in rising wages for those who already have those skills.

Fourth, higher exports do not correlate with higher aggregate employment (of local labor markets). If some towns experience rising exports, one might expect that the size of the local labor market and total local employment would increase. If moving is costly, however, total employment would not increase in response to rising demand for workers. Additionally, if people in local labor markets lack unemployment insurance or other income support, everyone in the local labor market will be employed in either the informal or formal sector, so an increase in labor demand would perhaps change the mix between formal and informal but not increase aggregate employment. Our results show that the increase in exports per worker does not show significant effect on aggregate employment, suggesting that either or both of these explanations might be at work. Other results we present suggest that workers in the informal sector may find formal sector opportunities when exports increase. Therefore, their wages may rise but their employment status may stay the same. We find that employment shifts between formality and informality but does not increase at the aggregate level.

RESULTS FOR SRI LANKA

The outcomes for Sri Lanka are similar to those for India, which is striking given the differences in these countries' sizes and economic conditions. Similar forces seem to be at play in both countries. We find that, if the OECD countries wanted to import more, the wage bill would rise significantly for most of the worker types. With a US$100 increase in exports per worker, average income would increase by SL Rs 206. Similarly, export shocks operate primarily through wages rather than employment, with the average wage increasing by about SL Rs 975 after a US$100 increase in exports per worker.

Which workers benefit most? The largest impact of exports on wage changes is for high-skilled workers, as in India. Plus, positive rising exports increase the standard deviation of wages; hence, income inequality between workers increases. But we did not find any statistically significant impact of changes in trade on formality of workers, unlike in India, although this is probably a result of the data limitations in Sri Lanka.

RESULTS FOR OTHER SOUTH ASIAN COUNTRIES

Preliminary findings for Bangladesh seem similar to India and Sri Lanka, and show that a positive trade shock affects localized labor markets through higher wages and reductions in informality, and the effects vary among different groups of workers. On the one hand, high-skilled, males, and urban workers seem to experience the largest wage increases.[1] Because of data limitations in Pakistan, we were unable to explore how higher exports would affect local labor markets in that country. Our findings from chapter 2, however, seem to indicate that a change in exports in Pakistan would likely increase wages as well.

Policies to Spread the Gains from Exports

The bottom line is that our results show the positive side of globalization in South Asia, which stems from higher exports. Indeed, rising wages and a shift from informal to formal employment are exactly the kinds of benefits governments hoped for when they opened up their economies to international trade. Our results also suggest that the key beneficiaries are mainly the more well-off groups—notably males, more-educated workers, and urban workers. What can be done to ensure that these benefits are more widely spread among the working population? We suggest the following three policy options:

FIGURE O.5 **As Exports Rise, So Do Wages, and Informality Lessens**

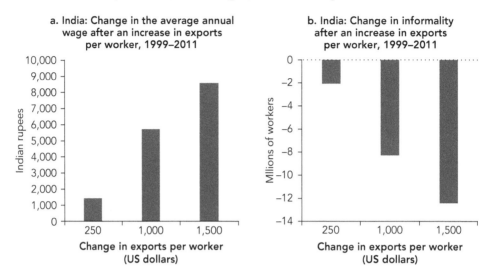

a. India: Change in the average annual
wage after an increase in exports
per worker, 1999–2011

b. India: Change in informality
after an increase in exports
per worker, 1999–2011

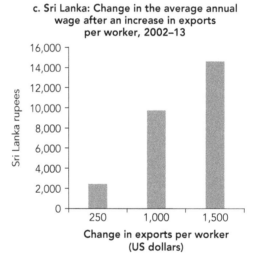

c. Sri Lanka: Change in the average annual
wage after an increase in exports
per worker, 2002–13

Source: Estimated using data from the Indian Labor Force Surveys.
Note: Results are shown at the significance level of less than 10 percent.

- **Increasing the scale of exports.** The degree to which exports might contribute to better labor market outcomes in general depends on the scale of export growth. Certainly, increasing exports in South Asian countries to the levels of Brazil and China would help greatly. We find that higher exports per worker in India increase wages on average between Rs 1,000 and Rs 8,000 and reduce informality between 2.1 million and 12.3 million workers, depending on the scale of export growth—that is, the more the better (figure O.5, panels a and b). In Sri Lanka, a similar pattern is evident for wages (figure O.5, panel c).

FIGURE O.6 **Different Types of Export Shocks Have Different Effects on Wages for Those with Different Skill Levels**

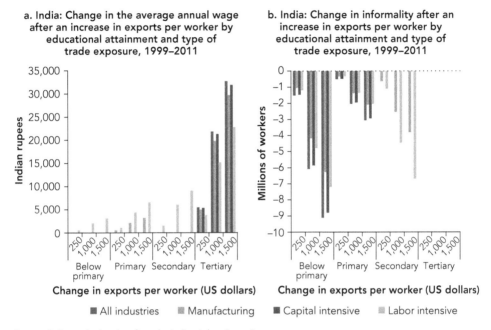

a. India: Change in the average annual wage after an increase in exports per worker by educational attainment and type of trade exposure, 1999–2011

b. India: Change in informality after an increase in exports per worker by educational attainment and type of trade exposure, 1999–2011

■ All industries   ■ Manufacturing   ■ Capital intensive   ■ Labor intensive

Source: Estimated using data from the Indian Labor Force Surveys.
Note: Results are shown at the significance level of less than 10 percent.

- **Changing the composition of exports to help disadvantaged groups.** The extent to which the increase in exports would benefit specific groups in society depends on the type of export shock. For example, an increase in labor-intensive (as opposed to capital-intensive) production is likely to have a broader impact on the wages of workers across all educational backgrounds, even those in rural areas—plus the bigger reduction in informality, particularly for those with educational levels secondary and below and in rural areas (figure O.6 and figure O.7).

- **Changing the composition of the workforce to help disadvantaged groups**. Increasing the participation of disadvantaged groups in the working-age population could also entail reductions in informal work. For example, we find that increasing the skills of workers and increasing the participation of rural and young workers in the labor force to the 75th percentile of their labor force participation rates across districts yield significantly substantial informality reductions if the export shock comes from labor-intensive industries. Similarly, increasing the share of women workers in the labor force to the 75th percentile of their labor force participation rates across districts could reduce informality substantially after an all-industry export shock (table O.1).

To make these gains from trade more inclusive requires complementary policies that could potentially address certain issues that restrict the scale and source of exports and

FIGURE O.7 **Different Types of Export Shocks Have Different Effects on Workers, Rural versus Urban Areas**

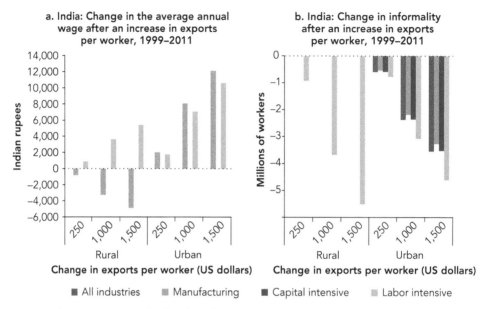

Source: Authors' estimates using data from the Indian Labor Force Surveys.
Note: Results are shown at the significance level of less than 10 percent.

the participation of certain groups in the labor force. Some of these policies could focus on (1) boosting and connecting exports to people (for example, by investing in infrastructure, better connectivity, and freer trade); (2) eliminating distortions in production (eliminating distortions in capital/labor inputs, increasing participation of women in merchandise exports, and improving worker mobility); and (3) protecting workers (for example, by investing in their education and skills).

Given that connectivity is imperative to ensure a trade-boosting environment, the region could increasingly focus policies on improving the quality of infrastructure—physical, institutional, and digital.[2] Removing policy distortions that limit the flexibility of labor, capital, and land markets could enable more-productive firms to grow. Greater participation of women in export-oriented industries could also improve labor market outcomes. Increasing women's participation would entail changing regulations that may discriminate against women in India and Sri Lanka—such as Maharashtra Shops and Establishments and the Factories Act (1948) in India and Employment of Females in Mines Ordinance No. 13 in Sri Lanka—as well as investing in gender-sensitive infrastructure at the workplace (Solotaroff, Joseph, and Kuriakose 2018). Economic and social obstacles that prevent women from joining the workforce would have to be reduced.

The region could also make progress in improving skills so that the workforce is prepared to handle the complexities of globalized production systems. Greater partnerships between the private sector and vocational institutes could be promoted to improve training—in both the formal and the informal sectors. Governments could

TABLE O.1 **Changing the Composition of the Labor Force Can Reduce Informality**

a. India: Simulated change in informality (workers) after a US$250 increase in exports per worker and increasing the share of a particular group to the 75th percentile of the labor force distribution across districts, 1999–2011

Types of affected workers	Type of export shocks			
	All industries	Manufacturing	Capital intensive	Labor intensive
Industry type				
Manufacturing				–2,395,590
Services		–2,105,168		–2,605,958
Capital intensive	–2,173,465	–2,043,600	–2,172,759	–1,734,539
Labor intensive	–2,394,692	–2,148,741	–2,336,100	–2,090,011
Gender				
Male	–1,830,565	–1,887,884	–1,832,601	
Female	–1,930,519	–1,806,992	–1,929,172	
Highest education				
Below primary	–2,737,130	–2,083,431	–2,641,574	–3,361,027
Primary	–3,007,457	–2,323,492	–2,900,994	–3,596,321
Secondary		–2,171,004		–3,837,770
Tertiary				
Age				
Young	–2,003,756	–1,971,068	–1,982,199	–2,433,261
Old	–2,085,805	–1,965,785	–2,064,933	–2,342,260
Location				
Rural				–1,897,343
Urban	–1,420,314	–1,166,794	–1,414,187	–2,143,424

b. India: Simulated change in informality (workers) after a US$250 increase in exports per worker and increasing the share of a particular group to 100 percent of the labor force, 1999–2011

Types of affected workers	Type of export shocks			
	All industries	Manufacturing	Capital intensive	Labor intensive
Industry type				
Manufacturing				–7,266,290
Services		–2,362,518		–3,917,234
Capital intensive	–2,280,871	–2,143,538	–2,288,397	–1,686,038
Labor intensive	–9,944,772	–6,860,260	–8,745,416	–9,142,427
Gender				
Male	–1,765,983	–1,940,149	–1,770,206	
Female	–2,333,303	–1,481,025	–2,318,320	
Highest education				
Below primary	–2,896,550	–1,990,076	–2,795,024	–3,042,541
Primary	–5,446,258	–3,713,413	–5,242,922	–4,209,027
Secondary		–2,306,787		–4,850,352
Tertiary				
Age				
Young	–1,697,741	–1,990,772	–1,673,628	–2,772,668
Old	–2,492,956	–1,939,570	–2,475,484	–1,890,681
Location				
Rural				–1,803,151
Urban	–1,918,975	–1,770,794	–1,905,149	–2,810,831

Source: Authors' estimates using data from the Indian Labor Force Surveys.
Note: Results are shown at the significance level of less than 10 percent.

also safeguard the interests of workers by providing suitable trade assistance programs for workers affected by trade.

Notes

1. The results for Bangladesh, however, are greater in magnitude, since a US$100 increase in exports per worker would raise the average annual wages by approximately US$20, while the effect on India and Sri Lanka would be of US$12.7 and US$10.2, respectively. On the other hand, female and younger workers seem to benefit the most from informality reductions.
2. For example, the government of India has launched ambitious infrastructure projects like Bharatmala, Sagarmala, and the Dedicated Freight Rail Corridors for improving the physical infrastructure and providing better connectivity. Similarly, the government of India is also directing efforts to improve road/rail connectivity between the neighboring countries such as Bangladesh and Nepal (Ministry of Commerce and Industry, Government of India, http://commerce.gov.in).

References

Autor, David H., David Dorn, and Gordon Hanson. 2013. "The China Syndrome: Local Labor Market Effects of Import Competition in the United States." *The American Economic Review* 103 (6): 2121–68.

Bartik, Timothy J. 1991. *Who Benefits from State and Local Economic Development Policies?* Kalamazoo, MI: Upjohn Institute for Employment Research.

Solotaroff, Jennifer L., George Joseph, and Anne Kuriakose. 2018. *Getting to Work: Unlocking Women's Potential in Sri Lanka's Labor Force.* Directions in Development—Countries and Regions. Washington, DC: World Bank.

Topalova, Petia. 2010. "Factor Immobility and Regional Impacts of Trade Liberalization: Evidence on Poverty from India." *American Economic Journal of Applied Economics* 2 (4): 1–41.

World Bank. 2017. *South Asia Economic Focus, Fall 2017: Growth Out of the Blue.* Washington, DC: World Bank.

———. 2018. *South Asia Economic Focus, Spring 2018: Jobless Growth?* Washington, DC: World Bank. https://openknowledge.worldbank.org/handle/10986/29650 License: CC BY 3.0 IGO.

CHAPTER 1

The South Asian Paradox

Key Messages

- South Asian economies face what some may perceive as a paradox: decades of very high and impressive growth rates have done (too) little to create job growth that is inclusive—and critical challenges, like low-quality jobs, remain.

- At the same time, decades of exponential trade growth in South Asia have left the region's economies less linked to international trade than economies in other regions.

- All of these developments are especially worrisome given that South Asia is still characterized by persistent—and, in places, extensive—poverty, a burgeoning youth population, and high levels of informal jobs.

- A greater export orientation is thought to be one way to improve the labor market picture—and the academic literature shows a strong link between trade and growth—but few studies provide estimates of the relationship between exports per worker and specific labor market outcomes.

- This report breaks new ground by developing an innovative approach to estimate the relationship between exports per worker, earnings, and employment in South Asia—and the results are promising.

Introduction

In South Asia, trade has been rising and poverty has been falling, and the combination of rising trade and falling poverty is no coincidence. Since 2010, however, trade growth has moderated, and South Asia's integration into world trade still lags behind other regions, such as East Asia and Pacific or Central Asia. This shortfall raises a critical question: To what extent could higher exports lead to a further reduction of poverty rates in the region? The key channel to reduce poverty is the labor market.

More and better jobs, as well as falling inequality, are often considered the most important labor market outcomes and as such are highly correlated with quality of life indicators, including poverty rates. Yet impressive economic growth rates have not fully translated into satisfactory employment growth, and labor markets in South Asia continue to face several (common) challenges that hold back the region.

Some analysts have even raised the question of jobless growth in South Asia (World Bank 2018). We describe this phenomenon of high growth rates accompanied by relatively low trade shares and—at best—moderate labor market performance as the "South Asian Paradox."

South Asia's economic growth remains the world's fastest. Growth in South Asia is forecast to pick up to 6.9 percent in 2018 and should further strengthen to 7.1 percent on average in 2019–20, reflecting an improvement across most of the region (World Bank 2018). South Asia could, therefore, maintain its position as the fastest-growing region and even extend its lead over East Asia and Pacific.

Economic growth has been correlated with positive job growth, which has contributed to rising living standards for South Asian workers (World Bank 2018). South Asia has witnessed a growth in wage and salaried workers as a total percentage of population, from 21.6 percent in 2008 to 26 percent in 2017. The region has been experiencing a slowly declining unemployment rate, falling from 4.1 percent in 2008 to 3.9 percent in 2017 (World Bank 2018).

Much of the growth is attributed to a favorable macroeconomic environment. Inflation in the region decelerated, mainly because of lower food and commodity prices. Remittance flows have stabilized in most countries. International reserves are at comfortable levels. In fact, among macroeconomic variables that might contribute to growth and to improving labor market outcomes, only international trade, specifically exports, is relatively low. South Asian trade as a fraction of total gross domestic product (GDP) is much lower than in other regions, and lately trade has been falling.

Why is there still a need for improving labor market outcomes in the region? First, improving labor market outcomes is a policy priority because the region remains home to millions of people living in extreme poverty. Informal employment is widespread, and earnings gaps between different demographic groups are still significant. As figure 1.1 shows, a large reduction in poverty has been achieved throughout the last years, halving the number of people living on less than US$1.90 a day since 2002. Nevertheless, there is still room for improvement. The proportion of people in South Asia living on less than US$1.90 a day was estimated at 12.4 percent, or about 216 million people, as of 2015—one-third of all the poor globally.

FIGURE 1.1 **Despite Falling Poverty Rates, Many South Asians Still Live on Less Than US$1.90 a Day**

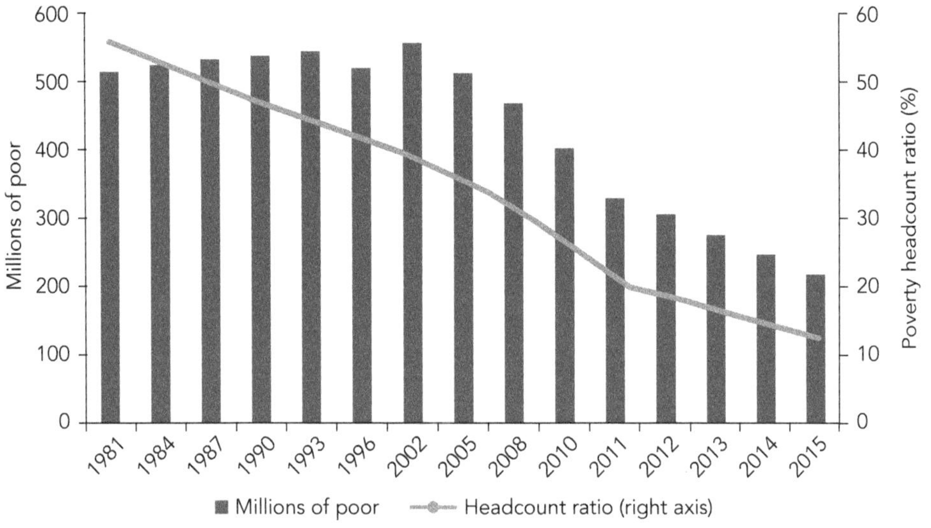

Source: Poverty & Equity Data Portal and PovcalNet.

Second, a big source of pressure on labor markets is the continued high population growth, which makes it necessary to improve labor market outcomes. South Asia's population increased by almost 60 percent between 1990 and 2018.[1] In particular, the fast growth of the working-age population can become problematic. Between 2005 and 2015, the number of South Asians aged 15 and above grew by 1.8 million per month, a trend that will moderate slowly in the next decade. In India, projections from 2012 to 2022 suggest that, on average, between 8 million and 9 million additional young people will join the labor force every year, producing an annual labor force growth rate of about 1.6 percent (ILO 2016a). In South Asia generally, projections from 2018 to 2025 suggest that, on average, the working-age population will increase by 1.3 million every month. Fast-growing populations and the rising share of young people offer prospects for attaining demographic dividends and strong economic growth—but only if sufficient numbers of new jobs are created.

Regular wage employment in the private sector has grown more slowly than total employment. The 2018 World Bank Report *Jobless Growth?* shows that the employment rate (the share of the employed among the working-age population) has been falling. Only part of this decline can be attributed to a shift in policies. The Right to Education (RTE) Act in India,[2] for example, helped increase school enrollment rates, and a corresponding decline in young workforce entrants followed. Another part of this decline can be explained by falling female labor force participation (FLFP).[3]

Even after accounting for this policy change and trends in FLFP, the simple fact is that the labor force is growing faster than the number of formal sector jobs. And, when the labor force grows more quickly than the number of jobs, labor market outcomes change in predictable ways. For example, fewer people enter the labor force because they do not believe a good job is available for them. Job quality also falls because workers have to accept any kind of job they find. In fact, many jobs are of low quality, and high informality is the norm (see, for example, ILO 2016a, 2016b; Srija and Shirke 2014; World Bank 2018). Like many developing regions, South Asia has labor markets that are therefore characterized by limited employment opportunities and earnings, as well as by wage inequality and informal employment (see box 1.1).

One potential solution to overcome these labor market challenges has been a stronger orientation toward globalization. International trade and growth can be a virtuous cycle, as we briefly discuss below; and usually the positive effects from more trade and higher growth spill over to the labor market. Trade volumes in South Asia, however, appear to be below their potentials, and the recent academic literature on trade and labor markets emphasizes that the effects of trade tend to be localized—that is, they do not always spread easily to everybody at the same pace. Could a greater export orientation of South Asia then result in better labor market outcomes? And, if so, what are the magnitudes that might be expected from different levels of increasing exports?

This report aims at rigorously estimating the potential impact from increasing South Asian exports per worker on wage employment and labor earnings (chapters 3 and 4). In the process, it breaks new ground because there have been few efforts to estimate the effects of exports on local labor market outcomes. The results suggest that this is a promising strategy—one that could result in higher wages and lower casual work (a reduction of informality). But it will also require complementary policies to amplify the positive effects for the working population (chapter 5).

BOX 1.1 Informality in South Asia

Informal employment means that workers either are hired by unregistered (informal) enterprises or have no employment contracts and no access to social protection, or that workers experience both situations simultaneously.

Informal workers are often less well paid and, in many cases, factually not covered by employment legislation. High rates of informality, although common in developing countries, are often a sign of low employment quality (see, for example, Giri and Verma 2017). A full discussion of the term informality, as well as technical definitions, can be found in chapter 2 and annex 2A of this report.

In India alone, the proportion of informal employment in total employment (the sum of workers in the unorganized [informal] sector and informal workers in the organized sector) ranges from 60 to 92 percent (Giri and Verma 2017; ILO 2016a; Papola 2017; Srija and Shirke 2014), depending on type of worker and activity (agriculture, manufacturing, services, or other industrial sector) (Shonchoy and Junankar 2014). Increased informal employment among formal firms can be observed recently in the manufacturing sector (Das, Choudhury, and Singh 2015; Goldar and Suresh 2017; Kapoor and Krishnapriya 2017; Sood, Nath, and Ghosh 2014).

South Asia: Low Trade Shares and Lower Integration into Global Value Chains

Given widespread trade liberalization throughout the developing world, including the spread of global value chains (GVCs), it is not surprising that countries' share of trade in GDP has increased worldwide, especially in upper-middle-income countries (figure 1.2). Note that the growth rate of trade's share of GDP seems to have increased in the early 1990s—which represents the beginning of the modern wave of globalization as Latin America and South Asia began to liberalize—although global international trade has stagnated since the economic and financial crisis of 2009, and it has declined in South Asia.

Since 1990, South Asia has adopted various trade liberalization policies to promote trade. However, trade still maintains a relatively low share of GDP in South Asian countries, especially when those countries are compared to developing nations in the East Asia and Pacific region (figure 1.3). Merchandise exports in South Asia account for less than 10 percent of GDP, compared to over 20 percent in East Asia and Pacific and 30 percent in Europe and Central Asia. At the country level, whereas exports in India and Sri Lanka have declined as a share of GDP, in Bangladesh they have increased.

Labor costs in South Asia's apparel industry are one-half to one-fourth of China's labor costs—and the region is a top cotton producer. Yet, although South Asia increased its share of the global market from 7.5 to 12.3 percent between 2000 and 2012, it has been outperformed by China, which accounts for 41 percent of the market (Lopez-Acevedo, Medvedev, and Palmade 2017). Even with its higher labor costs, China attracts

FIGURE 1.2 Share of Trade in GDP Has Increased Worldwide

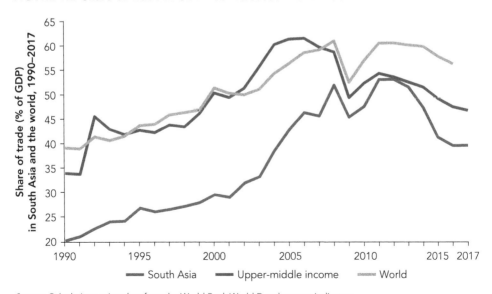

Source: Calculations using data from the World Bank World Development Indicators.
Note: Trade is the sum of exports and imports of goods and services measured as a share of GDP.

FIGURE 1.3 **South Asia Lags All Other Regions in Trade**

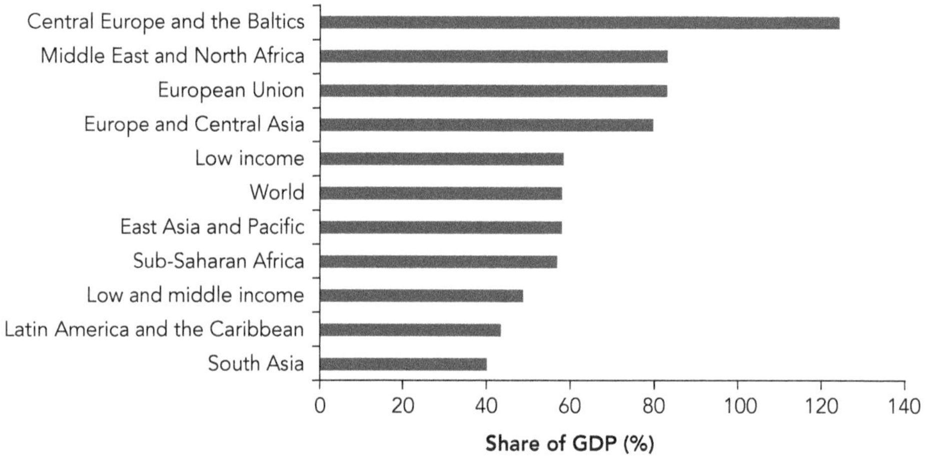

Source: Elaboration using data from World Bank World Development Indicators.
Note: Trade is the sum of exports and imports of goods and services measured as a share of GDP.

buyers by offering a wide range of apparel, produced at high levels of productivity with short lead times. No country in South Asia has thus far succeeded in offering the same overall package of goods and services.

South Asia is the second-most specialized region in GVC exports—a ranking based almost entirely on its strength as the most specialized region in both final and intermediate apparel: about half of GVC exports from South Asia are in final apparel (figure 1.4). On the import side, however, the region is relatively less integrated in GVCs than other regions (Lopez-Acevedo, Medvedev, and Palmade 2017). Bangladesh, India, Pakistan, and Sri Lanka run a substantial trade surplus in final GVC goods (US$68.0 billion of exports versus US$23.8 billion of imports) and have approximately balanced trade in intermediate goods (US$24.3 billion of exports versus US$25.1 billion of imports): they are net importers of intermediate electronics and autos and net exporters of intermediate apparel and footwear (Lopez-Acevedo, Medvedev, and Palmade 2017).[4] This pattern of trade is indicative of self-sourcing intermediates and therefore lower GVC integration.[5]

Trade and Growth: A Virtuous Cycle

Because jobs in the private sector, and especially in the formal private sector, are the main way out of poverty, understanding the economic conditions necessary to foster job and wage growth is critical for improving the standard of living of millions throughout the region.

The idea that international trade—both imports (which can compete with local production) and exports (which can increase local labor demand)—contributes to economic

FIGURE 1.4 **South Asia Global Value Chain Participation Focuses on Apparel**

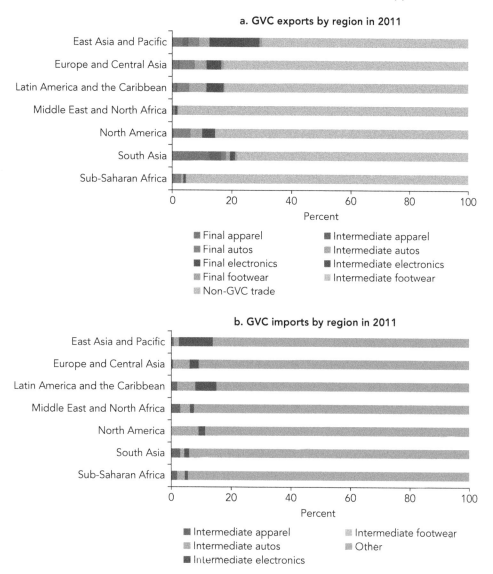

a. GVC exports by region in 2011

Source: Lopez-Acevedo, Medvedev, and Palmade 2017.
Note: GVC = global value chain.

growth is widely accepted. It can make this contribution in several ways. By definition, the world market is much larger than any domestic market. Having the opportunity to sell to a larger market gives firms the chance to take advantage of economies of scale. Access to global inputs can help improve products and production processes in ways that can make firms more productive, and higher productivity leads to growth. Exposure to foreign markets, through both imports and exports, can inspire new ideas for

FIGURE 1.5 **Economic Growth and More Trade Go Together**

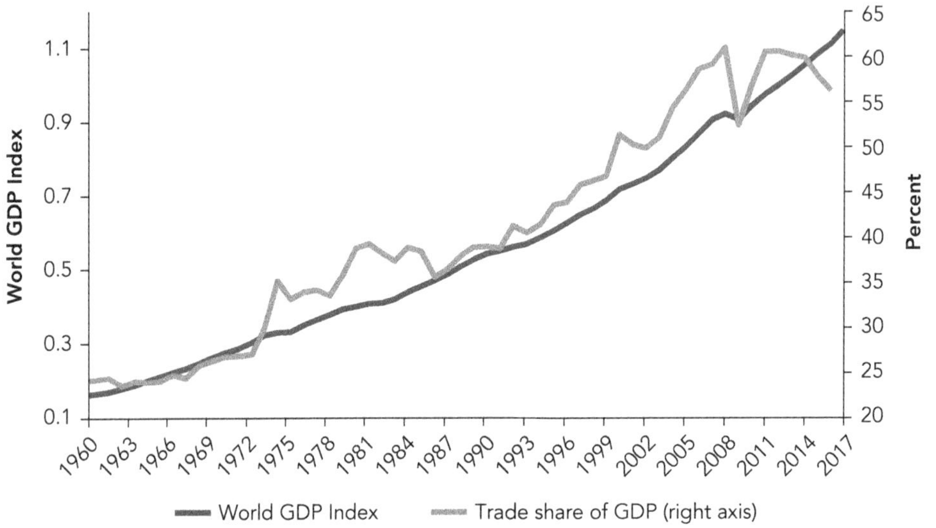

— World GDP Index   Trade share of GDP (right axis)

Source: World Bank World Development Indicators.
Note: The GDP Index is the total value of world GDP in constant (2010) U.S. dollars and normalized so that the value in 2012 is 1. Trade is the sum of exports and imports of goods and services measured as a share of GDP.

both products and production processes that can also increase domestic productivity. Competition from foreign markets also imposes discipline on firms and generates incentives to reduce waste and become more efficient.

There are many ways that trade can contribute to growth, so it is perhaps not surprising that casual observers can see that the poorest countries (such as the landlocked and politically isolated ones) tend to be those that trade the least. A review of international trade and economic growth also shows that the two are positively related. We can see this in figure 1.5, which shows a positive relationship between the world's total real GDP and trade as a share of GDP.

Of course, part of the positive relationship is due to the fact that rich countries can afford to buy more from the world. But rigorous academic studies that control for different factors that can affect both growth and trade—and therefore sort out causality—also have found support for the trade–growth relationship (for an overview, see Huchet-Bourdon, Mouël, and Vijil 2018). For example, to separate the effect of trade on income from the effect of income on trade, Frankel and Romer (1999) show a negative correlation between income and distance. They argue that, given that trade decreases with distance (a result shown in gravity models since the 1970s), it is difficult to explain the correlation without relying on trade. However, another oft-quoted study, Rodriguez and Rodrik (2001), differs, contending that several other factors might explain the negative correlation between income and distance. But Noguer and Siscart (2005) incorporate many of these explanations and show that the implied long-run relationship between trade and income does seem to be robust. More recently, Huchet-Bourdon, Mouël, and Vijil (2018) have reexamined the relationship between trade openness and growth for 169 countries; and they point out that the transition mechanisms can be complex and the relationship nonlinear. The variety and the product quality of countries' export baskets play a role, but overall their empirical results are in line with new international economics' insights that the relationship between trade and growth is positive.

In East Asia especially, trade has been associated with very rapid economic growth. The World Bank report *The East Asian Miracle* (Birdsall and others 1993)—which contrasts high-performing Asian economies (HPAEs) with other developing countries—demonstrates that countries that successfully promoted exports, such as those in East Asia, have enjoyed rapid and sustained growth. It also argues that engaging with the global economy, along with good macroeconomic management and other policies, brings benefits that contribute to growth.

Possibly inspired by the high growth rates of export-oriented East Asia and Pacific, developing countries in the 1980s and 1990s turned away from the inward-focused import-substitution industrialization (ISI) paradigm. The ISI strategy relied on quantitative restrictions on imports along with high-tariff and nontariff barriers to help protected industries grow faster than unprotected industries. It also contributed to macroeconomic instability and debt, acting as a drag on growth. In many cases, the protected industries were what economists call "capital intensive"—that is, they included larger-scale industries (such as steel and petroleum refining) and used less labor per unit of output than "labor-intensive" industries (such as apparel and assembly). In the end, countries with ISI policies grew less, on average, than HPAEs.

By contrast, modern globalization in developing countries embraces participating in GVCs and focusing on labor-intensive goods. GVCs are characterized by the division of the production process into stages and the distribution of these stages across different countries, along with globally dispersed production networks that are coordinated by lead firms. These chains make it possible for firms in developing countries to participate in the gains from producing the world's most complex and sophisticated products by specializing in tasks where they have a comparative advantage and to produce at the necessary large scale to be competitive globally. As a result, developing countries have become full-fledged participants in international production—importing labor-intensive inputs that they process and reexport in the form of goods, parts, components, and services used in some of the most sophisticated products on the planet (Lopez-Acevedo, Medvedev, and Palmade 2017).

Potential South Asian Gains from Greater Export Orientation

To what extent could globalization help address the labor market concerns described above? To answer this question, we need to know how local exports are related to employment, wages, and informality—especially, how a change in exports over time would be associated with changes in earnings, employment, and informality. The goal of this report is to generate these estimates by adapting the latest empirical methods to South Asia's exports and labor markets.

USING THE LATEST METHODS

In advanced economies, a new literature has emerged that credibly assesses the response of employment and wages to a greater exposure to imports—the so-called China Shock (see appendix A for a discussion of trade shocks). One of the seminal studies comes from Topalova (2010), who studies the effects of tariff changes on poverty rates across India's districts. The author measures the effective changes in tariff rates for districts (*zila*) by weighting industry-level changes with the number of workers in each district—and shows that poverty rates increased (or decreased more slowly) in districts that were more exposed to the trade shocks.

One of the author's key contributions is to implement an approach proposed by Bartik (1991). This approach takes advantage of a concentration of production and local labor markets to identify the relationship between globalization and local labor market outcomes. It has been used in other developing countries as well, with the results showing that local labor markets matter.

A methodology similar to Topalova (2010) and Bartik (1991) was later adopted by Autor, Dorn, and Hanson (2013) (henceforth ADH) to study the impact of China's rapid growth (the China Shock) on local labor markets in the United States, which are defined as commuting zones. ADH contributed to the research on trade and local labor markets in two important aspects. First, it is virtually impossible to argue against the exogeneity of their instrument because ADH use growth of China (measured by the change in exports of China to countries other than the United States) as the main instrument, rather than a potentially endogenous policy variable such as tariffs. Second, ADH identify one of the largest negative exogenous shocks to labor demand in recent history, that is, China's rapid growth. This discovery has attracted a great deal of attention. ADH find that the U.S. regions with a high concentration of import-competing industries experienced a significant decline in employment levels but not much of a decrease in wages.

The ADH methodology relies on the fact that workers are not fully mobile across localities, because of labor market frictions and mobility costs, with the result that import shocks differ depending on the structure of the local economy. If workers were fully mobile across locations or industries, the labor markets in all districts would be fully integrated into the national labor market. In other words, if workers were freely mobile, a trade shock would impact all workers similarly, independent of their location or region.

Which localities suffer most? It turns out that it is those localities where production is more specialized in goods that suddenly become cheaper to import. In measuring the effective changes in tariff rates, Topalova (2010) calculates the effective change in import protection for Indian districts after the 1991 trade reform. The variation in the author's sample comes from differences among districts in their industry and import compositions. The districts with a larger share of import-competing sectors and sectors with larger tariff reductions are exposed more severely to the trade liberalization shocks. Topalova assumes that tariff reductions are exogenous to the districts, because they were planned by the central government through international agreements. Several studies have used variations of this approach but have reached different conclusions. Topalova (2010) shows that poverty rates increased (or decreased more slowly) in districts that were more exposed to the trade shocks.

These papers typically exploit the variation in the trade exposure of districts on the basis of employment shares. For example, regions with high shares of import-competing industry employment are exposed to more-intensive trade shocks than districts with high shares of nontraded or export industry employment. Our approach differs from these studies by focusing on exports.

OUR APPROACH

For the most part, previous research on trade and local labor markets focuses on certain kinds of shocks, such as increasing competition due to growth of China, automation, exchange rates, or tariff reduction. One significant exception to that focus of the literature is Hasan and others (2012)—who use a measure based on protection to discuss the role of export sector employment shares on trade shocks, with a partial focus on export shocks. The authors find that trade protection is negatively correlated with state-level unemployment; this correlation is especially strong for states that have high employment in exporting industries. Hasan and others (2012) find that lower tariffs reduced unemployment rates by about 41 percent in states with flexible labor markets and large export shares.

We also focus on exports to answer the question of whether higher exports in South Asia can resolve the "paradox" and lead to a more satisfying labor market performance. For our methodology, we follow Topalova (2010), ADH, and Hakobyan and McLaren (2016) in applying the "Bartik" approach to understanding the local labor market effects of exports on workers in India (box 1.2). We use instruments to control for the potential endogeneity of exports. We also apply another novel empirical approach to Sri Lanka. For these two countries we combine household-level or worker-level surveys with trade data at the sectoral level to construct a dataset that is unique (at least to our knowledge) and that allows us to estimate the local labor market effects of exports (box 1.3).

This report seeks to estimate the link between exports and labor market outcomes. The few studies that examine the effects of exports suggest that it is possible that exporting countries experience positive effects through reallocation and rising productivity (Harrison 2007; McCaig and Pavcnik 2018), as well as rising wages. This prediction of rising wages follows from neoclassical economic theory. The Heckscher–Ohlin theorem, for example, suggests that labor-abundant countries, such as today's developing

BOX 1.2 **Our Methodology**

Our methodology follows the "Bartik" (1991) approach that has been applied to assess the effects of globalization on labor market outcomes. To illustrate, we can use the variable y to denote different labor market outcomes (employment, wages, and informality in our case). The outcomes are observed for different regions i at time t. Each of these regions at time t is associated with a change in exports, which we can denote using the variable x. Unfortunately, we do not observe the specific quantity of exports from any given region, but we do observe the share of employment in industry j in each region i. If we define the employment in region i in industry j at time t as L_{ijt} and the total employment of region i at time t as L_{it}, then we can define the employment share as

$$\lambda_{ijt} = \frac{L_{ijt}}{L_{it}}.$$

Thus, the estimated effect of exports is calculated as

$$y_{it} = \beta \lambda_{ijt} x_{jt}.$$

Our main interest is the coefficient β, which is what we estimate. Of course, our actual estimation is more complicated. Exports might be driven by workers in the exporting country, which means exports could be endogenous. Therefore, in the actual estimation, we add different controls and use the changes in labor market outcomes as a function of changes in exports, and then use instruments to control for the potential endogeneity of exports. Accordingly, the results should be interpreted as, for example, the change in average wages after a change in exports per worker. Hence, if the effect is negative, it means that there is a reduction in wages.

BOX 1.3 **Our Data Sources**

Bangladesh provides household-based sample surveys through the Bangladesh Bureau of Statistics beginning in 1980. We use labor force surveys conducted in 2005 (10th round), 2010 (11th round), and 2013 (12th round). These are combined with the first round of the Quarterly Labor Force Survey 2015. We select similar variables as in the India and Sri Lanka datasets for our analysis. The survey questionnaire and reported variables have witnessed dramatic changes within this period that hinder effective cross-temporal analysis. To ensure compatibility over time, we reaggregate the "marital status" variable from 5 to 4 categories, the "relationship to household head" variable from 9 to 6 categories, and the "education" variable from 19 to 6 categories. The "informality" variable is created from multiple categories of the "principle activity status" variable. The number and description of categories change over time, but efforts were made to ensure that the coverage includes self-employed, contributing family members, and day laborers across years. In addition, concordances for the geographic and industrial classifications were created to ensure that changes from the Bangladesh Standard Industrial Classification (SIC) 2002 and SIC 2009 are harmonized to ISIC Rev 3.1 for further merging with the trade data coming out of the World Bank's World Integrated Trade Solutions and the United Nations' Comtrade databases.

(Box continues next page)

Box 1.3 Our Data Sources *(continued)*

India collects data on its labor force through the quinquennial National Sample Survey (NSS), administered by the Ministry of Statistics and Programme Implementation. We use the section of the NSS titled "Schedule 10—Employment and Unemployment." Our empirical approach covers surveys conducted in 1999 (55th round), 2004 (61st round), 2007 (64th round), 2009 (66th round), and 2011 (68th round). Variables selected for analysis include sex, age, wage, occupational status, earnings, educational attainment level, school status, daily activities, activity intensity, marital status, informality indicator, activity status, caste, religion, employment status, and vocational training. To ensure comparability of geographic variables over time, we harmonize district variables according to the status of 1993. To maximize state-level analysis, the districts that were carved out to form the states of Chhattisgarh, Uttarakhand, and Jharkhand are grouped to recreate these new states in the 1993 dataset. Subsequently, the industry information from the dataset is harmonized over time using the ISIC Rev 3.1 classification to ensure concordance with trade data from the United Nations Comtrade database at the 4-digit commodity level (see appendix B for details on the database's construction).

Pakistan provides labor market information through several national surveys like the Pakistan Social and Living Standards Measurement Survey, the Pakistan Integrated Household Survey/Household Integrated Economic Survey/Household Integrated Income and Consumption Survey, and the Labor Force Survey. We use the labor force surveys conducted in 2005–06 and 2014–15 through the Pakistan Bureau of Statistics. Because of data limitations, only a limited analysis of descriptive labor market statistics was carried out.

Sri Lanka has a quarterly Labor Force Survey (LFS) from the Department of Census and Statistics, which provides labor market and socioeconomic information to measure the levels and trends of employment and unemployment in the country. We include annual data points from 1992 through 2015, with a few exceptions. We select similar variables as in the India dataset for our analysis. Significant revisions were made to the survey questionnaire in 1996, 2006, and 2013. To ensure compatibility over time, we aggregate 18 categories of education variables from 1996 to 2015 to 8 categories; sectoral classification is also simplified from 1996 onward to include estates as part of rural areas. Analysis on informality is conducted for the period after 2006, when it was added to the survey. Industrial classification, which changes from SLIC Rev 3.1 in 2002 to SLIC Rev 4 in 2013, is harmonized to ISIC Rev 3.1 before merging with the trade data. Because the LFS lacked official documentation on industrial classification prior to 2002, these observations are dropped from any industry-based analysis.

countries including most of South Asia, would export labor-intensive goods. As exports increase, the demand for, and therefore wages of, labor would increase. In addition, it is well established that exporting firms, at the micro level, pay higher wages (Bernard and others 2007). These results seem to come through at the industry level as well. Robertson and others (2009), for example, show that export sectors in developing countries, particularly apparel, pay higher wages than workers are likely to earn in other sectors.

Additionally, focusing on the local effects of exports, we show that South Asian industry tends to be very concentrated. In India, for example, industry is concentrated in only a few states (figure 1.6). We also show that the wage gap across states has been rising

FIGURE 1.6 India's Industry Is Concentrated in a Few States

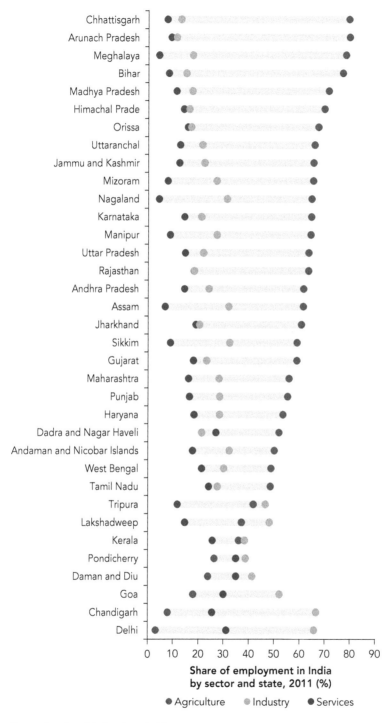

Share of employment in India
by sector and state, 2011 (%)

● Agriculture ● Industry ● Services

Source: Based on data from household surveys.

over time, with the highest-wage states experiencing the largest increases in wages. This area of research is vital, given that economists have recently gained renewed appreciation for the importance of adjustment costs. Furthermore, convergence of living standards across states is usually a policy priority.

EXPORTS AND BETTER LABOR OUTCOMES

The results, which are detailed in chapters 4 and 5, illustrate the estimated relationship between long-run export growth and labor market outcomes. The very small share of workers in export sectors means that the effects of exports on local labor markets are small. That said, even with the very small shares of workers in the exporting industries, we find statistically significant effects on local labor markets. For example, as exports increase, informality declines. Rising exports per person in the sector are associated with rising wages per worker. And rising exports seem to be more strongly associated with wages than with employment, which is also consistent with a labor market in which worker-level adjustment costs are particularly high.

What the South Asian Paradox Portends

In recent decades, South Asia has been characterized by policy measures to increase trade openness, and exports and imports have grown very strongly. At the same time the region has shown impressive economic growth rates and made significant progress in reducing poverty. So it seems obvious to link the latter successes with the former steps to increase trade openness.

However, some puzzles remain, which we have labeled the "South Asian Paradox." Improvements in South Asia's labor market outcomes have been moderate, at least compared to the size of the challenges ahead. Working-age populations in our four sample countries—Bangladesh, India, Pakistan, and Sri Lanka—are growing quickly, and the quality of many existing jobs is rather poor. Furthermore, significant gender gaps exist. To what extent South Asia's trade integration is conducive to better and more inclusive labor market outcomes is unclear. At the same time, exports have decelerated over the last few years. In the rest of the report, we attempt to unveil the potential between different export strategies and better labor market outcomes, a link that has rarely been quantified in previous studies for South Asia (see appendix A).

The following chapter analyzes in detail the situation in South Asia's labor markets and looks at the export patterns for each country.

Notes

1. More information about South Asian's population growth can be found at the United Nations Population Division database, https://population.un.org/wpp/DataQuery.

2. RTE is an Act of the Indian Parliament enacted in 2009 that supports free and compulsory education for children aged 6 to 14 years old.

3. Gender challenges in South Asia are high and persistent. At 32 percent, the South Asian FLFP rate is the second lowest of all regions. In India, between 2005 and 2015, female employment rates decreased by nearly 5 percent per year. In Bangladesh, female employment remained constant. In Pakistan, female employment even increased—though from a very low level—with women almost three times less likely to be employed in full-time jobs than men. In Sri Lanka, FLFP fell from 41 percent in 2010 to 36 percent in 2016 (Solotaroff, Joseph, and Kuriakose 2018). Women report having difficulty finding high-skill and high-paying jobs.

4. Some share of imported inputs, particularly in autos, is likely to be for maintenance and repair. Similarly, some reported electronics intermediates are likely to be delivered to sectors other than electronics—including the automotive sector.

5. Such self-sourcing would mainly be domestic commerce in India and Pakistan, which do not show up in trade data. This pattern of trade could also be explained by significant barriers to imports of final goods.

References

Autor, David H., David Dorn, and Gordon Hanson. 2013. "The China Syndrome: Local Labor Market Effects of Import Competition in the United States." *The American Economic Review* 103 (6): 2121–68.

Bartik, Timothy J. 1991. "Who Benefits from State and Local Economic Development Policies?" Upjohn Institute for Employment Research, Kalamazoo, MI.

Bernard, Andrew B., J. Bradford Jensen, Stephen J. Redding, and Peter K. Schott. 2007. "Firms in International Trade." *Journal of Economic Perspectives* 21 (3): 105–30.

Bown, Chad P., Daniel Lederman, Samuel Pienknagura, and Raymond Robertson. 2017. *Better Neighbors: Toward a Renewal of Economic Integration in Latin America.* Latin America and Caribbean Studies. Washington, DC: World Bank.

Birdsall, Nancy M., Jose Edgardo L. Campos, Chang-Shik Kim, W. Max Corden, Lawrence MacDonald [editor], Howard Pack, John Page, Richard Sabor, and Joseph E. Stiglitz. 1993. *The East Asian Miracle: Economic Growth and Public Policy: Main Report (English).* A World Bank Policy Research Report. New York: Oxford University Press. http://documents.worldbank .org/curated/en/975081468244550798/Main-report.

Das, Deb K., Homagni Choudhury, and Javir Singh. 2015. "Contract Labour (Regulation and Abolition) Act 1970 and Labour Market Flexibility: An Exploratory Assessment of Contract Labour Use in India's Formal Manufacturing." ICRIER Working Paper No. 300, Indian Council for Research on International Economic Relations, New Delhi.

Frankel, Jeffrey A., and David Romer. 1999. "Does Trade Cause Growth?" *American Economic Review* 89 (3): 379–99.

Giri, Rahul, and Rubina Verma. 2017. "Informality in Indian Manufacturing." Working Paper, February. International Monetary Fund and Department of Business Administration, Instituto Tecnológico Autónomo de Mexico. https://editorialexpress.com/cgi-bin/conference/down load.cgi?db_name=SED2017&paper_id=1566.

Goldar, Bishwanath, and R. Suresh. 2017. "Contract Labour in Organized Manufacturing in India." In *Labour and Development—Essays in Honour of Professor T. S. Papola*, edited by K. P. Kannan, Rajendra P Mamgain, and Preet Rustagi. New Delhi: Academic Foundation.

Hakobyan, Shushanik, and John McLaren. 2016. "Looking for Local Labor Market Effects of NAFTA." *Review of Economics and Statistics* 98 (4): 728–41.

Harrison, Ann. 2007. *Globalization and Poverty*. National Bureau of Economic Research and University of Chicago Press.

Hasan, Rana, Devashish Mitra, Priya Ranjan, and Reshad N. Ahsan. 2012. "Trade Liberalization and Unemployment: Theory and Evidence from India." *Journal of Development Economics* 97 (2): 269–80.

Huchet-Bourdon, Marilyne, Chantal Mouël, and Mariana Vijil. 2018. "The Relationship between Trade Openness and Economic Growth: Some New Insights on the Openness Measurement Issue." *The World Economy* 41 (1): 59–76.

ILO (International Labour Office). 2016a. "India Labor Market Update." ILO Country Office, India.

———. 2016b. "Global Wage Report 2016/17." ILO, Geneva.

Kapoor, Reddick, and P. P. Krishnapriya. 2017. "Informality in the Formal Sector: Evidence from Indian Manufacturing." Working Paper F-35316-INC-1, International Growth Centre. https://www.theigc.org/wp-content/uploads/2017/05/Kapoor-and-Krishnapriya-working-paper-2017.pdf.

Kathuria, Sanjay. 2018. *A Glass Half Full: The Promise of Regional Trade in South Asia*. Washington, DC: World Bank.

Lopez-Acevedo, Gladys, Denis Medvedev, and Vincent Palmade. 2017. *South Asia's Turn: Policies to Boost Competitiveness and Create the Next Export Powerhouse*. South Asia Development Matters. Washington, DC: World Bank. doi:10.1596/978-1-4648-0973-6. License: Creative Commons Attribution CC BY 3.0 IGO.

McCaig, Brian, and Nina Pavcnik. 2018. "Export Markets and Labor Allocation in a Low-Income Country." *American Economic Review* 108 (7): 1899–941.

Noguer, Marta, and Marc Siscart. 2005. "Trade Raises Income: A Precise and Robust Result." *Journal of International Economics* 65 (2): 447–60.

Papola, T. S. 2017. "Towards Promoting Decent Employment." *Indian Journal of Human Development* 7 (2): 353–55.

Robertson, Raymond, Drusilla Brown, Gaëlle Pierre, and Laura Sanchez-Puerta, eds. 2009. *Globalization, Wages, and the Quality of Jobs: Five Country Studies*. Washington, DC: World Bank.

Rodriguez, Francisco, and Dani Rodrik. 2001. "Trade Policy and Economic Growth: A Skeptic's Guide to the Cross-National Evidence." In *NBER Macroeconomics Annual 2000. Volume 15*, edited by Ben S. Bernanke and Kenneth Rogoff, 261–325. Cambridge and London: MIT Press.

Shonchoy, Abu S., and P. N. (Raja) Junankar. 2014. "The Informal Labour Market in India: Transitory or Permanent Employment for Migrants?" IDE Discussion Papers 461, Institute of Developing Economies, Japan External Trade Organization.

Solotaroff, Jennifer L., George Joseph, and Anne Kuriakose. 2018. *Getting to Work: Unlocking Women's Potential in Sri Lanka's Labor Force*. Directions in Development—Countries and Regions. Washington, DC: World Bank.

Sood, Atul, Paritosh Nath, and Sangeeta Ghosh. 2014. "Deregulating Capital, Regulating Labour: The Dynamics in the Manufacturing Sector in India." *Economic and Political Weekly* 49 (26–27): 58–68.

Srija, A., and S. Shirke. 2014. "An Analysis of the Informal Labour Market in India." Special Feature (Confederation of Indian Industry). http://www.ies.gov.in/pdfs/CII%20EM-october-2014.pdf.

Topalova, Petia. 2010. "Factor Immobility and Regional Impacts of Trade Liberalization: Evidence on Poverty from India." *American Economic Journal of Applied Economics* 2 (4): 1–41.

World Bank. 2017. *South Asia Economic Focus, Fall 2017: Growth Out of the Blue.* Washington, DC: World Bank.

———. 2018. *South Asia Economic Focus, Spring 2018: Jobless Growth?* Washington, DC: World Bank. https://openknowledge.worldbank.org/handle/10986/29650 License: CC BY 3.0 IGO.

CHAPTER 2

Labor Market Challenges and Export Patterns in South Asia

Key Messages

- South Asia's growing youth workforce offers a major demographic dividend, but only if the region can create enough good jobs to employ everyone—and that means increasing wages, reducing informal employment, and promoting equality.

- Exporting holds the potential to improve labor market outcomes, but South Asia has a relatively low engagement with global markets: its merchandise exports account for less than 10 percent of gross domestic product (GDP), compared to over 20 percent in East Asia and Pacific, and 30 percent in Europe and Central Asia.

- Making matters worse, exports are concentrated in a few goods and destinations (Europe and the United States), with export firms concentrated in a few geographical areas.

- In Bangladesh and Sri Lanka, labor-intensive export industries (like textiles and apparel) have benefitted workers, but the benefits of India's capital-intensive export industry (like chemicals and fabricated metals) for workers are less obvious.

Introduction

Having introduced the South Asian Paradox in the previous chapter, we now explore in depth the puzzling conditions of high growth and unsatisfactory labor market performance, coupled with declining trade in the South Asian region. The labor market challenges in all four South Asian countries that we examine (Bangladesh, India, Pakistan, and Sri Lanka) are in fact multifaceted, but they can be grouped into three kinds. There is first a challenge to create a sufficient quantity of jobs. We will see that this challenge is largely driven by demographic factors, but it also includes an important gender aspect: significantly fewer women than men have jobs. Investigating which economic sectors create more jobs than they lose is closely linked to the second major challenge faced by South Asian economies: job quality. Many new jobs are informal rather than formal, and they are therefore less well paid and without social protection. The third labor market challenge that can be detected for all four countries is the threat of rising inequality, measured as wage gaps between different groups of workers depending on geographical location or gender. These challenges are by and large similar across the four economies, but we also highlight specific country differences.

After demonstrating the magnitude of these common labor market challenges, the chapter describes the main characteristics and trends of the export sectors in Bangladesh, India, Pakistan, and Sri Lanka. We want to answer two key questions on exports: Which kinds of goods are exported? And who are the trading partners? Although South Asia as a whole does not integrate as much into global trade as other developing regions in the world, the chapter identifies several differences across countries. Bangladesh and Sri Lanka, for example, export labor-intensive products such as apparel and textiles, and India exports capital-intensive goods such as chemicals and fabricated metals. All South Asian countries depend heavily on Europe and the United States as customers for their products. Moreover, the export sectors for all countries in the region are geographically concentrated.

Labor Market Conditions and Policy Priorities

South Asia faces three significant labor market challenges: (1) creating a sufficient number of jobs for its large and rapidly growing populations; (2) improving the quality of jobs, which are mostly informal, often lacking access to basic social security; and (3) correcting the relatively unequal distribution of jobs and earnings, especially across gender but also across spatial dimensions.

CHALLENGE 1: LARGE POPULATIONS AND SIGNIFICANT POPULATION GROWTH

South Asia's population increased by almost 60 percent between 1990 and 2018.[1] These fast-growing populations and the rising share of young people reaching the working age are not necessarily bad developments. They can be turned into opportunities because they offer prospects for attaining demographic dividends and strong economic growth. However, those prospects will only be realized if South Asian countries can create a sufficient number of new jobs that are both productive and well paid; if that fails to occur, those same demographics could become a burden.

Working-age populations grow faster than overall populations, which can reduce the dependency ratios; but at the same time labor forces and employment have grown more slowly than working-age populations (aged 15+). In addition, labor force participation rates (LFPRs) have been declining and are well below averages for Organisation for Economic Co-operation and Development (OECD) countries, where rates between 65 and 75 percent are common. All of our four sample countries now face this predicament (figure 2.1). Declining LFPRs mean that smaller and smaller proportions of the overall working-age population work or are looking for work—a possible sign of an insufficient number of good job opportunities (see also Challenge 2). A closer look at gender differences shows that the reason for the overall low LFPR in South Asia can be traced to the extremely low and declining LFPR for women.

A look at *India,* with the second-largest population and labor force in the world, demonstrates the close links between population growth, labor markets, and prosperity. India's population grew by 55 percent from about 870 million in 1990 to more than 1.3 billion people in 2018—and it is projected to continue growing at a rate of 1.6 percent

FIGURE 2.1 Demographic Dividend or Demographic Bomb?

Evolution of total population, working-age population, dependents, and the accumulated increase of the labor force in South Asian countries, 1999–2030

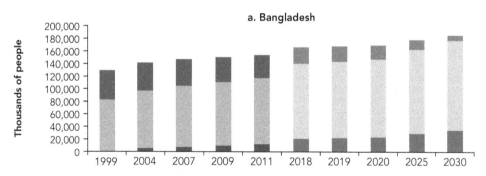

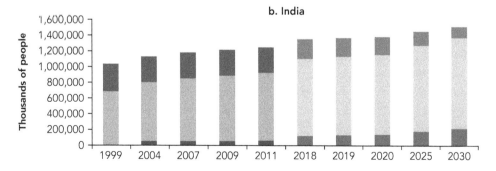

(Figure continues on next page)

FIGURE 2.1 **Demographic Dividend or Demographic Bomb?** *(continued)*

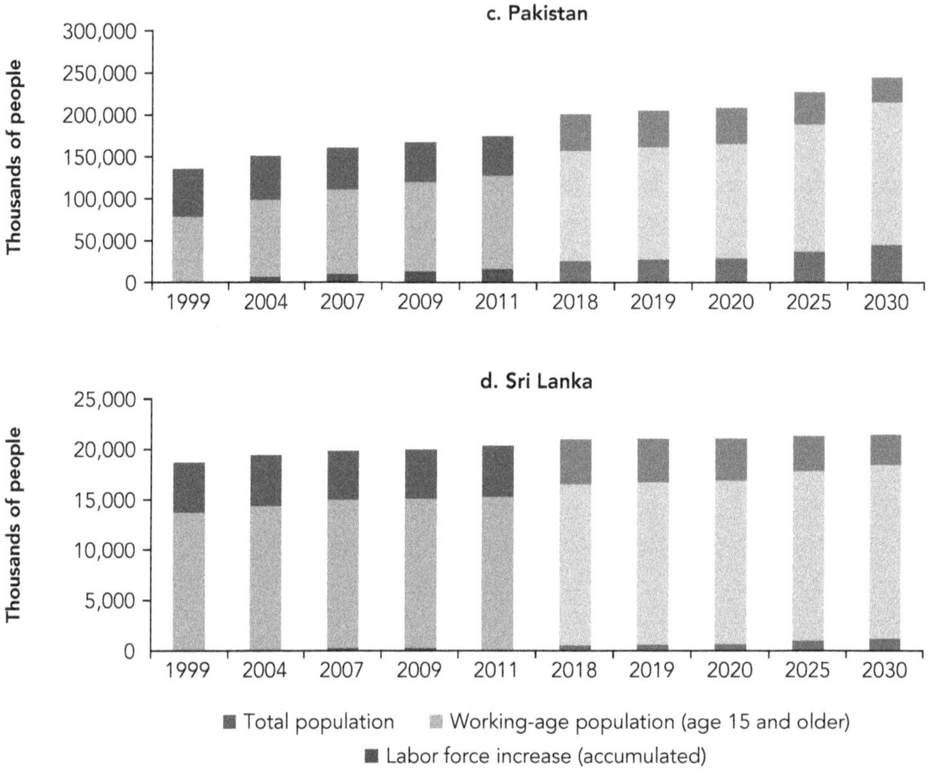

c. Pakistan

d. Sri Lanka

■ Total population   ■ Working-age population (age 15 and older)
■ Labor force increase (accumulated)

Source: Calculations based on data from Labor Force Surveys for Bangladesh, India, Pakistan, and Sri Lanka, and from the United Nations Population Division.
Note: The charts depict the total populations (full size of the bar) relative to working-age populations (green) and dependents, that is, people under the age of 15 or above 70 (blue). The shrinking size of the blue bar (dependents) over time relative to the green bar (potential workers) illustrates the demographic dividend. At the same time the red bar depicts the accumulated increase of the labor force, which needs to be accommodated with new jobs if the dividend is to be seized. Because labor force participation rates are relatively low, the size of the red bar can be seen as the lower end of the number of jobs that need to be created by the respective year.

annually between 2018 and 2030. Roughly 61 million people entered the labor market over the 1999–2011 period. Annually, the labor force increased by 5.1 million people on average, with the number of entrants to the labor market rising to about 8.8 million annually. By 2030, the labor force will have increased by 216 million people since 1999, of which 100 million are still expected to join the labor market between now and 2030. At an LFPR of about 54 percent, this means that the Indian economy has to generate 5 million to 9 million new jobs every year. However, the overall LFPR has declined from 59 percent in 1999 to 54 percent in 2011—with the female rate dropping from 34.0 percent to 27.7 percent in 2011 (OECD average for women in 2016 was 63.6 percent).

Sri Lanka's much smaller population has not increased as fast as India's. It grew by about 21 percent—from 17.3 million in 1990 to 21 million people in 2018—and it is expected to swell to 21.5 million people in 2030. But the average past population growth rate of 0.7 percent is going to slow down. Thus, Sri Lanka's labor market is under less pressure than India's to create a high number of new jobs. Although the working-age population is also growing faster than the average population, the future decline in dependency ratios is less pronounced than for India. The overall LFPR has declined from 58 percent in 1999 to 53 percent in 2011; with the male LFPR down from about 77 percent to 74 percent in 2011, and the female rate down from 39 percent to 34 percent.

Pakistan's population almost doubled between 1990 and 2018, rising from about 107 million people to more than 200 million, with the working-age population and the labor force in Pakistan growing faster than the overall population.[2] But the past average population growth rate of roughly 2.1 percent is expected to slow down slightly by 2030. These dynamics mean that Pakistan has to create between 1.3 million and 1.6 million new jobs every year—about 20 million more jobs by 2030—to keep employment and unemployment rates stable at current LFPRs. At this point, Pakistan's labor force is expected to reach 85 million people in 2030. Although Pakistan's LFPR has not declined, it is at the lower end in South Asia, with only every second person being active. Moving the LFPR closer to OECD averages, for example, to 65 percent, would result in an even larger labor force of 110 million people in 2030, or in 50 million additionally needed jobs compared to today. Gender differences are similar to those in India and Sri Lanka. Our estimates show a female LFPR of only 23 percent in 2014.

In *Bangladesh,* the population increased by 56 percent, from 106 million in 1990 to 166 million people in 2018—a rate that is expected to slow down now but remain below growth rates of the working-age population. At the same, the LFPR has dipped from 60 to 58 percent. These dynamics mean that the labor force would require about 34 million additional jobs by 2030. The gender gap is similar to others in the region, with a male LFPR of between 82 and 89 percent, and a female LFPR of between 23 and 36 percent. However, a striking difference in Bangladesh is that the female LFPR rose from 23 percent in 2005 to 36 percent in 2015. This increase illustrates how even a slightly higher female LFPR can significantly boost prospects for a demographic dividend.

CHALLENGE 2: PERSISTENT INFORMALITY AND LOW-QUALITY JOBS

Although at least some progress, albeit not sufficient, has been made to generate the sheer numbers of jobs, South Asia's economies lack productive, good-quality jobs. Many existing jobs and many recently created jobs are of relatively poor quality. We measure job quality along two lines: (1) whether jobs are informal (as measured by workers' employment status), and (2) if they provide decent wages or have at least experienced decent wage increases.

The term informality was first coined in the early 1970s and has always contained some ambiguity. The International Labour Organization defines work as informal employment if a worker's "employment relationship is, in law or in practice, not subject to labor legislation, income taxation, social protection or entitlement to certain employment benefits." Providing a formal and precise definition can be challenging and become complex (see ILO 2013, 2015, 2018) (see annex 2A for a fuller discussion). The key point about informality in our context is that the vast majority of informal workers share a basic vulnerability, given that they lack protection from abuses, such as nonpayment of wages and risky working conditions, and lack social benefits (such as pensions, sick pay, and health insurance).

In South Asian economies, as in many other developing and emerging ones, the labor markets are dominated by informal employment relationships. In India, the proportion of informal employment in total employment (the sum of unorganized sector workers and informal workers in the organized sector) ranges from 60 to 92 percent (ILO 2016a; Papola 2017; Srija and Shirke 2014; Giri and Verma 2017), depending on sector and type of worker (Shonchoy and Junankar 2014). In 1994–95, an estimated 91 percent of all Indian workers were informal, according to the National Commission for Enterprises in the Unorganized Sector. Estimates in 2004–05 show a similarly high rate: 92 percent of all Indian workers are informal—largely due to a rise in informal employment in the formal (organized) sector.

This high level can be explained by a growing propensity of formal sector employers to offer no contract and by other forms of casual labor (with as much as 79 percent of nonagricultural workers holding no written contract) (ILO 2016a, 2016b; Srija and Shirke 2014). In fact, from 1994 to 2004, formal employment in the formal sector grew by only 6 percent, whereas informal employment in the formal sector increased by 25 percent (Giri and Verma 2017). The widespread use of casual labor in the booming construction industry has played an important role (Shonchoy and Junankar 2014). The share of informal firms accounted for about 86 percent of employment in 2004–05, and dropped to 82 percent in 2011–12 (ILO 2016a, 2016b; Sengupta 2009; Shonchoy and Junankar 2014).

There are also discrepancies geographically and socially. Informality is generally more widespread in rural areas than in urban areas. In 2007, about 69 percent of those employed and living in urban areas were engaged in informal work. At the same time, an astounding 81 percent of those employed and living in rural areas were informally employed. Plus, there is a growing gap between the share of men and women in informal employment.

What might the typical informal worker look like? According to our estimations of informality in India (2011), the average informal worker is employed in the agriculture sector, where roughly 60 percent of all informal workers are employed. He is male and 37.4 years old, even though women are more likely to be employed informally (85 percent of women are in informal employment relationships compared to 74 percent of men). Informal workers are also poorly educated: 46 percent possess only below primary education, and only 5 percent of informal workers have tertiary education. They suffer a wage discount of about 15–30 percent compared to formal workers with the same socio-demographic characteristics. In summary, these estimates confirm that many informal jobs are low-skilled jobs and of lower quality.

As for the other South Asian economies, they also feature high levels of informality. In Bangladesh, we estimate that 85 percent of all workers are employed informally. In Sri Lanka, we find similarly high rates of informality from 2007 to 2015—accounting for about 80 percent of employment—which show no signs of abating. In the private sector, about 75 percent of the 2.3 million workers had informal arrangements in 2007. Meanwhile the semigovernment sector, which accounted for 8.9 percent of all jobs, retained 34.7 percent of jobs informally. Even the public sector had 10 percent of its 700,000 workers working informally.

This widespread occurrence of informality is also reflected in our estimations of job creation and destruction by sector. In India, most new jobs (1999–2011) are informal ones—especially in the construction sector, which has been the main engine of job growth over the last two decades (figure 2.2). By contrast, some other sectors with a positive job balance (like manufacturing, education, or health and social work) produce relatively large numbers of formal jobs. A result worth noting is that the informality rate

FIGURE 2.2 **Most New Jobs in India Are Informal**

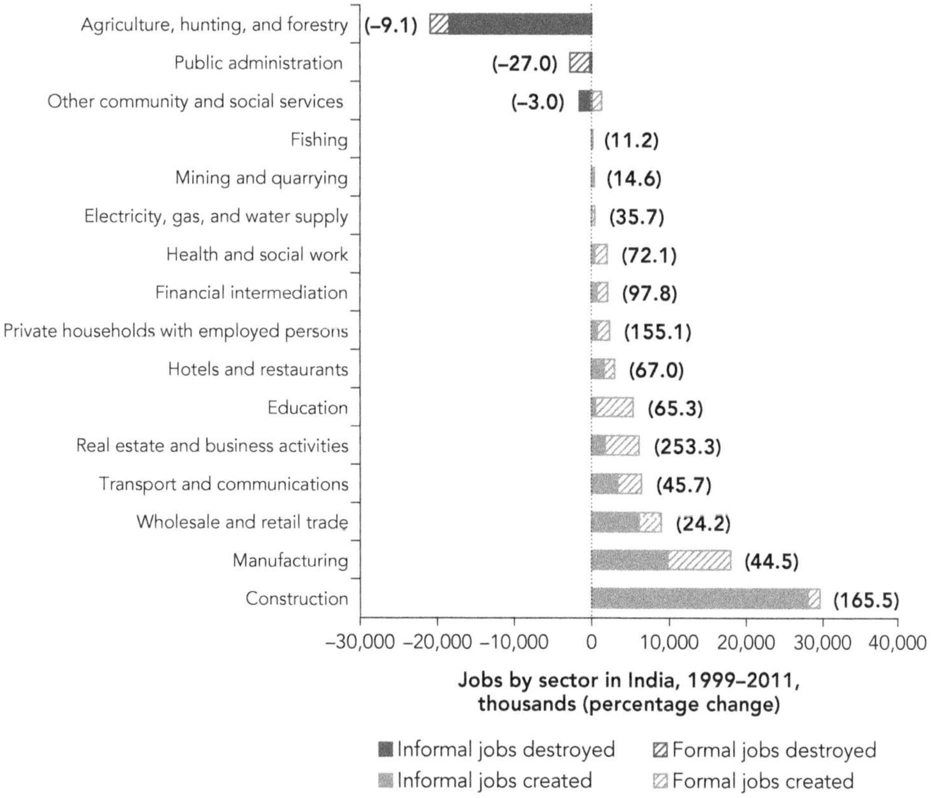

Jobs by sector in India, 1999–2011,
thousands (percentage change)

■ Informal jobs destroyed ☒ Formal jobs destroyed
▨ Informal jobs created ☑ Formal jobs created

Source: Calculations based on data from Labor Force Surveys for India and from the United Nations Population Division.

in India's trading sector lies at 63 percent, lower than the national average. However, this effect comes only from excluding the agricultural sector from our definition of the exporting sector, which has a large share of informal employment. The national average for informality would also lie at about 63 percent if the agricultural sector is excluded (2011).

In Bangladesh, Pakistan, and Sri Lanka, we see a similar picture (annex 2B, figure 2B.1). The vast majority of jobs that have been created are informal. The agricultural sector and the construction sector, two large employers in South Asia, create mostly informal employment. In the manufacturing sector, the situation is a bit more balanced, and up to 50 percent of the newly created jobs in India in manufacturing have been formal jobs. Hence, a shift to more manufacturing jobs in South Asia could lead to lower informality rates. Formal employment relationships are commonly found in the public sector, which can lead to a situation where downsizing of the public sector and expansion of the private sector result in higher informality rates. This situation is demonstrated by the example of Pakistan where formal jobs have been replaced by informal jobs in agriculture and manufacturing.

This (re-)emergence of many low-quality jobs in South Asia takes place in an environment in which these economies are undergoing a massive structural transformation. As part of the normal development process, many jobs in the agricultural sector are shifted to manufacturing and services. Ideally, these new jobs should be more productive, better paid, and of better quality. Exposure to international trade can be an accelerator of this process. Our estimates in figures 2.2 and 2B.1 show, however, that South Asian economies do not fully succeed in moving this transformation process into a direction in which enough good-quality jobs outside agriculture are being created.

CHALLENGE 3: SIZABLE WAGE GAPS

Our second indicator of job quality is the level of real wages (real incomes) and the distribution of wages across groups. Here "wages" refers to all forms of incomes, including self-employed incomes and nonmonetary incomes derived by formal or nonformal workers. Hence, the term "wages" is not restricted to a narrow interpretation in which it refers only to wage incomes derived by formal employees.

How has South Asia been doing on this indicator? Since the 1990s, and especially since 2004, our four sample countries have enjoyed a significant rise in real wages. In India, average (annual) real wages in our sample went up from Rs 47,424 to Rs 76,908 between 1999 and 2011, an average growth rate of about 4 percent per annum—and wages have continued to grow at a similar pace since then (ILO 2016b).[3] But there are large deviations from these averages depending on socioeconomic background. For example, whereas men earned about Rs 83,720 in 2011, females earned only Rs 53,508. Workers in urban areas earned Rs 124,384 compared to Rs 52,312 for workers in rural areas. The biggest differences are based on education: people with tertiary education earned on average Rs 213,668 in 2011, whereas workers with below primary education earned only Rs 38,636.

A first look at the differences among groups shows that some of these differences seem to have become smaller over time. For example, formal workers earned 4.0 times more than informal workers in 1999 and only 3.2 times more in 2011, and workers with tertiary education earned 7.1 times more than workers without primary education in 1999, compared to 5.5 times more in 2011. However, the problem with such one-dimensional comparisons is that we cannot account for composition effects. It might be that other wage-determining factors have led to a reduced pay gap between formal and informal workers. Once we control for all observable factors and run a standard Mincer regression on wages for all years, we find that the wage premiums for specific worker characteristics remain virtually unchanged over time (annex 2C, table 2C.1). All other factors equal, being a man is rewarded with a premium of about 30 to 38 per-cent higher wages compared to women with the same profile. The premiums for higher education also appear to remain stable over time, with completed tertiary education leading to a 70–80 percent increase in wages. In summary, highly educated men in urban areas in formal employment maintained their preeminence as the highest salary demographic over the past two decades. Wages clearly do not equalize across different demographic and regional groups, even when observationally equivalent workers are compared.

How about deviations reflecting a particular industry or working in a particular state? As figure 2.3 shows, all states in India have experienced wage increases since 1999, although there are variations across states for both the levels and growth rates of wages. Not surprisingly, states dominated by the agricultural sector (like Chhattisgarh or Bihar) are at the lower end of the wage distribution, whereas states with a large ser-vices sector (like Delhi and Chandigarh) are at the higher end.

The key here is that such state and industry premiums can be indicators of "seg-mented" labor markets. A lack of labor mobility across sectors and across industries would result in premiums for industries and states. If labor is perfectly mobile, these premiums should decline over time, because workers with the same characteristics would move to states and industries offering higher wages. The correlation of the pre-miums over time should then be small and decline. The reality, however, is that in India industry and state premiums are highly correlated and persist over time. Given that not all industries participate in international trade and industries are not equally dispersed across states, localized trade shocks and a lack of mobility may play a role.

As for the other three South Asian economies, where we have less data, a few trends stand out:

- In Sri Lanka, national weekly real wages rose by more than 113 percent between 1992 and 2015, and 54 percent between 2000 and 2015. Urban males with higher education earn the most, as in India, although the gender pay gap (at 22–30 percent) is a bit smaller.

FIGURE 2.3 **Wage Gaps Vary by Industries and States**

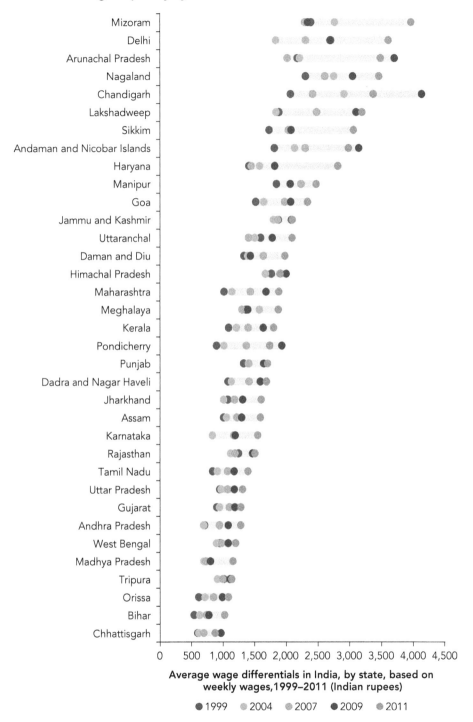

Average wage differentials in India, by state, based on
weekly wages,1999–2011 (Indian rupees)

● 1999   ● 2004   ● 2007   ● 2009   ● 2011

Source: Calculations based on Labor Force Surveys for India.

- In Bangladesh, wages have been growing at a significant and fast rate throughout the last decade. For example, the nominal wages of low-paid skilled and unskilled workers increased by 170 percent between 2004–05 and 2014–15 (BBS 2017).

Trends in South Asian Trade

Although South Asian economies have wrestled with the three major labor market challenges, they have also tried to position themselves to take advantage of globalization. Our four sample countries all opened up to international trade over the past three decades, with exports increasing exponentially.[4] The two main drivers have been (1) trade openness as a matter of public policy, and (2) improvements within comparative advantage. India has tended to specialize in capital-intensive goods, whereas the others have specialized in labor-intensive goods. The big question we take up now, and in the next chapters, is whether international trade has helped lift up the boats of all South Asian workers— and, if not, what can be done to ensure this happens in the future?

INITIAL STRONG EXPORT GROWTH AND RECENT SLOWDOWN

South Asia began to liberalize trade in the 1980s and 1990s, and by 2016 its import tariffs had fallen to close to 10 percent from a high of nearly 100 percent in the early 1990s. As expected, trade increased quickly after liberalization: between 1990 and 2016, Bangladesh's exports shot up by 2,000 percent, India's by 1,500 percent, and Pakistan's and Sri Lanka's exports by 300 percent (figure 2.4). This upswing lost some of its momentum, however, following the 2008 global financial crisis, with its short-lived dip in global trade, and the resulting slow recovery. Still, 2016 marks a historical high for the region.

India. From 1970 to 1990, the Indian economy did not rely deeply on the external sector, which used to represent less than 10 percent of GDP. In fact, India has run a persistent trade deficit since 1980, with imports growing faster than exports as a share of GDP. Exporting sectors grew during the 1990s and even during the 2008 financial crisis, with textiles and chemicals industries the standout beneficiaries. The benefits of trade spread to industries supplying inputs to exporters, and higher export shares went hand in hand with bigger employment shares. Nevertheless, India exports mainly capital-intensive goods, meaning that the direct benefits for employment have been moderate. The 2008 trade shock saw an increase in India's trade deficit, but exports and imports revived shortly, contributing to one-third of economic activity in 2012.

How about employment in trading industries? To answer this, we split the Indian economy into those industries that can trade and those that cannot. We define an industry on a 4-digit level as "tradable" if total global imports of OECD countries in this industry were larger than US$1 million in all five years for which we have employment data.[5] This definition includes industries that may not actually export from India and

FIGURE 2.4 India and Bangladesh Lead the Region's Dramatic Export Growth, 1990–2017

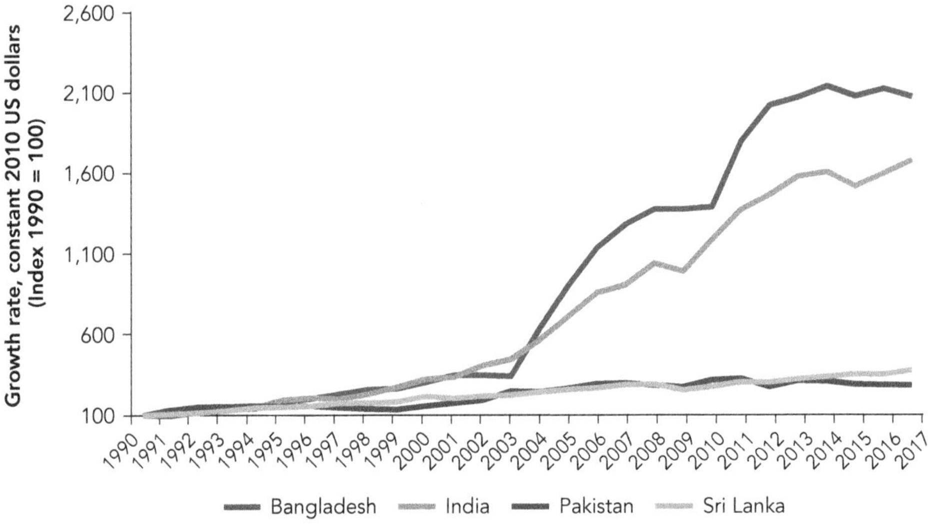

Source: World Bank World Development Indicators, https://data.worldbank.org/data-catalog/world-development
-indicators.

therefore renders as "tradable" most subsectors in agriculture, where most of India's employment is found. Figure 2.5 shows the evolution of employment in tradable sectors in India between 1999 and 2011, excluding the whole agricultural sector (which saw employment fall by more than 20 million workers).

We find that between 1999 and 2011 the total number of workers in tradable industries (excluding agriculture) increased from 45 million (of which 11 million were women) to 63 million (of which 16 million were women). But, compared to overall employment numbers, the share of workers in the tradable sector is relatively small and has increased only from 12 percent to 14 percent. As for the share of women working in the tradable sector, it has increased from 10 percent to 14 percent—which is now in line with the national average of workers in the tradable sector.

Sri Lanka. The economy has enjoyed a significant contribution from international trade even before the large-scale economic liberalization policies were introduced in 1977, which only furthered the predominance of the external sector—especially the import-to-GDP ratio. The 1990s witnessed a steady progression following a second wave of economic liberalization in the country in the late 1980s—with Sri Lanka's exports reaching a high of 39 percent of GDP in 2000. But this share has since declined, and in 2016 exports accounted for only 21.4 percent of GDP.

Domestic factors have played an increasing role in this decline: Sri Lanka—which was entrenched in civil conflict until 2009—has focused on infrastructure development in the postconflict period. External factors have also mattered, including (1) the global financial crisis, which weakened demand in the main export markets; (2) the phasing

FIGURE 2.5 **Employment Rose in India's Tradable Industries, 1999–2011**

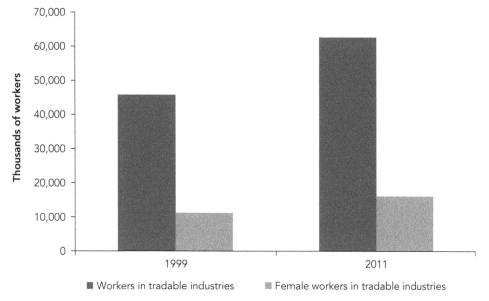

■ Workers in tradable industries   ▨ Female workers in tradable industries

Source: Calculations based on data from Labor Force Surveys for India and from United Nations Population Division, agricultural sector excluded.

out of the Multi-Fiber Arrangement in 2004, which led to reduced access to U.S. markets; (3) the elimination of the GSP-plus (Generalized System of Preferences) scheme in 2010, which resulted in reduced access to European markets; and (4) an overvalued domestic currency, which weighed heavily on Sri Lanka's export performance.[6] Similarly, imports, which had long exceeded exports, also dropped in significance during this period.

On the job front, manufacturing of apparel remains an important employer; it hired 46 percent of all workers in the exporting industries, of which 72 percent were women (2002). However, the relative size of the sector has decreased from 46 percent in 2002 to 34 percent in 2015. New industries in manufacturing and food processing sectors have sprung up in this period with higher export values than in 2002. The second-highest earning sector in 2015 was the growing of fruit, nuts, beverage, and spice crops. Export processing zones have played a large role in absorbing low-skilled manufacturing jobs, with the number of workers in export processing zones increasing from under 10,000 in 1980 to 120,000 in 2012 (Karunaratne and Abayasekara 2013).

Bangladesh. Trade liberalization measures during the early 1980s marked a shift from import-substitution toward an export-led industrialization strategy. In the 1990s, Bangladesh stepped up its efforts, launching a wide-ranging trade reform strategy (including exchange rate policy reform) aimed at easing imports and expanding exports for rapid industrialization, led by the private sector. The result has been a dramatic

FIGURE 2.6 **Bangladesh's Exports and Imports Have Risen Sharply Since 1970**

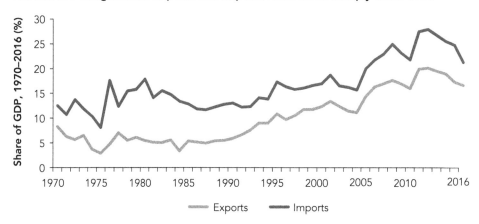

Source: World Development Indicators, https://data.worldbank.org/data-catalog/world-development-indicators.

increase in trade. Between 1984 and 2012, exports grew steadily from 3.4 to 20.2 percent of GDP, whereas imports surged from 13 to 28 percent of GDP (figure 2.6)—although by 2016, exports as a share of GDP dropped to 16 percent.

However, while the export-oriented garment sector has been the main driver of the structural transformation and a main source of employment, only 60,000 jobs have been created annually since 2010 compared to an annual 300,000 new jobs during the previous decade (Farole and others 2017). And domestic demand is increasingly shaping job creation in the manufacturing sector.

Pakistan. After decades of import-substitution policies, Pakistan began adopting export-promotion policies in the late 1980s. Overall, these policies have shown an improvement in absolute terms—thanks to a rapid increase in imports—but not much impact as a share of GDP. In the early 2000s, imports and exports increased as a share of GDP, but much of the import increase was wiped out even before the 2008 global financial crisis (figure 2.7). The key reasons for the poor performance stem from domestic structural issues, including a shortage of human capital; a disparity between electricity generation and consumption, leading to rolling blackouts; and the high cost of doing business (Mahmood and Ahmed 2017), driven by regulatory and security factors.

RELATIVELY LOW TRADE-TO-GDP RATIOS

Despite these political moves toward more trade openness and the successes in rising exports, the economic significance of trade is still low in South Asia, compared to other regions. Merchandise exports in South Asia account for less than 10 percent of GDP, whereas in East Asia and Pacific they account for over 20 percent of GDP, and in Europe and Central Asia 30 percent (figure 2.8). Local spending and consumption have fueled higher growth in South Asia, unlike in East Asia and Pacific, where the emphasis has

FIGURE 2.7 Pakistan's Exports Have Slipped in Recent Years

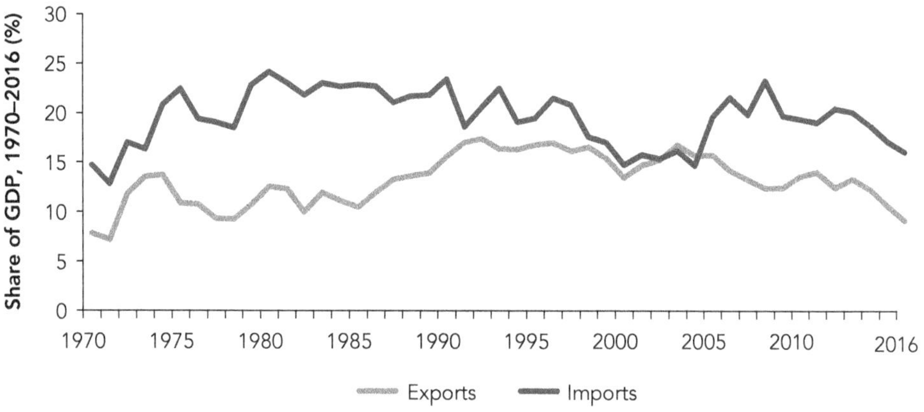

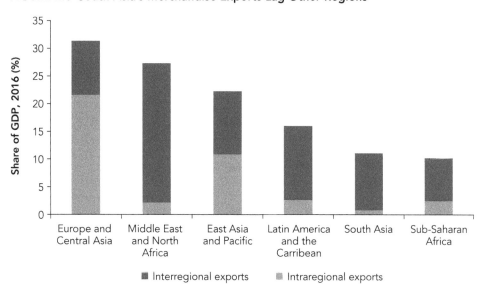

Source: World Development Indicators, https://data.worldbank.org/data-catalog/world-development-indicators.

FIGURE 2.8 South Asia's Merchandise Exports Lag Other Regions

Source: World Development Indicators, https://data.worldbank.org/data-catalog/world-development-indicators.

been on private investment and higher exports. As a result, East Asia and Pacific has enjoyed much higher integration into global value chains and larger trade flows.

However, recent developments suggest a possible improvement in South Asia's trade balance. Import growth in the region is expected to peak in 2018, and moderate to about 6 percent in 2020. Export growth, which underperformed in 2017, is expected to strengthen to 6 percent in 2019. Growth in India is projected to accelerate to 7.3 percent in 2018, and to 7.5 percent in 2019 and 2020, reflecting stronger private spending and export growth.[7] Similarly, Sri Lanka's GDP growth is expected to average about 4.5 percent over the medium term, reflecting robust consumption and investment growth.

GREATER IMPORTANCE FOR INDUSTRY AND SERVICES

South Asia's trade liberalization, export surge, and labor market shifts must be seen against a backdrop of the fast structural transformation that began in the 1990s (Srinivasan 2013) (box 2.1).

BOX 2.1 Structural Transformation and Reallocation of Jobs in South Asia

For South Asia's labor market, this transformation is characterized by a massive reallocation of workers from the agricultural sector to the manufacturing and services sectors, including exporting industries. But the transition is far from complete. Although agriculture's share in total employment has been steadily declining, agriculture is still the largest employer in Bangladesh, India, and Pakistan. But in Sri Lanka services already dominate, employing 3.83 million people, which is almost 47 percent of the total labor force.

In **Bangladesh**, the past 15 years have seen rapid job creation in both the industry and services sectors, resulting in a transformation in employment's share away from agriculture, even within rural areas. Between 2003 and 2013, services (and especially commerce-focused) microenterprises accounted for 90 percent of all new firm entries but just 60 percent of employment; industry accounted for 9 percent of net new firm creation and 40 percent of jobs (Farole and others 2017). Despite this large growth, the overall share in the industrial sector has remained low, hinting at the untapped potential for a further transformation in the economy. And, like in other South Asian countries, most industries (and jobs) remain concentrated at the subnational level—notably, in the Dhaka and Rajshahi markets.

In **India,** about 21 million jobs were lost between 1999 and 2011 in the agricultural sector, reducing the sector's share in total employment by 13 percentage points to 47 percent in 2011. Another sector in which many jobs were destroyed was the public sector, where 2.8 million jobs disappeared. The biggest providers of new jobs were the construction sector and manufacturing, with 29.6 million and 18.0 million new jobs, respectively. Within the manufacturing sector, industries with notable employment increases were textiles and apparel, tobacco, and furniture manufacturing. In the services sector, wholesale and retail trade, as well as transportation, remain big employers in India, creating 9 million jobs and 6.5 million jobs, respectively.

This transition away from agriculture as the most dominant sector has continued (ILO 2017). Services acccounted for 54 percent of GDP in 2017 (CSO 2017), followed by industry (including manufacturing and construction) at 31 percent, and agriculture at about 15 percent. The services sector has been the most successful at creating jobs in urban areas.

In **Sri Lanka**, a similar economic transformation is under way. One major policy initiative was the 200 Garment Factory Program, spearheaded by the Board of Investments in 1992, to encourage garment manufacturers to invest in rural areas (Central Bank of Sri Lanka 2006). Following the success of the program, *Nipayum Sri Lanka* (300 Enterprise Program) was introduced in 2006, which provided tax holidays and duty exemptions on the import of new equipment (Byiers and others 2015). Construction is leading the way for industry (as in India) with the highest increase in employment numbers. It has benefitted from public investment, spurred by the government's decision to prioritize infrastructure development as part of the nation's rebuilding effort.

The South Asian region is an agricultural powerhouse, and our sample countries are ranked among the world's largest producers of many agricultural commodities and agri-based manufacturing industries. From 1990 to 2015, Bangladesh and India doubled their crop yields, and Pakistan managed an annualized growth of over 2.5 percent. Sri Lanka struggled to keep pace with its neighbors because of political economy factors, but still managed to expand crop yields by 36 percent. Similarly, Bangladesh, India, and Pakistan doubled both food production and livestock population, while Sri Lanka boosted food production by 43 percent and livestock production by 71 percent. And, although these countries have had to contend with a burgeoning population and a rapidly increasing internal demand for agri-output, they have still managed to translate higher production into higher export earnings. Even so, agriculture is no longer the dominant force it once was in South Asia, with industry and services increasingly driving the economy.

Although each South Asian country opened up its market in different ways, there are some similarities. Notably, the textiles and apparel sectors have played a leading role in the growth of exports since 1990, whereas traditional exporting sectors, such as agriculture, have played a steadily declining role. What then sets these countries apart is their individual export profiles and how they have responded to the two major trade shocks of recent decades. The first occurred in the early 1990s with first-generation liberalization policies in South Asia—a shock that was internally driven. The second came with the 2008 financial crisis, which began in the United States and triggered a significant collapse in trading activity across the world. The liberalization of trade led to dramatic gains in exports that, for some countries, were coupled with a changing composition of export baskets. The second global financial crisis resulted in a greater concentration of exports in the textile-related sectors.

India. Capital goods production increased by up to 40 percent per year in the mid-2000s, but the collapse in global trade originating from the 2008 financial recession resulted in a slowing down of the expansion. In addition, over 1990–2016, basic goods, intermediate goods, and consumer nondurables witnessed a steady increase of 14 percent per year on average. Chemicals and fabricated metal industries saw the largest gains after the 1991 trade liberalization. Even though the gains from trade were spread across various industries, these two sectors stand alone, accounting for almost half of India's total export growth since the 2000s (figure 2.9). After the 2008 financial crisis, the clear winners have been the textiles and chemicals industries. The share of textile exports grew an average 3.4 percent per year postcrisis (2008–11), and the export share of chemicals rose an average 0.2 percent. However, the exports of all other industries declined.

Sri Lanka. Since its trade liberalization in 1977, Sri Lanka's composition of exports changed considerably, moving away from a reliance on agriculture and into manufacturing sectors (Athukorala and Jayasuriya 2004). In fact, from 1970 to 2007, the share of industrial exports grew to 75 percent of total exports from just 1.7 percent. The textiles and apparel sectors were the most important exporting industries, accounting for one-third of Sri Lankan total exports growth, followed closely by agriculture and mining, and chemicals with 20.9 and 18.0 percent, respectively. In fact, Sri Lanka ranks third in the region in terms of value (US$4.4 million) and global market share (1.2 percent

FIGURE 2.9 **Capital and Consumer Durable Goods Drive India's Industrial Production Rise**

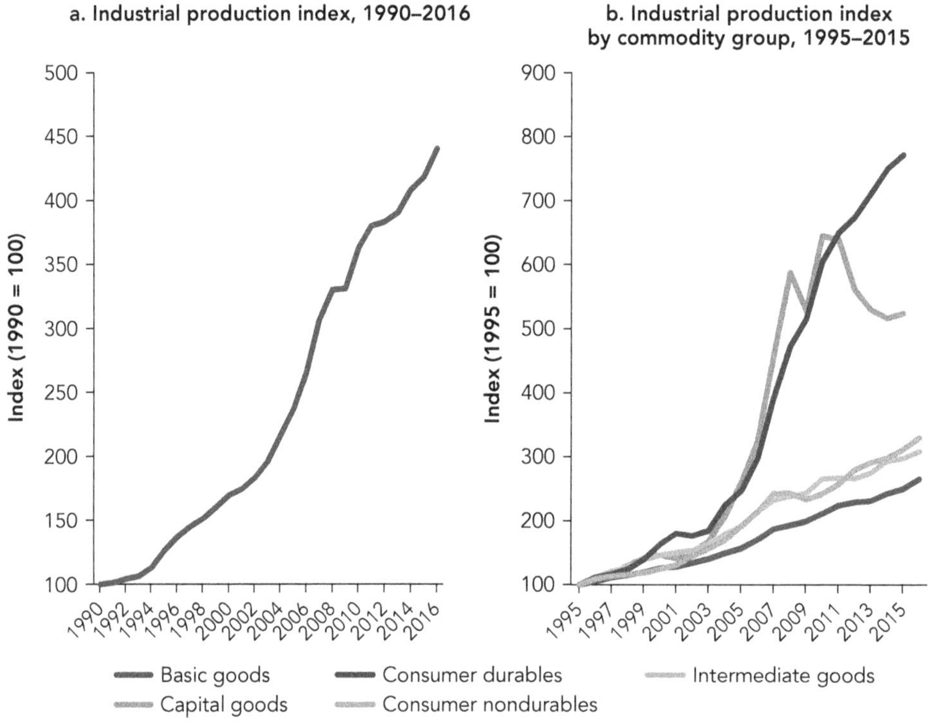

a. Industrial production index, 1990–2016

b. Industrial production index by commodity group, 1995–2015

Basic goods — Consumer durables — Intermediate goods
Capital goods — Consumer nondurables

Source: Haver Analytics database (data provided by national authorities).

in 2012), although the apparel industry has a relatively high share of total merchandise exports at 45 percent (Lopez-Acevedo and Robertson 2016).

Bangladesh. Like other South Asian countries, Bangladesh has a composition of exports that witnessed a dramatic shift as the economy underwent a major economic transformation from agriculture to manufacturing. In particular, the garment sector has been the most crucial industry by a large margin for the external sector, given that it has contributed more than 90 percent of the export gains since 2000. Bangladesh has the largest apparel export industry of all South Asian countries in terms of value (US$22.8 billion) and global market share, accounting for 6.4 percent of global apparel exports in 2012 (Lopez-Acevedo and Robertson 2016). Bangladesh's exports of final apparel in 2013—which have nearly tripled since 2007—amounted to over US$26 billion, making it the second-largest exporter of final apparel in the world next to China (Lopez-Acevedo and Robertson 2016). As a result, this economy's exports are highly concentrated in textiles and apparel sectors.

Pakistan. It also experienced substantial gains in trade during the 1990s, mainly driven by trade liberalization policies. As in Bangladesh, textiles and apparel sectors have been the main drivers of Pakistan's exports, experiencing an increase from US$5.8 billion in 1995 to US$11 billion one decade later. Similarly, agricultural goods, mainly rice, registered significant increases in their exports. Since 2000, more than half of Pakistan's total exports growth is explained by these industries, whereas 18.1 percent was contributed by food, beverages, and tobacco.

EXPORTS HIGHLY CONCENTRATED IN GOODS AND DESTINATIONS

South Asia has tended to send more of the same products to the same destinations. The lack of substantial transformation in the export bundle, a symptom of sluggish innovation, is also revealed by the fact that almost 80 percent of the export growth observed between 2000 and 2014 is explained by selling more of the same goods to the same destinations (figure 2.10).

FIGURE 2.10 **Changes in Export Market Shares by Country, 2000/04–2010/14**

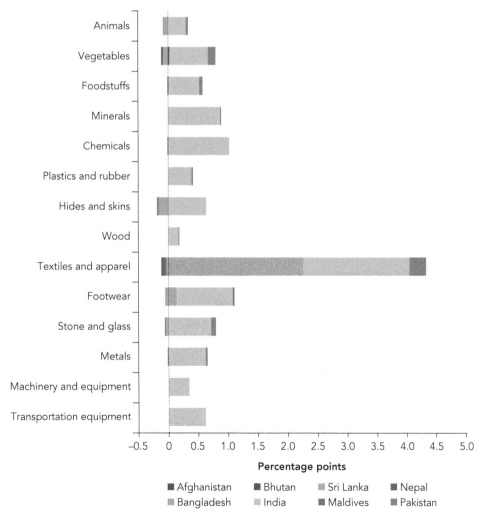

Source: Lopez-Acevedo, Medvedev, and Palmade 2017.

FIGURE 2.11 **South Asia's Export Portfolio Is Less Diversified Than Those of Other Regions**

Country exports from South Asia and upper-middle-income and high-income countries, by sector, 2016

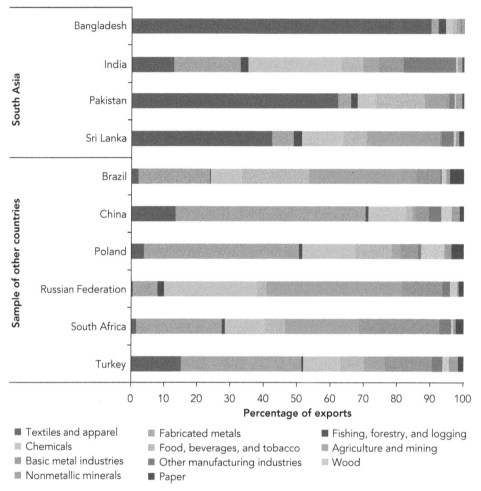

Legend:
- Textiles and apparel
- Chemicals
- Basic metal industries
- Nonmetallic minerals
- Fabricated metals
- Food, beverages, and tobacco
- Other manufacturing industries
- Paper
- Fishing, forestry, and logging
- Agriculture and mining
- Wood

Source: World Integrated Trade Solution database, https://wits.worldbank.org/.

Although traditional trade theory expects, or even encourages, countries to maintain or nurture a certain degree of specialization in sectors where there are definitive comparative advantages—such as fabricated metals in China, or agriculture and mining in the Russian Federation—South Asian export baskets are comparatively less diversified than those of several upper-middle-income countries within other regions (figure 2.11). Given that South Asia is abundant in labor, it would be expected that exports would be labor intensive. However, India, for example, uses more capital-intensive techniques of production in manufacturing than countries at similar levels of development (and similar factor endowments), including China.

South Asia's economies are united by their continued reliance on only a handful of trading partners—and a strong overlap in terms of the main trade destinations. Europe, East Asia and Pacific, and North America are the primary trading partners for the region (figure 2.12). Together, these three regions account for 80, 65, and 55 percent of the exports of Bangladesh, Sri Lanka, and Pakistan, respectively.

As mentioned above, export growth during the last decades has been concentrated in a few industries, which has led to little diversification in export baskets for almost all South Asian countries. Export concentration reveals the extent to which South Asian nations have focused on a small number of export categories in their production matrixes. It is well acknowledged that the lack of diversification in export baskets exacerbates a country's vulnerability to external economic shocks. South Asian nations' trade portfolios differ substantially among themselves, except for the preeminence of

FIGURE 2.12 Europe and North America Are the Key Export Markets for South Asia
Destination of exports by region (%)

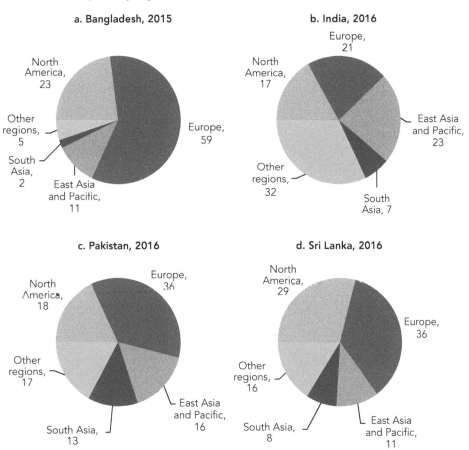

Source: World Integrated Trade Solution database, https://wits.worldbank.org/.

FIGURE 2.13 **Textiles and Apparel Lead South Asian Export Growth**
Industry contribution to export growth in South Asia

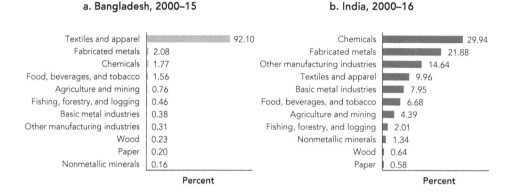

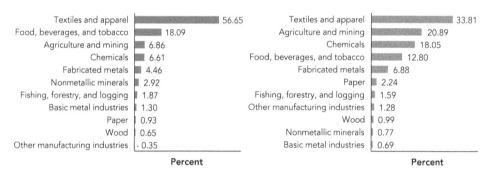

Source: World Integrated Trade Solution database, https://wits.worldbank.org/.

textiles (figure 2.13). India's exports have always been much more diversified than those of other countries in the region. Except in India, the textiles and apparel sector is, by far, the dominant sector in the region's exports, reaching more than 90 percent in Bangladesh, 62 in Pakistan, and 42 percent in Sri Lanka (figure 2.11). In India, textiles come in third after chemicals and fabricated metals. This sector's preeminence reflects the large agrarian sectors and extensive agri-processing industries.

Conclusion

This chapter discusses several facets of the South Asian Paradox. In particular, we highlight key labor market challenges for Bangladesh, India, Pakistan, and Sri Lanka that past periods of strong economic growth have not been able to overcome. We identify the fastest-growing economic sectors in each of the countries and which types of jobs (formal or informal) have been created. Trading sectors have been identified and the chapter shows how countries in the region have chosen different export paths, with India exporting more capital-intensive goods than the others. The role of trade in terms of job creation and other labor market improvements appears to be modest in all four countries, and this raises the question of the further potential of trade to improve labor market outcomes. Geographic concentration of export sectors substantiates the hypothesis that export shocks have local labor market impacts. The next chapter will introduce the methodology with which exports can be linked to various features of local labor markets that have been discussed and described in this chapter.

Annex 2A. Informality

Employment in the informal economy consists of (1) employment in the informal (unorganized) sector, (2) informal employment in the formal sector, and (3) informal employment in households.

The first concept, employment in the informal sector, is determined through the economic unit, that is, the enterprise in which a person works. If this enterprise is informal, the respective worker is employed in the informal sector. As a working definition, we consider enterprises informal if they are not officially registered, have no bookkeeping system, and are not legal entities apart from their owners (see also ILO 1993). Other, similar definitions have been used in the literature: for example, Giri and Verma (2017) estimate the informal economy in India by defining the unorganized sector as unincorporated private enterprises that employ fewer than 10 workers. We do not have original data on enterprises and, accordingly, we cannot base our own estimations of informality on this definition.

The second and third concepts of informal employment are based on the employment status of the worker, not on the firm. Unpaid family workers are usually classified as informal workers. Workers in other employment statuses like own-account workers, employers, or casual workers can usually be classified as informal workers only if additional information is available—for example, whether or not contributions are made to social security systems, and whether workers are entitled to sick leave and paid annual leave. If the answer to these questions is no, the respective workers can be considered in an informal employment relationship. Because of a lack of comparable data, our own estimations on informality are based only on employment status, without taking any additional information into account. The technical definitions for each country are summarized in box 2A.1.

Although informal employment is quite common in most developing and emerging economies, it constitutes a challenge for development and shared prosperity because it correlates with low-productivity activities, low or no social protection, poor working conditions, and limited application of the rule of law including tax and labor legislation.

BOX 2A.1 Technical Definitions of Informality for Each South Asian Country

For *Bangladesh*, the Labor Force Surveys categorize informal employment as a combination of the informal characteristics of an individual job and employment within the informal sector. These constitute (1) all wage and salaried workers with no pension or contribution to a retirement fund, (2) all contributing family workers, (3) all own-account workers and employers in the informal sector (private unincorporated enterprises), (4) all own-account workers employed in a private household, and (5) day laborers. For this report, informality encompasses all employment within the informal sector as defined above as well as all informal jobs (using a proxy of jobs without a written contract), thereby overinflating the number of informally employed. This ensures comparison across years because older rounds of our Bangladesh Labor Force Survey data do not include detailed information on benefits and firm registration.

For *India*, the National Sample Survey data enable us only to approximate the rate of informal employment. By focusing solely on workers' employment status, we can calculate the sum of the shares of own-account workers, family-unpaid workers, and casual workers in the labor force—including employee informal employment in both the formal (organized) and informal (unorganized) sectors. However, this sum does not cover informal employment in its entirety. That is, the employer element of our informal employment definition is likely to be overestimated because we include own-account workers operating in both the formal and the informal sectors. The available National Sample Survey data do not allow us to distinguish between formal and informal enterprises (sectors).

For *Pakistan*, the Labor Force Surveys classify status in employment as (1) employees, (2) employers, (3) own-account workers, and (4) unpaid family workers. For this report, informality encompasses all own-account workers—people working on own-account or with one or more partners at a self-employment job, without any employee engaged on a continuous basis—and unpaid family workers—people working without pay in cash or in kind on an enterprise operated by a member of their household or other related persons.

For *Sri Lanka*, the Labor Force Survey categorizes status in employment as (1) employee, (2) employer, (3) own-account worker, and (4) unpaid family worker. Information on informal institutions is collected from employers and own-account workers. As for paid employees, they are considered to be working informally if they work for an employer that does not contribute to a pension scheme or provident fund on their behalf, or if they are not entitled to paid leave or leave encashment. Unpaid family workers are always considered to be in the informal sector. For the purpose of this report, informality encompasses employers and own-account workers who operate informal institutions, as well as paid employees and unpaid family workers who work under informal conditions.

Annex 2B. Job Creation in Bangladesh, Pakistan, and Sri Lanka

FIGURE 2B.1 **Job Creation and Destruction, by Sector, in Bangladesh, Pakistan, and Sri Lanka, 2001–15**

a. Bangladesh

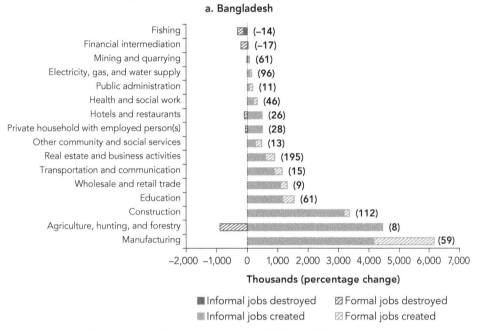

Source: Calculations based on Bangladesh's Labor Force Survey 2005 and 2015.

b. Pakistan

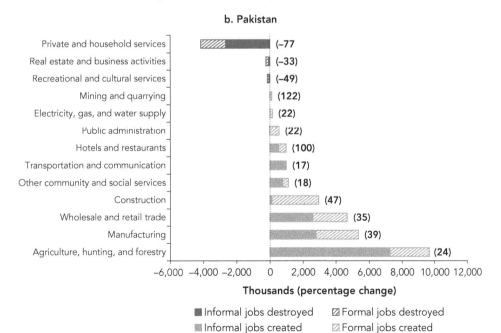

Source: Calculations based on Pakistan's Labor Force Survey 2005–06 and 2014–15.

(Figure continues on next page)

FIGURE 2B.1 **Job Creation and Destruction by Sector in Bangladesh, Pakistan, and Sri Lanka, 2001–15** *(continued)*

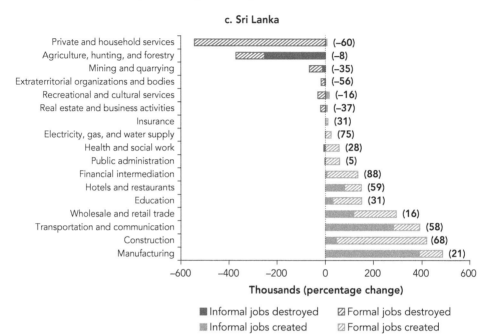

c. Sri Lanka

Source: Calculations based on Sri Lanka's Labor Force Survey 2002 and 2015.

Annex 2C. Wage Regressions for India

Table 2C.1 provides the results of standard Mincer earning regressions for India. We regress the logarithm of real wages on observable worker characteristics such as age, gender, working time, education, geographical location, industry, and sector. We include indicator variables for industries and states and run a standard ordinary least squares regression for each year, using a Heckman selection model. The coefficients can be interpreted as marginal effects on real wages. Industry and state coefficients (not shown) are significant and relatively stable over time.

TABLE 2C.1 **Results from an OLS Mincer Earnings Regression with State and Industry Dummies, India, 1999–2011**

	1999	2004	2007	2009	2011
Male	0.322***	0.381***	0.335***	0.320***	0.348***
	–0.00875	–0.00872	–0.00963	–0.0135	–0.0138
Age	0.0292***	0.0325***	0.0255***	0.0272***	0.0283***
	–0.00126	–0.00144	–0.00133	–0.00178	–0.00212
Age^2	–0.000285***	–0.000325***	–0.000237***	–0.000258***	–0.000274***
	–0.0000161	–0.0000185	–0.0000165	–0.0000217	–0.0000263
Working time	0.0197***	0.0205***	0.0215***	0.0209***	0.0207***
	–0.000178	–0.000184	–0.000184	–0.000299	–0.000332
Urban	0.200***	0.224***	0.244***	0.229***	0.196***
	–0.00953	–0.00852	–0.00814	–0.0109	–0.00917
Married	0.0828***	0.106***	0.0740***	0.0733***	0.0917***
	–0.00683	–0.0074	–0.00744	–0.0099	–0.0107
Primary education	0.0823***	0.0698***	0.0757***	0.0418***	0.0526***
	–0.00864	–0.00776	–0.00814	–0.01	–0.0104
Secondary education	0.230***	0.203***	0.140***	0.169***	0.154***
	–0.00799	–0.00765	–0.00656	–0.00929	–0.00901
Tertiary education	0.768***	0.810***	0.680***	0.811***	0.789***
	–0.0181	–0.0167	–0.0146	–0.0229	–0.0174
Informal worker	–0.287***	–0.191***	–0.178***	–0.188***	0.156***
	0.0106	–0.0104	–0.0109	–0.0153	–0.0135
In the tradable sector	0.0411**	–0.139***	–0.00319	–0.0534*	–0.0656**
	–0.0136	–0.0204	–0.024	–0.0267	–0.0223
Constant	4.025***	3.842***	4.155***	4.386***	4.440***
State indicators	Yes	Yes	Yes	Yes	Yes
Industry Indicators	Yes	Yes	Yes	Yes	Yes
N	392,156	404,090	398,322	325,254	326,650

Source: Calculations based on National Sample Survey for India, 1999–2011.
Note: The table shows the coefficient estimates of an ordinary least squares (OLS) regression as well as the standard errors below. We estimate the informality earnings gap following Tansel and Khan (2012).
* $p < 0.1$; ** $p < 0.05$; *** $p < 0.01$.

Notes

1. More information about South Asian's population growth can be found at the United Nations Population Division database, https://population.un.org/wpp/DataQuery.

2. Labor force survey data for Pakistan are available only for the period 2005 to 2014. We use the first available estimate for the LFPR in 2005 for all calculations pertaining to the period 1999–2004 and the last available estimate of the LFPR for all calculations, including the projections, between 2015 and 2030.

3. We use the Indian Consumer Price Index (CPI) to transform nominal wages into real wages (all India base: 2010 = 100), and we estimate annual wages on the basis of weekly wages reported in the labor force survey for the respective years.

4. Our trade analysis is based on a wide cross-section of data, including comprehensive datasets of national labor force surveys, the United Nations Comtrade Database, trade statistics from the World Bank World Integrated Trade Solution database, World Bank World Development Indicators, estimates for employment modeled by the International Labour Organization, official statistics from national authorities, and the Atlas of Economic Complexity from the Center for International Development at Harvard University.

5. We verified with actual export values from India that these industries of the Indian economy have indeed positive exports.

6. During the 2008–11 period, the Sri Lankan rupee was held constant against the U.S. dollar by the Central Bank, despite a weak current account position.

7. India's cumulative value of exports for the period April–November 2018–19 (projected) was US$217.10 billion versus US$194.94 billion, registering a positive growth of 11.36 percent over the same period last year. In fact, India's merchandise exports reached a level of US$303.53 billion during April–March 2017–18, registering a positive growth of 10.03 percent over the previous year (Directorate General of Commercial Intelligence and Statistics), http://dgciskol.gov.in).

References

Athukorala P.-C., and S. Jayasuriya. 2004. "Complementarity of Trade and FDI Liberalization in Industrial Growth: Lessons from Sri Lanka." 10 Years of ASARC—An International Conference, The Australian National University, Canberra.

BBS (Bangladesh Bureau of Statistics). 2017. "Consumer Price Index (CPI), Inflation Rate and Wage Rate Index (WRI) in Bangladesh." BBS, Bangladesh.

Byiers, B., F. Krätke, P. Jayawardena, L. Rodríguez-Takeuchi, and A. Wijesinha. 2015. "Manufacturing Progress? Employment Creation in Sri Lanka." Overseas Development Institute Case Study Report: Employment. https://www.odi.org/publications/9313-manufacturing-progress-employment-creation-sri-lanka.

Central Bank of Sri Lanka. 2006. *Annual Report 2006.* Colombo: Central Bank of Sri Lanka.

CSO (Central Statistics Office of India). 2017. *National Accounts Statistics 2018.* Ministry of Statistics and Programme Implementation. http://www.mospi.gov.in/node/17651.

Farole, Thomas, Yoonyoung Cho, Laurent Loic Yves Bossavie, and Reyes Aterido. 2017. "Bangladesh Jobs Diagnostic: Overview" (English). Jobs Series, Issue 9, World Bank, Washington, DC.

Giri, Rahul, and Rubina Verma. 2017. "Informality in Indian Manufacturing." Working Paper, February. International Monetary Fund and Department of Business Administration, Instituto Tecnológico Autónomo de Mexico. https://editorialexpress.com/cgi-bin/conference/download.cgi?db_name=SED2017&paper_id=1566.

Government of Sri Lanka. 1995. *Trade Policy Review.* Colombo: World Trade Organization.

ILO (International Labour Organization). Various years. ILOSTAT. http://www.ilo.org/ilostat.

———. 1993. "Resolution Concerning the Measurement of Employment in the Informal Sector, adopted by the Fifteenth International Conference of Labour Statisticians." International Labour Office, Geneva.

———. 2013. "Measuring Informality: A Statistical Manual on the Informal Sector and Informal Employment." International Labour Office, Geneva.

———. 2015. "Recommendation 204. Recommendation Concerning the Transition from the Informal to the Formal Economy, Adopted by the Conference at Its One Hundred and Fourth Session, Geneva, 12 June 2015." International Labour Office, Geneva.

———. 2016a. "India Labour Market Update." ILO Country Office, India.

———. 2016b. "Global Wage Report 2016/17." ILO, Geneva.

———. 2017. "India Labour Market Update." ILO Country Office, India.

———. 2018. *Women and Men in the Informal Economy: A Statistical Picture,* Third Edition. Geneva: International Labour Office.

Karunaratne, C., and A. Abayasekara. 2013. "Impact of EPZs on Poverty Reduction and Trade Facilitation in Sri Lanka." In *Impacts of Trade Facilitation Measures on Poverty and Inclusive Growth: Case Studies from Asia,* edited by R. Ratnayake, R. Ratna, and F. A. Francesca, 275–309. Bangkok: Artnet.

Kathuria, Sanjay. 2018. *A Glass Half Full: the Promise of Regional Trade in South Asia.* Washington, DC: World Bank.

Lopez-Acevedo, Gladys, Denis Medvedev, and Vincent Palmade. 2017. *South Asia's Turn: Policies to Boost Competitiveness and Create the Next Export Powerhouse.* South Asia Development Matters. Washington, DC: World Bank.

Lopez-Acevedo, Gladys, and Raymond Robertson, eds. 2016. *Stiches to Riches: Apparel Employment, Trade, and Economic Development in South Asia.* Directions in Development. Washington, DC: World Bank.

Mahmood, A., and W. Ahmed. 2017. "Export Performance of Pakistan: Role of Structural Factors." SBP Staff Notes 02/17, State Bank of Pakistan.

Papola, T. S. 2017. "Towards Promoting Decent Employment." *Indian Journal of Human Development* 7 (2): 353–55.

Sengupta, A. 2009. "The Challenge of Employment in India: An Informal Economy Perspective." Report of the National Commission for Enterprises in the Unorganised Sector, Government of India.

Shonchoy, Abu S., and P. N. (Raja) Junankar. 2014. "The Informal Labour Market in India: Transitory or Permanent Employment for Migrants?" IDE Discussion Papers 461, Institute of Developing Economies, Japan External Trade Organization.

Singh, Harsha Vardhana. 2017. "Trade Policy Reform in India since 1991." Brookings India Working Paper, The Brookings Institution, Washington, DC, March.

Srija, A., and S. Shirke. 2014. "An Analysis of the Informal Labour Market in India." Special Feature (Confederation of Indian Industry). http://www.ies.gov.in/pdfs/CII%20EM-october-2014.pdf.

Srinivasan, P. V. 2013. "Dynamics of Structural Transformation in South Asia." *Asia–Pacific Development Journal* 20 (2): 53–88.

Tansel, Aysit, and Elif Oznur Khan. 2012. "The Formal/Informal Employment Earnings Gap: Evidence from Turkey." IZA Discussion Paper No. 6556, IZA, Bonn, Germany.

CHAPTER 3

The Methodology

Key Messages

- When it comes to estimating the relationship between globalization and labor market outcomes, the big focus in economic research has been on the impact of falling tariffs or rising imports—whereas hardly any studies have been done on the impact of rising exports.

- Yet many countries have relied on a major export push to boost growth and improve labor market outcomes.

- Our study tries to begin filling this research gap with a new analysis—based on the Bartik approach—that estimates the relationship between exporting and labor market outcomes (like wages, employment, and informality).

- In effect, we look at the flipside of globalization to see how the size of the drawbacks of import competition on labor market outcomes might compare with the potential benefits of higher exports.

Conceptual Underpinnings

Globalization, in the form of falling tariffs or rising imports, has been shown to have significant negative effects on local labor markets in both developed and developing countries. But what happens when the other side of globalization—that is, higher exports—occurs?

This question matters greatly because the most successful developing countries have sought to accelerate growth by encouraging exports—and there is potentially a strong correlation between exports, growth, and labor market outcomes. However, most of the previous empirical studies on trade and labor markets have focused on shocks different from rising exports, such as increasing competition due to China's growth, automation, exchange rates, or tariff reductions.

In our report, we try to deepen our knowledge by exploring what happens when shocks, such as higher exports, occur. This chapter explains how we break new ground by estimating the relationship between exports and local labor market outcomes, such as employment and wages. The challenge is that, when observing simultaneous changes in employment and exports, it is not possible to tell which one drives the other, or whether they are both driven by something else. This means that we need to identify a truly exogenous source of variation to reveal the direction of causality and the precise size of impact. In particular, this variation should be exogenous to local labor markets (such as at the district level in India).

Identifying these effects requires variations across the units that are affected in the localities. If labor was fully mobile, all regions in a country would constitute a single unified labor market, and the regions would not exhibit variation in any labor market outcomes. As it turns out, it is possible to observe variations in local labor market outcomes as a result of changes in export because of the existence of labor mobility barriers—such as commuting costs, language differences, value of local networks, and weak portability of social benefits.

Specifically, we propose a strategy to estimate how local labor markets are affected by exogenous demand shocks to South Asian exports. We ask the following question: How does higher demand from Organisation for Economic Co-operation and Development (OECD) countries (the "trade shock") affect economic outcomes across districts (the subnational level) in South Asian countries?

To answer this question, we use a two-stage econometric analysis (figure 3.1). In the first stage, we estimate the contribution of OECD's import demand to the increase in South Asia's exports. Having an independent (exogenous) variable, such as OECD's imports from the rest of the world, ensures that the chain of causality is flowing in the right direction. The higher demand for exports is measured as rising exports per worker. Because exports can be affected by local conditions, we propose a way to isolate the part of rising demand that is not caused by economic conditions in South Asia. Without the first stage, our estimates would show only correlation, not causation, and they would be biased.

In the second stage, we estimate the effect of an increase in exports on local economic outcomes. These economic outcomes would include informality rates, wages, employment, and wage variance for different worker types (male, female, rural, skilled, unskilled, young, and old). In performing this two-stage econometric analysis, we emphasize two aspects: first, we allow for the endogeneity of exports by using OECD

FIGURE 3.1 Illustration of the Two-Stage Econometric Analysis

OECD import demand affects South Asia's exports, but it is unaffected by economic conditions in local labor market conditions (at the sub-state level) in South Asia. Using an independent (exogenous) variable, such as OECD imports from the rest of the world, determines the direction of causality.

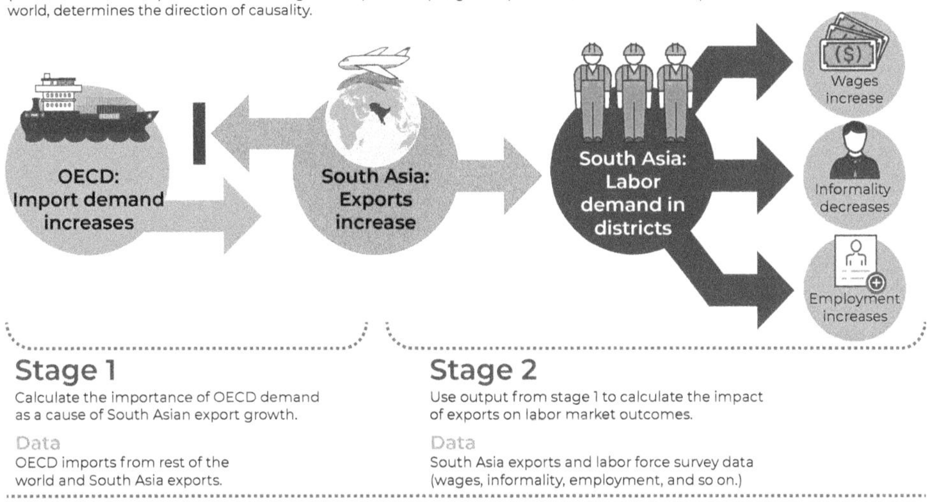

Stage 1	Stage 2
Calculate the importance of OECD demand as a cause of South Asian export growth.	Use output from stage 1 to calculate the impact of exports on labor market outcomes.
Data	Data
OECD imports from rest of the world and South Asia exports.	South Asia exports and labor force survey data (wages, informality, employment, and so on.)

Note: OECD = Organisation for Economic Co-operation and Development.

demand from non-South Asian countries as instruments; and, second, we exploit the spatial variation to estimate the local labor market effects of exports.

Our empirical approach has deep roots in the current economic literature (for a complete list see appendix A). The next section discusses some of that literature, and is followed by an explanation of how our methodology will work, using an empirical example. We conclude by describing how the approach is applied to South Asia.

Literature Review of Methodology

STUDIES ON SOUTH ASIA

Our approach builds upon several recent empirical papers. Pioneering research by Topalova (2010) studies the effects of tariff changes on poverty rates across India's districts (*zila*). The author measures the effective changes in tariff rates for districts by weighting industry-level changes with the number of workers in each district. One of Topalova's (2010) key contributions is to implement an approach proposed by Bartik (1991). This approach takes advantage of a concentration of production and local labor markets to identify the relationship between globalization and local labor market outcomes. More specifically, Topalova calculates the effective change in import protection for Indian districts after the 1991 trade reform. The variation in the author's sample comes from differences among districts in their industry and import compositions. The districts with a larger share of import-competing sectors and sectors with larger tariff reductions are exposed more severely to the trade liberalization shocks. Topalova assumes that tariff reductions are exogenous to the districts, because the reductions were planned by the central government through international agreements.

Several studies have used variations of this approach but have reached different conclusions. Topalova (2010) shows that poverty rates increase (or decrease more slowly) in districts that are more exposed to trade shocks. One concern about the Topolova (2010) study, however, is that the study assumes zero tariffs for nontraded sectors such as services, and includes those sectors in the analysis. In reality, however, nontraded sectors face trade costs that are prohibitive, which is more consistent conceptually with infinite tariffs than with zero tariffs. Hasan, Mitra, and Ural (2007) argue that changing the zero tariffs to prohibitive levels generates results suggesting that trade shocks potentially reduced poverty in India. Although their results contrast with Topalova (2010), in their research they use a similar instrument based on Bartik (1991).

Other studies have also found that local labor markets play an important role in understanding the effects of globalization on labor market outcomes. Using an empirical approach suggested by Hasan, Mitra, and Ramaswamy (2007), Krishna, Mitra, and Sundaram (2010) show that the positive impact of trade liberalization on poverty reduction is less significant in lagging regions in Bangladesh, India, Nepal, Pakistan, and Sri Lanka. In a related study, Hasan and Jandoc (2012) show that trade protection is negatively correlated with state-level unemployment; this correlation is especially strong for states that have high employment in exporting industries.

STUDIES ON OTHER DEVELOPING COUNTRIES

The Bartik (1991) approach has been used in other developing countries as well, and the results show that local labor markets matter. Kovak (2013) uses an instrument based on tariff changes, similar to Topalova (2010), to analyze the impact of trade liberalization on Brazil's labor markets. Unlike previous research, the study uses a semistructural approach based on a general theoretical model. Kovak shows the exact specification for the instrument that is consistent with the economic theory. The author argues that the effects of trade shocks on local labor markets are larger when localities are more exposed to trade through higher producer prices, larger employment shares in import-competing sectors, and higher elasticities of labor demand.

Dix-Carneiro and Kovak (2017) show that the negative impact of trade shocks can have persistent effects that are larger in the long run than in short and medium runs. Pierce and Schott (2016) show the impact of trade shocks on manufacturing employment, and Utar (2015) looks at the wage impacts.

A parallel line of research in the international trade literature focuses on trade liberalization shocks using matched employer–employee data rather than geography-based data. Autor and others (2014) show the effect of the China Shock using both micro-level worker data and firm-level data. A similar methodology was implemented previously by Menezes-Filho and Muendler (2011) to show the impact of trade liberalization in Brazil on employment.

STUDIES ON DEVELOPED COUNTRIES

The Bartik (1991) approach used in these studies has also been applied to developed countries. Hakobyan and McLaren (2016) apply the Topalova (2010) instrument to local labor markets in the United States, using the change in tariffs due to the North American Free Trade Agreement (NAFTA). They find that the impact of NAFTA shocks to the industry-level labor market was as important as the agreement's impact on the local-level labor market. Unlike previous research, they base the analysis on worker data directly via Mincer-like wage regressions with instruments (see Mincer 1958). This modification allows them to specify very sophisticated and detailed regression equations. A follow-up paper by Hakobyan and McLaren (2017) uses a similar empirical methodology (and additional theoretical analysis) to study the differential impact of NAFTA on male and female wages and employment. They find that this gender differential is extremely difficult to explain with standard economic theory or as labor market discrimination.

A methodology similar to Topalova (2010) and Bartik (1991) has been adopted by Autor, Dorn, and Hanson (2013) (henceforth ADH) to study the impact of China's rapid growth on local U.S. labor markets that were defined as commuting zones. ADH contribute to the research on trade and local labor markets in three important ways. First, it is virtually impossible to argue against the exogeneity of their instrument because ADH use growth of China (measured by the change in Chinese exports to countries other than the United States) as the main instrument, rather than a potentially endogenous policy variable such as tariffs. Second, their unit of analysis, commuting zones, is the smallest geographical unit with significant labor mobility barriers. Use of this unit lets them identify trade shocks more precisely compared to previous research. Third, ADH identify one of the largest negative exogenous shocks to labor demand in recent history, that is, China's rapid growth. This discovery attracted a great deal of attention.

Following the success of these papers, the Bartik (1991) methodology, as revised by ADH, has become the gold standard in empirical trade literature for analyzing labor market effects of trade shocks. (See Autor, Dorn, and Hanson [2016] for a detailed literature review of the China Shock.)

Many prominent papers have followed some variations of the ADH methodology. Acemoglu and Restrepo (2017) analyze the impact of automation on local labor markets. Feler and Senses (2017) show the impact of the China Shock on provision of local public goods. Although the focus is employment and earning losses in this line of research, any local outcome—such as mortality rates, poverty, marriage rates, and political polarization—can be analyzed with this methodology.

STUDIES ON LABOR MOBILITY AND IDENTIFICATION OF TRADE SHOCKS

The fundamental implicit assumption behind these studies is that workers are essentially entangled by labor market frictions and mobility costs. Other papers, however, focus explicitly on these costs. One of the first papers about labor market frictions in the trade literature is Artuc, Chaudhuri, and McLaren (2010). They show that workers incur very large costs when they try to change industries after trade shocks. Follow-up work by Artuc and McLaren (2015) shows large frictions for occupational mobility as well. Caliendo, Dvorkin, and Parro (2015) combine the Artuc, Chaudhuri, and McLaren (2010) framework with Caliendo and Parro's (2015) input–output linkage analysis and show that a model with labor mobility frictions can explain the ADH model findings on local labor markets. This paper is critical for understanding the mechanism behind the ADH approach.

If workers were perfectly mobile, labor markets in all districts would be fully integrated into the national labor market. In other words, if workers were not entangled, a trade shock would affect all workers similarly independent of their location or region. Accordingly, we focus on how a change in exports may affect workers in a given region. The effect of a change in exports would be (mostly) contained within the region because the factors cannot move freely from import-competing, industry-intensive regions to export industry-intensive regions.

These papers usually exploit the variation in the trade exposure of districts on the basis of employment shares. For example, regions with high shares of import-competing industry employment are exposed to more intensive trade shocks than districts with high shares of nontraded or export industry employment. This research calculates the impact of tariff changes or export shocks weighted by the employment shares for each district. The employment share of industries in each district is taken from a time prior to the shock to ensure the exogeneity of the shares. Then the papers look at the impact of trade shocks on employment and wage outcomes for districts, with an instrumental difference-in-difference approach.

Quantifying a Positive Demand Shock to Exports: The Case of India

Our empirical approach is similar to these previous studies because we also employ the geography-based Bartik (1991) approach. But our main research question and focus differ because we focus on exports. One significant exception to the traditional focus of the literature (that is, increasing competition due to growth of China, automation, exchange rates, or tariff reduction) is Hasan and others (2012). Although the authors use a measure based on protection (rather than exogenous export shocks), they also discuss the role of export sector employment shares in trade shocks, with a partial focus on export shocks. From this perspective, our study is closely related to Hasan and others (2012) and provides evidence consistent with their findings, despite the use of a different methodology and the focus on different economic outcomes.

How do we quantify exogenous import demand shocks from OECD countries for South Asian exports? Let us take the case of India. A reduction in transportation costs or growth of trading partners' gross domestic product (GDP) could induce an increase

FIGURE 3.2 Illustration of a Demand Shock to India's Exports

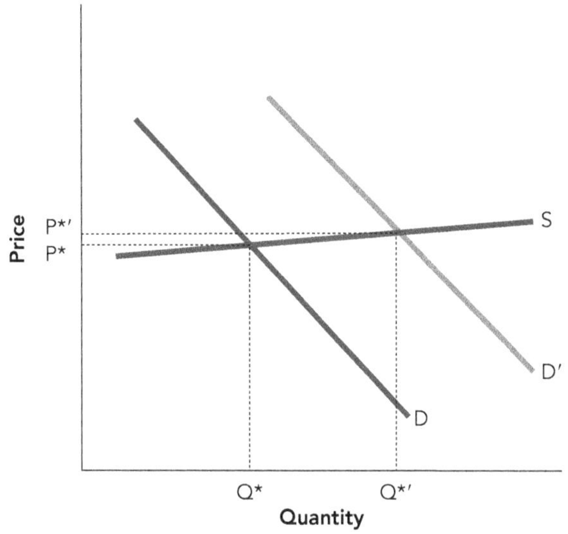

Note: S and D are the supply and demand curves, respectively. After a demand shock to India's exports, the demand curve shifts to the right (D'). P* is the equilibrium price of a representational Indian export good faced by Indian producers before the demand in OECD countries increases from Q* to Q*' and reaches a new, higher equilibrium price P*'.

in the demand for India's exports. This positive exogenous trade shock would material-ize as a shift in the demand curve faced by Indian producers (figure 3.2).

This demand shock has two important characteristics. First, because the shock origi-nates from trading partners, such as OECD countries trading with South Asia, it is exog-enous to local conditions in the districts. Thus, it can serve as a right-hand-side variable in regressions without causing any endogeneity bias. Second, the shock's impact will vary by district because each district has different industry compositions. For example, if the shock is especially prominent for the textiles sector, then the districts with a large share of textiles employment will be more affected than other districts. Therefore, the variation in the exposure of districts to this shock can serve as an identification tool.

In the trade data, this demand shock can potentially be measured by the increase in exports of different industries. For example, if exports increase by Rs 1,000,000 in a specific industry, and there are 2,000 workers attached to that industry, then we can approximate the amount of increase per worker as Rs 1,000,000/2,000 = Rs 500. After calculating this change for every possible industry, we can calculate the effective change for districts using the employment numbers for each industry in each district. There-fore, it is easy to calculate the effective trade shock relevant for a local economy using trade data, national employment data, and regional employment data.

However, there is an important problem with the calculation method described above: exports can increase because of local shocks (such as a decrease in wages, gov-ernment policies, rain, or simply lack of local demand). In this case, using the change in exports can cause a bias in the regression analysis due to endogeneity. To solve this problem, we calculate the change in imports of OECD countries (net of imports from the country of interest), and use this change as an instrument to calculate the exogenous portion of the variation in exports. South Asian exports are relatively small compared to total imports of all OECD countries, and exports of districts are even smaller. Therefore, it is unlikely that the imports from other countries would be affected by local market conditions in the small districts of South Asia.

To explain this with a concrete example, we assume that local market conditions in a given district of West Bengal do not affect total OECD imports from other countries (excluding India). Thus, if exports of a given district in West Bengal show a correlation to total OECD imports, it is attributed to a shock originating from OECD rather than a shock originating from the given district.

In each district, we expect the regional GDP, average wages, and the number of employees to increase after a greater exports-induced demand shock. The mechanism is simple: After a greater demand for exports shock, prices increase. New firms then enter the market, and existing firms increase their capital through investments. As a result, output, wages, and employment increase.

The main goal of the econometric analysis is to find the relation between exports and economic outcomes. In the regressions, each district will constitute an observation. We will calculate the average economic outcome for a given worker type (such as average wage for women) and the change in exports for each district. Then we will show how much of the change in the economic outcome can be attributed to export shocks using the exogenous instrument.

Trade Exposure Index

Consider an economy with many regions, indexed with r; many industries, indexed with i; and many worker types, indexed with s (see box 3.1). The total number of workers

---

BOX 3.1 Slicing the Data by Worker Types

Our rich household-level data allow us to examine the changes in outcomes for many different worker types. Specifically, we consider the following worker types in the empirical analysis:

- Manufacturing and services workers
- Males and females
- Four education groups (below primary, primary, secondary, and tertiary)
- Young and mature (younger and older than 35 years old)
- Urban and rural

in region r attached to industry i at time t is denoted as $L_t^{i,r}$. The industry i imports of OECD from the South Asian country at time t are denoted as M_t^i. We would like to calculate the change in exports per worker driven by an exogenous demand shock originating from outside. Because the export data for regions are not available for the countries of interest, we must approximate regional exports using the number of workers in each industry and the volume of national industry exports. To this end, we adopt the ADH trade exposure index without any modifications.

The change in industry i exports of India to OECD (or imports of OECD from India) between time t and $t + n$ can be expressed as $Q_{t+n}^i - Q_t^i$. Then the change in exports per worker for industry i is equal to $(Q_{t+n}^i - Q_t^i)/(\sum_r L_t^{i,r})$. Thus, we can calculate the effective change in exports to OECD weighted by the labor shares for each region as

$$x_{t,t+n}^r = \sum_i \frac{L_t^{i,r}(Q_{t+n}^i - Q_t^i)}{(\sum_j L_t^{j,r})(\sum_d L_t^{i,d})}. \tag{3.1}$$

Alternatively, we can express the exposure formula as in ADH

$$x_{t,t+n}^r = \sum_i \frac{L_t^{i,r}(Q_{t+n}^i - Q_t^i)}{L_t^r L_t^{i,India}}, \tag{3.2}$$

where L_t^r is the total number of workers assigned to any industry in district r and $L_t^{i,India}$ is the total size of industry i. (We used India as an example, but it can be Sri Lanka). The trade exposure variable $x_{t,t+n}^r$ can be interpreted as the change in exports per worker in district r measured in real U.S. dollars.

Then we apply the same formula using OECD total imports from all countries except India, instead of imports from India, to generate the instruments $z_{t,t+n}^r$. For example, in the districts in both Delhi and Goa, the increase in exports per worker is more than US$900. Conversely, in the districts in Meghalaya, the increase in exports per worker is less than US$25. The underlying data, aggregated at state level, are presented in annex 3A, table 3A.1. The change in manufacturing exports per worker is presented in annex 3A, table 3A.2.

Similar to India, Sri Lanka shows significant variation in the increase in exports per worker across districts. For example, the change in Gampaha is approximately US$100 per person per year, whereas the change in Ampara is approximately zero. The underlying data are presented in annex 3A, table 3A.3. In annex 3A, table 3A.4 presents the change in manufacturing exports per worker.

We find that the correlation between the trade exposure index and the instrument is equal to 0.80—which means that India's exports are highly correlated with the demand in OECD countries (see annex 3A, table 3A.1). How about if we isolate manufacturing as the main traded industry? Here, too, we find that the correlation between the manufacturing trade exposure and the instrument is equal to 0.95 (see annex 3A, table 3A.2). In other words, the manufacturing exports of India are almost perfectly correlated with the manufacturing demand shocks in OECD countries.

DEPENDENT VARIABLES

Consider an economic outcome variable $y_t^{s,r}$ for type s worker in region r at time t. The type of a worker could be male, female, urban, rural, young, old, and so forth. The dependent economic outcome variable can be total wage income (average wage multiplied by employment) in real local currency, average annualized wage in real local currency, wage employment probability, informality probability, and variance of wages in real local currency. We express the change in the economic outcome between t and $t + n$ as $y_{t,t+n}^{s,r}$. Informality is defined as described in chapter 2 and annex 2A. Employment is defined as being attached to an industry with positive reported wage.

REGRESSION EQUATION

We consider a simple linear regression equation using only the sample of type s workers, such as

$$y_{t,t+n}^{s,r} = \beta_0^s + \beta_1^s x_{t,t+n}^r + \beta_2^s y_t^{s,r} + \epsilon_{s,r}, \tag{3.3}$$

where $y_{t,t+n}^{s,r}$ is the dependent variable as described above, β_0 is the intercept, β_1 is the coefficient of the trade exposure variable, and β_2 is the coefficient of the control variable. The district-level trade exposure change, $y_{t,t+n}^r$ is the main independent variable. By controlling time t levels of the dependent variable, we make sure that possible trends unrelated to the trade shock are purged from regressions. The number of observations in this regression equation is equal to the number of regions or districts. We employ a simple instrumental variable specification (which is equivalent to two-stage least squares) using $z_{t,t+n}^r$ as an instrument for $y_{t,t+n}^{s,r}$. The regression tells us how much of the change in $y_t^{s,r}$ between years t and $t + n$ can be attributed to the change in exports per worker driven by exogenous demand in OECD countries.

ALTERNATIVE REGRESSION EQUATION BASED ON INDUSTRIES

It is possible to slice the data on the basis of industries, rather than regions. Because exports of industries are easily available from United Nations Comtrade data,[1] the trade exposure based on industries is simple to calculate. The change in India's exports to OECD countries per worker for industry i between time t and $t + n$ is simply equal to

$$x_{t,t+n}^i = \frac{(Q_{t+n}^i - Q_t^i)}{(\sum_r L_t^{i,r})}. \tag{3.4}$$

As in the previous section, we apply the formula using OECD countries' total imports from all countries except India, instead of imports from India, to generate the instruments, $z_{t,t+n}^i$. The regression equation is

$$y_{t,t+n}^{s,i} = \beta_0^s + \beta_1^s x_{t,t+n}^i + \beta_2^s y_t^{s,i} + \beta_3^s D_t^i + \epsilon_s, \tag{3.5}$$

where D_t^i is a dummy variable equal to one if industry i is tradable, zero otherwise. We define an industry as tradable if OECD countries' total imports are larger than US$1 million (in real terms) at time t.

ALTERNATIVE APPROACH FOR SRI LANKA

The Bartik (1991) approach found in the literature and described above requires many identifiable regions within a country because it takes advantage of differences across local labor markets. For countries with fewer districts (such as Sri Lanka), we modify the regression equation to allow observations for different years to be pooled together. In other words, we group several years together to form time periods. The regression described in the earlier section captures long-run effects of trade shocks, where $n > 5$. The specification with pooled data, where $n = 1$, may not capture the impact of the shock fully because the impact is probably unobservable in the short run. To accommodate a potentially slow response of the dependent variable, we allow lags for the dependent variable.

Consider the following simple linear regression equation using only the sample of type s workers,

$$y_{t+m.t+n+m}^{s,r} = \beta_0^s + \beta_1^s x_{t.t+n}^r + \beta_2^s y_{t+m}^{s,r} + \epsilon_{s,r,t+m},\qquad(3.6)$$

where β_0 is the intercept, β_1 is the coefficient of the trade exposure variable, and β_2 is the coefficient of the control variable. By controlling time t levels of the dependent variable, we make sure that possible trends unrelated to the trade shock are purged from regressions. The number of observations in this regression equation is equal to the number of regions multiplied by the number of time periods minus one.

SAMPLE AND VARIABLE SELECTION

We consider the following dependent variables: the total wage bill divided by the working-age population (as a proxy for regional GDP) employment probability, average wage, informality probability, and standard deviation of wages. The average wage bill, average wage, and standard deviation of wage variables are measured in real rupees (normalized with the 1999 consumer price index). The other variables are measured as probabilities.

The trade exposure index can be calculated on the basis of regions or industries as explained above. We consider a slightly modified exposure index calculated with only manufacturing industries, rather than all industries, to investigate if nonmanufacturing trade drove the results. The exposure variables are measured in real U.S. dollars (normalized with the 1999 consumer price index).

We drop all workers who are younger than 15 years old from the sample. When calculating the trade exposure index, we include all individuals who reported an industry for their main activity. The reported industries of individuals in the National Sample

Survey are mapped to the ISIC3[2] industry codes at the 4-digit level so that the trade data can be merged with the labor data. When calculating the average wage, informality probability, and standard deviation of wage variables, we restrict the sample to the individuals who reported weekly wages larger than Rs 100.

HOW TO READ THE RESULTS

The average wage bill, average wage, and standard deviation of wage variables are measured in weekly frequency. Before reporting the results, we convert wage variables to annual levels by multiplying them by 5,200, so that the results can be interpreted as the predicted change in annual wage due to a US$100 increase in exports per worker. In other words, we report $\tilde{\beta}_1^s = 5200\hat{\beta}_1^s$ for the average wage bill per person of working-age population, average wage, and standard deviation of wage variables. Because we instrument the exposure variables with OECD countries' import data (net of Indian exports to OECD countries), the results are purely driven by import demand shocks originating from OECD countries.

The employment probability and informality probability variables are converted to the number of people, to make the interpretation easier, with the following equation:

$$\tilde{\beta}_1^s = \hat{\beta}_1^s \sum_r 100 \, L_t^{s,r}. \tag{3.7}$$

Therefore, we can see how many more people can be employed if exports per worker increase by US$100.

IMPUTING THE STATE-LEVEL IMPACT

After estimating the coefficient $\hat{\beta}_1^s$, we can calculate the change in the dependent variable that can be attributed to the exogenous import demand shock as

$$\hat{y}_{t,t+n}^{s,r} = \hat{\beta}_1^s x_{t,t+n}^r. \tag{3.8}$$

Then we can calculate the state-level change in the dependent variable due to the exogenous shock as

$$\hat{y}_{t,t+n}^{s,State} = \frac{\sum_{r \in State} \hat{\beta}_1^s x_{t,t+n}^r L_t^{s,r}}{\sum_{r \in State} L_t^{s,r}}. \tag{3.9}$$

Conclusion

Workers are imperfectly mobile both within their regions and within their industries because of significant adjustment costs. A wave of new research takes advantage of labor market segmentation that stems from frictions to identify how globalization might contribute to labor market outcomes—although, to date, nearly all of the studies have focused on the effects of falling tariffs or rising imports. This chapter illustrates how we break new ground by extending this approach to analyze the relationship between exports and local labor market outcomes. It also illustrates how we modify this approach for countries with very concentrated labor markets, like Sri Lanka, and countries with fewer data. The next chapter discusses the results that come out of applying this approach to household survey data in South Asian countries.

Annex 3A. Trade Exposure

TABLE 3A.1 **Trade Exposure of India, by State, 1999–2011**

State	Change in exports per worker (US$)	Instrument z
Andaman and Nicobar Islands	66	2,011,557
Andhra Pradesh	267	12,333,423
Arunachal Pradesh	20	2,060,345
Assam	65	49,373,182
Bihar	49	1,907,329
Chandigarh	548	37,340,151
Chhattisgarh	378	15,581,434
Dadra and Nagar Haveli	1,176	45,230,148
Daman and Diu	845	54,170,240
Delhi	944	49,030,668
Goa	968	60,944,011
Gujarat	525	45,592,547
Haryana	259	16,734,288
Himachal Pradesh	69	3,999,924
Jammu and Kashmir	107	4,236,611
Jharkhand	1,114	52,965,114
Karnataka	354	18,787,627
Kerala	324	14,140,387
Lakshadweep	15	1,746,997
Madhya Pradesh	144	7,172,676
Maharashtra	538	22,057,612
Manipur	73	4,093,908
Meghalaya	22	1,905,724
Mizoram	31	2,012,896
Nagaland	572	−1,605,294
Orissa	176	9,400,889
Pondicherry	762	22,978,829
Punjab	295	12,537,352
Rajasthan	151	7,007,463
Sikkim	42	2,506,310
Tamil Nadu	285	13,376,619
Tripura	31	1,799,578
Uttar Pradesh	137	7,446,280
Uttaranchal	107	5,137,588
West Bengal	580	24,179,006

Note: The table shows the change in exports per worker in U.S. dollars between 1999 and 2011, and the corresponding instrument z.

TABLE 3A.2 **Manufacturing Trade Exposure of India, by State, 1999–2011**

State	Change in exports per worker (US$)	Instrument z
Andaman and Nicobar Islands	0	0
Andhra Pradesh	251	10,239,845
Arunachal Pradesh	0	0
Assam	0	0
Bihar	44	1,678,888
Chandigarh	547	37,035,483
Chhattisgarh	361	14,742,351
Dadra and Nagar Haveli	1,174	45,092,332
Daman and Diu	841	53,700,863
Delhi	920	36,515,216
Goa	913	43,915,612
Gujarat	522	16,776,097
Haryana	258	16,519,479
Himachal Pradesh	63	3,074,562
Jammu and Kashmir	0	0
Jharkhand	1,099	45,969,328
Karnataka	349	18,200,639
Kerala	285	11,652,040
Lakshadweep	12	933,190
Madhya Pradesh	131	6,169,846
Maharashtra	534	19,342,548
Manipur	65	3,528,276
Meghalaya	0	0
Mizoram	23	1,337,953
Nagaland	0	0
Orissa	160	6,900,798
Pondicherry	761	22,545,627
Punjab	293	12,159,664
Rajasthan	148	6,721,400
Sikkim	37	1,376,049
Tamil Nadu	277	12,252,741
Tripura	26	1,392,006
Uttar Pradesh	134	7,238,119
Uttaranchal	102	4,528,669
West Bengal	574	22,362,961

Note: The table shows the change in manufacturing exports per worker in U.S. dollars between 1999 and 2011, and the corresponding instrument z.

TABLE 3A.3 **Trade Exposure of Sri Lanka, by District, 2012–13**

District	Change in exports per worker (US$)
Ampara	0
Anuradhapura	–6
Badulla	19
Batticaloa	–55
Colombo	46
Galle	81
Gampaha	100
Hambantota	20
Jaffna	14
Kalutara	28
Kandy	24
Kegalle	49
Kilinochchi	4
Kurunegala	51
Mannar	–49
Matale	35
Matara	43
Moneragala	13
Mullaitivu	–6
Nuwara Eliya	26
Polonnaruwa	–6
Puttalam	83
Ratnapura	34
Trincomalee	32
Vavuniya	–39

Note: The table shows the change in exports per worker in U.S. dollars between 2012 and 2013.

TABLE 3A.4 **Manufacturing Trade Exposure of Sri Lanka, by District, 2012–13**

District	Change in exports per worker (US$)
Ampara	10
Anuradhapura	3
Badulla	24
Batticaloa	–42
Colombo	48
Galle	81
Gampaha	101
Hambantota	27
Jaffna	17
Kalutara	46
Kandy	25
Kegalle	50
Kilinochchi	49
Kurunegala	47
Mannar	–41
Matale	40
Matara	45
Moneragala	13
Mullaitivu	6
Nuwara Eliya	26
Polonnaruwa	10
Puttalam	87
Ratnapura	35
Trincomalee	37
Vavuniya	–29

Note: The table shows the change in manufacturing exports per worker in U.S. dollars between 2012 and 2013.

Notes

1. For more information, visit https://comtrade.un.org.
2. ISIC3 stands for International Standard Industrial Classification Rev. 3.

References

Acemoglu, Daron, and Pascual Restrepo. 2017. "Robots and Jobs: Evidence from US Labor Markets." NBER Working Paper 23285, National Bureau of Economic Research, Cambridge, MA.

Artuc, Erhan, Shubham Chaudhuri, and John McLaren. 2010. "Trade Shocks and Labor Adjustment: A Structural Empirical Approach." *American Economic Review* 100 (3): 1008–45.

Artuc, Erhan, and John McLaren. 2015. "Trade Policy and Wage Inequality: A Structural Analysis with Occupational and Sectoral Mobility." *Journal of International Economics* 97 (2): 278–94.

Autor, David H., David Dorn, and Gordon Hanson. 2013. "The China Syndrome: Local Labor Market Effects of Import Competition in the United States." *American Economic Review* 103 (6): 2121–68.

———. 2016. "The China Shock: Learning from Labor-Market Adjustment to Large Changes in Trade." *Annual Review of Economics* 8: 205–40.

Autor, David H., David Dorn, Gordon Hanson, and Jae Song. 2014. "Trade Adjustment: Worker Level Evidence." *Quarterly Journal of Economics* 129 (4): 1799–1860.

Bartik, Timothy J. 1991. "Who Benefits from State and Local Economic Development Policies?" Upjohn Institute for Employment Research, Kalamazoo, MI.

Caliendo, Lorenzo, Maximiliano Dvorkin, and Fernando Parro. 2015. "The Impact of Trade on Labor Market Dynamics." NBER Working Paper 21149, National Bureau of Economic Research, Cambridge, MA.

Caliendo, Lorenzo, and Fernando Parro. 2015. "Estimates of the Trade and Welfare Effects of NAFTA." *Review of Economic Studies* 82 (1): 1–44.

Dix-Carneiro, Rafael, and Brian Kovak. 2017. "Trade Liberalization and Regional Dynamics." *American Economic Review* 107 (10): 2908–46.

Feler, Leo, and Mine Senses. 2017. "Trade Shocks and the Provision of Local Public Goods." *American Economic Journal: Economic Policy* 9 (4): 101–43.

Hakobyan, Shushanik, and John McLaren. 2016. "Looking for Local Labor Market Effects of NAFTA." *Review of Economics and Statistics* 98 (4): 728–41.

———. 2017. "NAFTA and Gender Wage Gap." Working Paper 17-270, Upjohn Institute for Employment Research, Kalamazoo, MI.

Hasan, R., and K. R. L. Jandoc. 2012. "Labor Regulations and the Firm Size Distribution in Indian Manufacturing." Program on Indian Economic Policies Working Paper 2012–3, Columbia University, May 2.

Hasan, Rana, Devashish Mitra, and K. V. Ramaswamy. 2007. "Trade Reforms, Labor Regulations, and Labor-Demand Elasticities: Empirical Evidence from India." *Review of Economics and Statistics* 89 (3): 466–81.

Hasan, Rana, Devashish Mitra, Priya Ranjan, and Reshad N. Ahsan. 2012. "Trade Liberalization and Unemployment: Theory and Evidence from India." *Journal of Development Economics* 97 (2): 167–518.

Hasan, Rana, Devashish Mitra, and Beyza Ural. 2007. "Trade Liberalization, Labor-Market Institutions, and Poverty Reduction: Evidence from Indian States." *Indian Policy Forum* 3 (1): 71–122.

Hummels, David, Rasmus Jorgensen, Jakob Munch, and Chong Xiang. 2014. "The Wage Effects of Offshoring: Evidence from Danish Matched Worker-Firm Data." *American Economic Review* 104 (6): 1597–1629.

Kovak, Brian. 2013. "Regional Effects of Trade Reform: What Is the Correct Measure of Liberalization?" *American Economic Review* 103 (5): 1960–76.

Krishna, Pravin, Devashish Mitra, and Asha Sundaram. 2010. "Trade Liberalisation and Lagging Regions in South Asia." Vox, February 13. http://voxeu.org/article/trade-liberalisation -and-lagging-regions-south-asia.

Menezes-Filho, Naercio A., and Marc-Andreas Muendler. 2011. "Labor Reallocation in Response to Trade Reform." Unpublished manuscript, University of California at San Diego.

Mincer, Jacob. 1958. "Investment in Human Capital and Personal Income Distribution." *Journal of Political Economy* 66 (4): 281–302.

Pierce, Justin R., and Peter K. Schott. 2016. "The Surprisingly Swift Decline of U.S. Manufacturing Employment." *American Economic Review* 106 (7): 1632–62.

Topalova, Petia. 2010. "Factor Immobility and Regional Impacts of Trade Liberalization: Evidence on Poverty from India." *American Economic Journal of Applied Economics* 2 (4): 1–41.

Utar, Hale. 2015. "Workers Beneath the Floodgates: Impact of Low-Wage Import Competition and Workers' Adjustment." Unpublished manuscript, University of Bielefeld, Bielefeld, Germany.

CHAPTER 4

How Export Shocks Affect Local Labor Markets

Key Messages

- Our analysis shows that higher demand from Organisation for Economic Co-operation and Development (OECD) countries for imports from India would go hand in hand with higher wages for India's export workers, but would not necessarily mean more jobs.

- If the value of India's exports increases by US$100 per worker, average annual wages would increase by Rs 572 per worker—with the biggest beneficiaries being college graduates, urban workers, and males—but the effects vary greatly among states.

- Rising exports are also associated with falling informality in India—especially for unskilled workers, who benefit less from wage increases compared to others.

- For Sri Lanka, the same pattern holds as in India, with higher demand from OECD countries for Sri Lankan imports boosting wages, but not necessarily creating more jobs.

Introduction

South Asia needs more jobs, better jobs, and higher wages. But, as the 2018 World Bank report *Jobless Growth* suggests, the region's spectacular economic growth over the past decade has not generated enough jobs. In fact, the employment rate has been growing more slowly than the labor force, and informality rates remain stubbornly high. One way to help increase the rate of job creation in the formal sector would be to focus on exports. However, South Asia lags behind other regions in trade—in recent years, trade growth, as a share of gross domestic product (GDP), has been falling.

Against this backdrop, this chapter tries to shed more light on how much of an impact higher exports would have on South Asia's labor markets and which groups of workers would benefit most. In particular, we estimate the relationship between exports and wages, employment, informality, and inequality for different groups—with the focus on the local labor markets.

Why the local and not the national level? We would argue that, because workers are tied to local labor markets, local economic conditions would contribute significantly to local labor market outcomes. In particular, there will be separate (but potentially correlated) labor demand and supply curves in each location, and there will be different equilibrium wages and employment levels. Trade shocks will affect these local labor markets differentially because of variations in the composition of traded industries. The locations with a higher concentration of tradable industries will be more exposed to trade shocks, whereas other locations will be more isolated. Then, one can look at the changes in equilibrium wages and employment levels by district and map them to changes in trade shocks to infer the impact of trade on workers.

Our estimation approach fills a gap in the academic literature. Research and policy papers on local labor markets in the international trade literature usually focus on imports (such as the rapid growth of China and falling tariffs). The independent variable in regressions, also known as the trade exposure variable, captures the growth of China's exports or changes in effective tariffs weighted by industry employment shares in each location. One can think of this exposure variable as the change in trade that is relevant for jobs in each location. For example, if the share of import-competing sectors is large in each location, the trade exposure variable is also high for that location.

For our study, we use a similar intuition but ask a different and novel question: What happens to labor market outcomes when a local labor market receives an export-oriented shock (such as higher demand for exports) rather than an increase in import competition? Specifically, we look at the changes in import demand from OECD countries for South Asian goods, and then calculate their impact on various local labor market outcomes. The independent variable is the change in exports per worker weighted by the industry employment in each location. This is equivalent to the trade exposure variable used by Autor, Dorn, and Hanson (2013) (henceforth ADH).

Our key finding is that a higher demand for South Asian goods from OECD countries should be closely associated with higher wages but not necessarily with more job creation. The benefits will flow especially to college graduates and urban workers. For example, in the case of India, an increase in the value of exports by US$100 per worker would boost wages by Rs 572 per worker. South Asian countries would also see less informality, although income inequality may increase.

How Exports Affect Income, Jobs, and Wages

We begin by trying to estimate the change in the district-level aggregate income in India due to the positive export shocks experienced in South Asia between 1999 and 2011. Because we do not have district-level production or income data, we use the wage bill as a proxy for district-level aggregate output. This proxy is a crude approximation but probably valid given that the wage bill is a constant share of the output in many standard economic models and is calculated by multiplying the average wage by the number of employed workers. We then divide the wage bill by the working-age population to get a number that has the same order of magnitude as average wages (see box 4.1). However, it is important to note that the wage bill divided by the working-age population is different from average wages: the former is a reliable indicator of total output, whereas the latter is an indicator of labor productivity.

For the time frame, we look at a period of 10 years, when the exports increased persistently and significantly almost every year. This significant and continuing increase of exports probably improved growth rates and had aggregate impacts. We can think of an increase in an economic outcome, for example wages, as an economy-wide general increase plus a region-specific increase. Our geography-based methodology identifies

---

BOX 4.1 Our Methodology in Brief

We apply the Bartik (1991) approach and adapt it to analyze exports. The dependent variable in the first regression is the increase in the wage bill by district divided by the working-age population, acting as an indicator of the output increase between 1999 and 2011. Our sample includes approximately 450 districts, and therefore we have at most 450 observations in the regressions. The independent variable is the imputed exports per district to Organisation for Economic Co-operation and Development (OECD) countries. Because the exports can depend on endogenous domestic or local policies, we use OECD imports from all countries (minus imports from India) as an instrument for the independent variable. It is unlikely that local policies in India have any effect on OECD imports from third countries, and therefore the exogenous variation in the demand shock can be identified.

In the first benchmark regression, we use the wage bill calculated with the wage data of all employed workers in our sample. Then we repeat the regression analysis using various subsamples of workers, including workers employed in manufacturing industries, workers employed in service industries, male workers, female workers, workers with education below primary school degree, workers with final degree of primary school, secondary school graduates, tertiary school graduates, workers below 35 years of age (classified as young), workers above 35 (classified as old), urban workers, and rural workers. In table 4.1 in the main text, we report the coefficients for the trade exposure variable (which is equal to a US$100 increase in exports per worker), the number of observations, and the t-statistics. When a coefficient is statistically significant at the 95 percent level, the t-statistics are presented in bold fonts. (For details on the methodology, see chapter 3).

It is important to note that, given that the identification in this methodology relies on differences in outcomes across locations, it does not capture nationwide or average impact of trade shocks.

only the region-specific part of this increase and not the aggregate effect; therefore, the estimated impact is probably the lower bound of the actual impact. If workers were perfectly mobile across districts, the positive impact would spread equally across districts, and we would not see any differential impact. Therefore, the sign of the aggregate impact should be the same as the differential impact, and the size of the aggregate impact should be negatively correlated to the moving costs. Similarly, when we compare the impact on two different worker types, such as males and females, we have to assume that the aggregate impact was the same for all worker types, otherwise the results would not be comparable.

Income. Our results show that average income increases about Rs 178 per person after a US$100 increase in exports per worker, which means that the output increases endogenously because of positive export shocks (table 4.1). Because we are using an exogenous

TABLE 4.1 **How a US$100 Increase in Exports Has Varied Effects on India's Labor Market**
Effect of US$100 increase in exports per worker in India, 1999–2011

		Average income		Employment		Wages	
		N	Estimate	N	Estimate	N	Estimate
All	Change	440	178	440	−488,379	430	572
	T-statistic	440	**(2.35)**	440	(−0.61)	430	**(1.97)**
Manufacturing	Change	312	589	312	627	187	551
	T-statistic	312	**(3.02)**	312	(0.38)	187	(1.76)
Services	Change	437	484	437	−24	412	543
	T-statistic	437	**(2.01)**	437	(−0.10)	412	(1.51)
Male	Change	440	318	440	−17,411	428	655
	T-statistic	440	**(2.54)**	440	(−0.05)	428	**(2.26)**
Female	Change	424	96	424	−314,795	324	361
	T-statistic	424	**(2.62)**	424	(−0.49)	324	(1.41)
Below primary	Change	435	20	435	−645,117	398	−100
	T-statistic	435	(0.47)	435	(−1.02)	398	(−0.74)
Primary	Change	423	169	423	−9,539	227	144
	T-statistic	423	**(2.23)**	423	(−0.07)	227	−0.80
Secondary	Change	437	62	437	−557,460	385	−131
	T-statistic	437	(0.95)	437	**(−2.15)**	385	(−0.42)
Tertiary	Change	373	1,817	373	84,258	239	2,180
	T-statistic	373	**(5.04)**	373	(1.25)	239	**(3.20)**
Young (< 35)	Change	438	137	438	387,575	421	319
	T-statistic	438	**(2.10)**	438	(0.68)	421	(1.54)
Old (> 35)	Change	438	349	438	−721,271	419	1,103
	T-statistic	438	**(3.21)**	438	(−1.88)	419	**(2.46)**
Rural	Change	432	−18	432	−550,512	414	−365
	T-statistic	432	(−0.31)	432	(−0.81)	414	(−1.46)
Urban	Change	401	700	401	164,257	355	546
	T-statistic	401	**(5.00)**	401	(0.87)	355	(1.49)

Source: Authors' calculations.
Note: The table shows the predicted change in total wage income divided by the working-age population in rupees, the number of employed people, and wages in rupees after a US$100 increase in exports per worker. T-statistics with significance at the 95 percent level are presented in bold.

instrument for exports, we are disciplining the direction of causality in our regressions. Thus, the results reflect causation rather than simple correlations. This increase is relatively small but statistically significant. The most prominent winners are tertiary school graduates who experience a significant increase in their income, an average of Rs 1,817 per person. The increase in the wage bill is significant for all age groups and for both men and women. However, it is significant only for urban workers and not for rural workers.

Jobs and wages. After establishing that income, or more precisely the wage bill, increases after positive export shocks, we need to look for the underlying reason: Which channel contributes to the increase in the wage bill—higher wages or more employment, or both?

Our results show that an increase in exports triggered by higher demand from OECD countries increases wages in India significantly for many worker types, but the employment levels stay approximately unchanged. Indeed, a US$100 increase in exports per worker would cause average wages to increase about Rs 572 (figure 4.1)—equivalent to about US$12.70 in 1999 exchange rates. This means that about 12.7 percent of the increase in output is transferred to workers through their wages. The biggest beneficiaries would be tertiary school graduates (Rs 2,180), older workers (Rs 1,103), and males (Rs 655). Females and young workers experience a wage increase, but the magnitudes are smaller compared to those for other workers. And the changes in wages are negative or negligibly small for workers below the tertiary education level and rural workers (see table 4A.3 for detailed regression results).

So why would we get higher wages but not higher employment when standard upward-sloping labor supply and downward-sloping labor demand curves would

FIGURE 4.1 **Largest Wage Rewards Go to the Most-Educated and Experienced Workers**

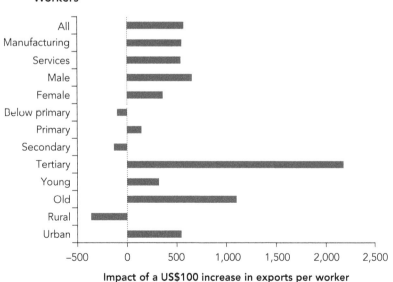

Impact of a US$100 increase in exports per worker on wages in India, 1999–2011 (Indian rupees)

Source: Calculations based on wage regressions.
Note: Detailed regression results are available in annex 4A.

predict both higher wages and more employment? We believe this phenomenon has two possible main explanations:

1. *Large frictions for labor mobility:* Workers may not be able to change their industries or locations. In this case, labor supply would be fixed and inelastic in every industry or district.

2. *Essentially full employment:* When workers have no income support, they have to find work to survive. If they are working in the informal sector, the rise in exports may create formal sector opportunities. As workers switch from informality to work in the formal sector, their wages may rise but their employment status may stay the same.

It is important to note that distortions due to minimum wages are inconsistent with our findings. If true undistorted equilibrium wage levels are lower than minimum wage levels, then a positive demand shock would increase only employment but not wages. Our findings suggest the opposite.

Informality. How about the impact of a positive export shock on informality? Our results show that higher exports reduce the level of informality, especially for male workers and low-skilled workers (those with below primary education) (figure 4.2). Increased exports can explain the conversion of about 800,000 jobs from informal to formal between 1999 and 2011, representing 0.8 percent of the labor force. Low-skilled

FIGURE 4.2 **Higher Exports Lead to Less Informality**

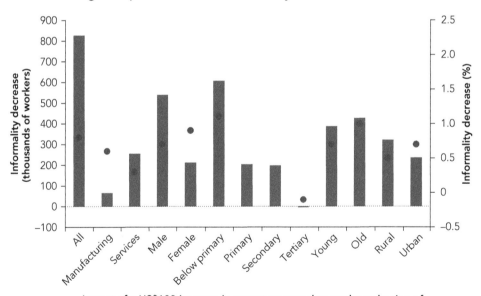

Impact of a US$100 increase in exports per worker on the reduction of informality levels for various worker types in India, 1999–2011 (thousands of workers and percentage)

■ Number of workers ● Percentage (right axis)

Source: Calculations based on informality regressions.
Note: Detailed regression results are available in annex 4A.

FIGURE 4.3 **Higher Exports Lead to Greater Wage Inequality, Especially for the Most Educated**

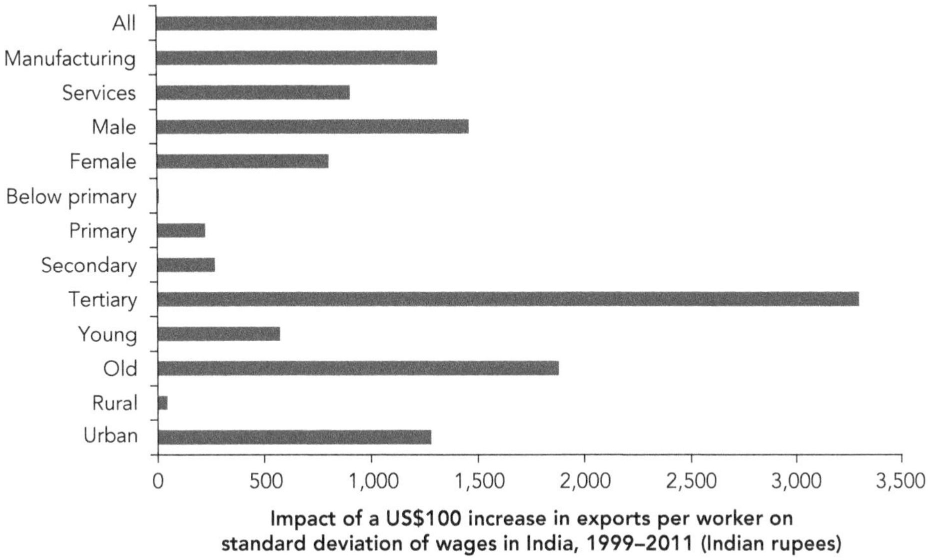

Impact of a US$100 increase in exports per worker on
standard deviation of wages in India, 1999–2011 (Indian rupees)

Source: Calculations based on standard deviation of wages regressions.
Note: Detailed regression results are available in annex 4A.

workers seem to benefit from exports through an increase in formality rates (possibly through social security and other nonwage benefits), whereas high-skilled workers seem to experience wage increases rather than increased formality levels (see table 4A.4 for detailed regression results). It should be noted that an increase in exports per worker leads to a greater formalization rate for females than for males (0.9 percent versus 0.7 percent). However, because the latter constitute a larger share of the workforce, a larger number of male workers is expected to transit to the formal sector after a positive export shock.

The informality results are consistent with the wage and employment results. In an environment without unemployment insurance, workers have very low reservation wages and have to find some employment to survive. As in many developing countries, workers in India who cannot find work in the formal sector often take jobs in the informal sector. Workers in the informal sector take formal sector jobs when employment opportunities arise. In our case, the increase in labor demand from the rise in exports increases wages and pulls workers into the formal sector of the economy. Because the informal workers who move into the formal sector were previously considered employed, there is little or no change in local employment when exports increase.

It is important to mention, however, that the increase in wages and reduction in informality do not seem to be a commonly shared experience by the entire population. Our results show that the impact of a US$100 increase in exports per worker worsens inequality, as measured in figure 4.3 by the standard deviation of wages. Those who experienced the largest increases in wages dispersion are males, tertiary school graduates, urban workers, and experienced (older) workers—whereas those who showed the least are the least-educated and rural workers (see table 4A.5 for detailed results). The increase in demand for workers from the boost in exports, combined with the availability of workers in the informal sector from which to draw, essentially allows formal sector firms to attract workers without having to offer higher wages. The most-educated workers are the least likely to be working in the informal sector and the most likely to be employed: increasing the demand for these workers, therefore, is more likely to translate into an increase in their wages.

Big Mobility Issues at the Industry Level

Next, we add another dimension to our local labor market analysis by moving away from a geography-based analysis to one based on industry. Rather than calculating average district-level economic outcomes and district-level trade exposure, we now calculate industry-level average economic outcomes and the industry-level trade exposure index.[1]

The results for industry-level regressions are consistent with the geography-based regressions. We do not find any evidence for an increase in employment and some evidence for an increase in wages due to the positive trade shocks (figure 4.4) (despite the smaller sample size compared to geography-based regressions). A US$100 increase in exports per worker increased average wages in that industry by Rs 177. The effects are

FIGURE 4.4 Positive Trade Shocks Lead to Better Wages at the Industry Level

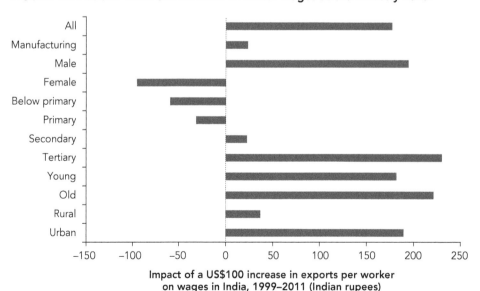

Impact of a US$100 increase in exports per worker
on wages in India, 1999–2011 (Indian rupees)

Source: Calculations based on wage regressions.
Note: Detailed regression results are available in annex 4A.

smaller compared to geography-based regressions, suggesting (although not conclusively) that the mobility barriers are larger across regions than across industries.

It is important to note that this finding can be an artifact of composition effects. The industries could be allocated across districts in such a way that industry-level immobility could be empirically equivalent to geographical immobility. Imagine that there are two industries, one located in region A and the other in region B. Even if workers were perfectly mobile between regions A and B, as long as they are immobile across industries, they cannot move across districts. Therefore, it is impossible to make a conclusive statement about labor mobility through reduced-form regressions. (See tables 4A.6 through 4A.8 for detailed industry-based regression results). We can, however, say that some sort of mobility cost plays an important role.

Exports Have a Bigger Impact in Some States

Yet another way to assess the relationship between positive export shocks and local labor markets is to ask what happens at the state level. This knowledge is important because many policies are determined at the state level, and those policies can magnify or diminish the effect of export shocks. We can perform this assessment by pooling districts that are in the same state. Note that the export shocks can explain more than 100 percent of the change because there are other factors affecting the economic outcomes. For example, exports can increase wages whereas a recession can reduce wages; in this case, the change in wages due to exports can be larger than the actual change, causing an effect larger than 100 percent.

Starting with wages, our results show that exports play a much bigger role in some of India's 27 states than in others (figure 4.5). At the high end, about 15 percent of the wage increase in Pondicherry and Jharkand can be attributed to more exports in response to higher OECD demand. In Gujarat and West Bengal, about 10 percent of the wage increase is associated with higher exports. In Chhattisgarh, Delhi, and Maharashtra, the export-related wage increase is larger than 5 percent. But, in the other 20 states, it is less than 5 percent.

As for informality, greater exports can explain all of the reduction in informality in Delhi (figure 4.6). In Maharashtra and Chandigarh, higher exports reduce informality about 40 percent relative to the total change in informality. But in the other 24 states, exports' role is less than 25 percent. (See annex 4A, tables 4A.9 and 4A.10 for detailed results by state.)

How Our Results Compare with Others

How do our results on India compare with those found by others who use a similar type of methodology to explore trade impacts on local labor markets? In the following

FIGURE 4.5 **Exports Play a Bigger Role in Wages in Some States Than Others**

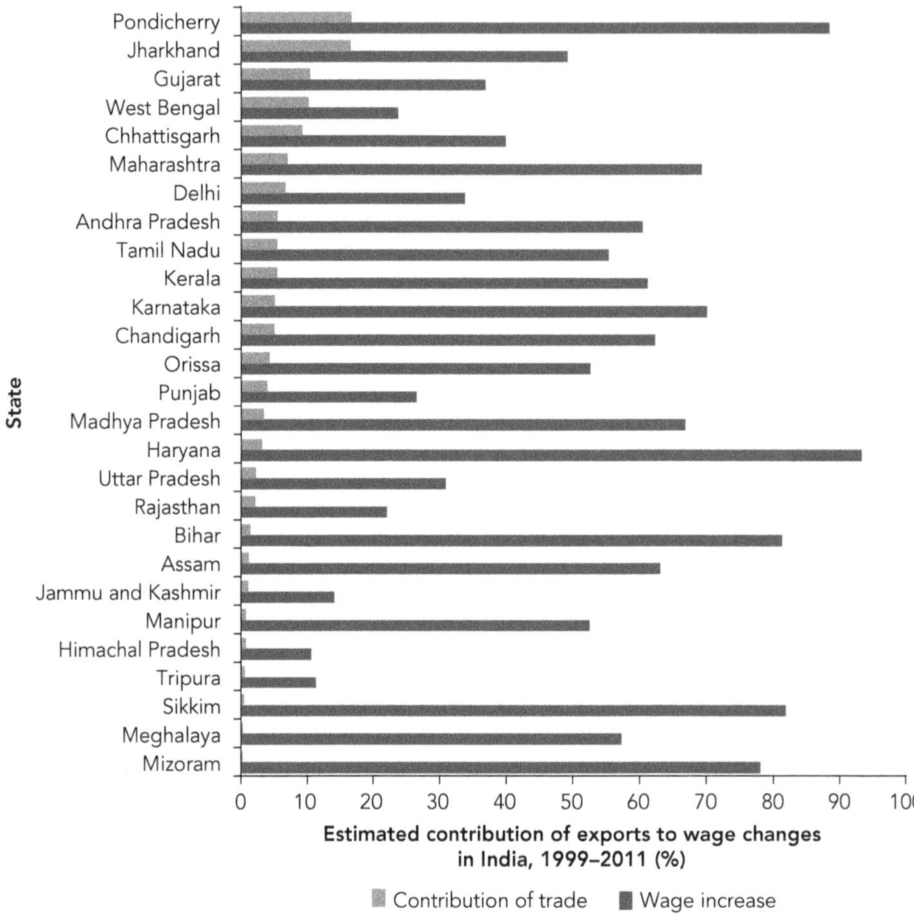

Estimated contribution of exports to wage changes
in India, 1999–2011 (%)

▓ Contribution of trade ■ Wage increase

Source: Calculations based on regressions.
Note: The blue bar shows the wage percentage change in each state between 1999 and 2011; the green bar
shows how much of the wage percentage change can be attributed to more exports in response to higher OECD
demand.

section we compare our methodology and results with those of other important studies,
such as ADH (Autor, Dorn, and Hanson 2013), Topolova (2010), and Hasan, Mitra, and
Ural (2007), among others. We also explain some caveats and important interpretation
issues of the methodology used.

A COMPARISON WITH ADH

We start with the study by ADH, which is the closest to our own but with some key differences. ADH look at an industrial country, the United States, and ask what happened
to local labor markets in response to higher imports from China (a greater import competition shock). Our study looks at the effects in a developing country (India) local labor

FIGURE 4.6 Exports Play a Bigger Role in Informality in Some States Than Others

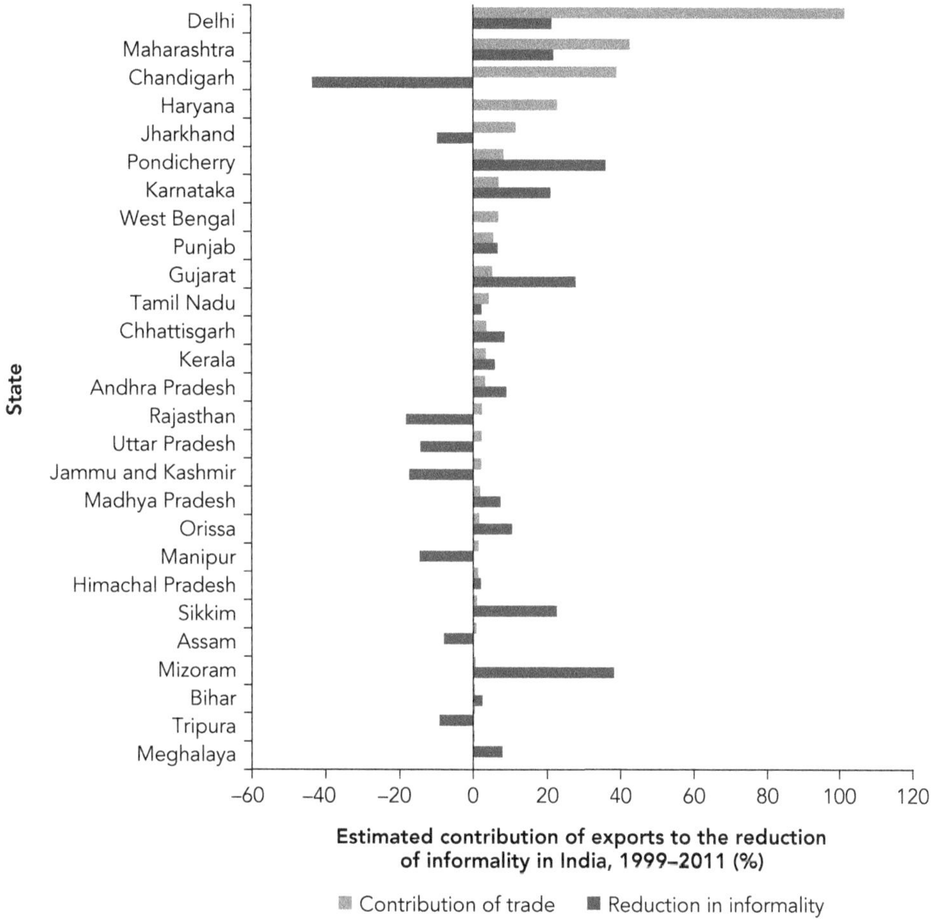

Estimated contribution of exports to the reduction
of informality in India, 1999–2011 (%)

▨ Contribution of trade   ■ Reduction in informality

Source: Calculations based on regressions.
Note: The blue bar shows the wage percentage change in each state between 1999 and 2011; the green bar
shows how much of the wage percentage change can be attributed to more exports in response to higher OECD
demand. A negative value in blue indicates an overall increase in informality for the state—although it should be
noted that export shocks (in green) decreased informality in all states.

market in response to higher exports (a greater demand for exports shock). In an effort
to compare our results with ADH, we divide the changes in income, wages, and employment by their average. We also multiply the coefficients by 10, so that the reference
change in exports is equal to the US$1,000 change in imports per worker as in ADH, as
shown in table 4.2.

ADH find that the U.S. regions with a high concentration of import-competing
industries experienced a significant decline in employment levels but not much of a
decrease in wages. These findings contrast with our own, which find little change in
employment but definite wage increases.

TABLE 4.2 How a US$1,000 Increase in Exports Has Varied Effects on India's
Labor Market
Effect of US$1,000 increase in exports per worker in India, 1999–2011

		Income (%)		Employment (%)		Wages (%)	
		N	Estimate	N	Estimate	N	Estimate
All	Change	440	31.91	440	−1.39	430	19.96
	T-statistic	440	**(2.35)**	440	(−0.61)	430	**(1.97)**
Manufacturing	Change	312	46.33	312	0.02	185	17.59
	T-statistic	312	**(3.02)**	312	(0.38)	185	(1.76)
Services	Change	437	21.85	437	0.00	412	13.02
	T-statistic	437	**(2.01)**	437	(−0.10)	412	−(1.51)
Male	Change	440	34.33	440	−0.07	428	21.55
	T-statistic	440	**(2.54)**	440	(−0.05)	428	**(2.26)**
Female	Change	424	52.2	424	−2.93	324	17.84
	T-statistic	424	**(2.62)**	424	(−0.49)	324	(1.41)
Below primary	Change	435	6.15	435	−3.38	399	−6.19
	T-statistic	435	(0.47)	435	(−1.02)	399	(−0.74)
Primary	Change	423	40.57	423	−0.24	228	6.79
	T-statistic	423	**(2.23)**	423	(−0.07)	228	(0.80)
Secondary	Change	437	8.94	437	−5.71	385	−3.54
	T-statistic	437	(0.95)	437	**(−2.15)**	385	(−0.42)
Tertiary	Change	373	64.07	373	4.29	240	27.32
	T-statistic	373	**(5.04)**	373	(1.25)	240	**(3.20)**
Young	Change	438	31.48	438	2.04	421	14.49
	T-statistic	438	**(2.10)**	438	(0.68)	421	(1.54)
Old	Change	438	47.39	438	−4.46	419	30.71
	T-statistic	438	**(3.21)**	438	(−1.88)	419	**(2.46)**
Rural	Change	432	−4.38	432	−2.04	414	−16.18
	T-statistic	432	(−0.31)	432	(−0.81)	414	(−1.46)
Urban	Change	401	65.01	401	2.18	355	11.89
	T-statistic	401	**(5.00)**	401	(0.87)	355	(1.49)

Source: Authors' calculations.
Note: The table shows the predicted percentage change in total wage income divided by the working-age
population, the number of employed people, and wages after a US$1,000 increase in exports per worker.
T-statistics with significance at the 95 percent level are presented in bold. N represents the number of observations
for each regression.

In particular, ADH find that a US$1,000 change in imports correlates to a decrease in manufacturing employment of 4.3 percent in the United States, whereas nonmanufacturing employment does not decrease significantly. They also find that services wages decline about 0.7 percent, whereas manufacturing wages do not respond significantly. In contrast, we find that neither manufacturing nor nonmanufacturing employment levels respond to a US$1,000 increase in exports per worker, and wages in both manufacturing and nonmanufacturing sectors increase significantly with positive trade shocks. With a US$1,000 increase in exports per worker, manufacturing wages increase about 17 percent while services wages increase about 13 percent.

We believe that the difference between our results and ADH's results is possibly due to the inelastic nature of India's labor supply. Between 1999 and 2011, labor market rigidities, such as lack of efficient social safety nets,[2] might have contributed to the inelastic nature of the labor supply—that is, the lack of responsiveness of the size of the labor force to changes in wages following higher imports from China. Moreover, follow-up work by Autor and others (2014) shows that wages indeed declined after the trade shock; in the later study, the authors focused on wages of individual workers rather than looking at average wages in regions without controlling for selection bias.

Another big difference between the original ADH study and our own is the channel by which the trade shock affects the local labor market. ADH find that the trade shock affects the labor market primarily through employment—and, although wage effects are likely to exist, they are harder to show econometrically. In contrast, we find the opposite: trade shocks affect the labor market primarily through wages. One potential explanation is that the United States has wage supports such as unemployment insurance and long-term disability. Alternative sources of income keep incomes from falling dramatically in times of falling demand, but come at the expense of falling employment. Workers in India, without these support programs, have to find work. The increase in wages we find in India could represent a shift from the informal to the formal sector, while leaving aggregate employment relatively unchanged.

COMPARISONS WITH OTHER STUDIES

Topalova (2010) finds that a 1 percent reduction in tariffs increases the poverty rate by a magnitude of between 0.2 percent and 0.7 percent and reduces consumption (used as an indicator for wages) at most by 0.58 percent in India. Because Topalova's independent variable is the tariff change, the author's results are not comparable with ours in any way. Moreover, Topalova finds that the reduction in consumption is significant in only one out of eight specifications at 95 percent statistical confidence level.

Hasan, Mitra, and Ural (2007) disagree with Topalova's (2010) results for India; they argue that, if one uses nontariff barriers in addition to tariffs and labor market flexibility measures, most of the findings can be reversed. Hasan and others (2012) find that lower tariffs reduced unemployment rates by about 41 percent in states with flexible labor markets and large export shares. Although our results are not perfectly comparable because we look at a different time period and trade shock, they also show positive impact of exports on labor markets, consistent with the findings of this report.

Hasan, Mitra, and Ramaswamy (2007) find that trade liberalization increases labor demand elasticity in India—a result that can be driven by a reduction in labor shares, as argued by Rodrik (1997), assuming the elasticity of substitution between capital and labor is constant. An increase in the labor share (that is, wage bill divided by total output) can be a result of technological upgrading, such as using a more capital-intensive technology and a higher share of skilled workers for production. Therefore, Hasan, Mitra, and Ramaswamy's results are perfectly consistent with our findings: an increase in demand for exported goods in India causes producers to employ more-productive workers or increase the capital-to-labor ratio without increasing employment significantly, which in turn would cause labor share in output to decline and labor demand elasticity to increase. In a related study, Hasan and others (2012) show that trade protection is negatively correlated with state-level unemployment; this correlation is especially strong for states that have high employment in exporting industries.

Pierce and Schott (2016) find that import competition causes labor shares to decline in the United States, which is in line with the elasticity increase suggested by Hasan, Mitra, and Ramaswamy (2007), and also consistent with our findings. Similar to this report, Kovak (2013) finds a significant effect on wages. He reports that a 10 percent decline in prices due to trade liberalization reduces wages about 4 percent in Brazil.

Overall, our results are consistent with studies with which they can be compared. Several other studies produce results that are somewhat different qualitatively, but they are not directly comparable to our study. As such, our results fill an important gap in the economic literature.

CAVEATS AND INTERPRETATION ISSUES

In the previous studies, such as ADH and Topalova (2010), the authors looked at a period with an extreme shock. Although we observe a significant increase in exports of many developing countries between 1999 and 2011, this global shock is probably smaller than the China-specific shock of the same period or the India-specific trade liberalization shock of 1991. Therefore, the variation required for identification is probably weaker in our study. With a stronger variation, we could estimate the coefficients more tightly and would get a larger number of significant coefficients.

If the workers were perfectly mobile, we would not see any impact of exports on labor markets with our methodology. When a positive trade shock hits a district with a relatively high concentration of export industries, wages increase in this particular district. Then workers move into this district from other districts, and the wages decrease slightly after the initial increase, as the marginal productivity of labor decreases. If workers are perfectly mobile, this process continues until the wages are equalized in all districts. Therefore, rather than a large export-concentrated region-specific wage increase, we would see a modest wage increase in all districts. If workers were immobile, then we would see the wage increase in only export-concentrated districts—and there would be some increase in wage differentials across districts. In reality, workers are partially mobile, and there is both an overall wage increase common to all districts and an export-concentrated region-specific wage increase. Our coefficient estimates identify only the changes in wage differentials—that is, the second channel—and thus should be considered as the lower bound.

The estimated coefficients are point elasticities; therefore, they capture the impact of marginal (such as US$1) change in exports per worker. When we calculate the impact of a US$100 increase in exports, we assume that the elasticity is constant, which is probably not true because of general equilibrium effects. However, it is impossible to calculate general equilibrium effects with an empirical analysis, so any assumption about general equilibrium effects would be speculative. Because of the fixed cost of investments (as in Cooper and Haltiwanger 2006) and exports (as in Melitz 2003), it is safe to assume that elasticities would increase as the magnitude of the export shock increases. Therefore, our results are probably lower bounds, yet for another reason.

To identify the import demand shocks, we use the change in exports from non-South Asian developing countries to OECD countries. This change can be driven by import demand shocks in OECD or technological shocks such as developments in communication and transportation technologies. In any case, as long as the shocks do not originate from districts in South Asia, our estimates are unbiased. We believe the policy implications are also roughly independent of the specific reason for the shocks: if South Asian countries were isolated from the rest of the world, they would not be subject to these shocks in the first place. It is impossible to think about global technology shocks without the international trade dimension.

Export Shocks and Labor Markets in Sri Lanka

When turning our analysis to Sri Lanka, we had to rethink the methodology that we used for India. Sri Lanka is not a large country—and thus does not offer a large number of districts, each of which would constitute an observation for the econometric analysis. A country with a small number of districts, and thus a limited number of local labor markets, does not provide enough observations (in other words, finely disaggregated geographical units) to allow us to perform regressions.[3]

We were, however, able to pool time-series data of Sri Lanka to construct a sufficient number of time-district observations, although that raises other issues. One is that export shocks spread within the local labor markets gradually because workers and employers do not adjust to these shocks instantaneously. For example, when OECD countries increase their demand for Sri Lankan apparel products, firms might invest in capital and hire new workers over a lengthy period of time to satisfy the increased demand. This process may take an uncertain number of years—in which case it would be best to look at the data around the time of shock and a few years later. So, when we pool the data of Sri Lanka, we restrict the analysis to short-run impacts, and we are unable to capture more prominent long-run effects. Another issue is that there are possible econometric problems, such as the correlation of residuals due to the pooling of years and districts.

Keeping these caveats in mind, we try to keep the specifications for Sri Lanka as close as possible to those for India for the sake of comparability. We consider various dependent variables such as income, employment, wages, informality, and wage variance. We limit the sample to a subset of workers in alternative specifications to explore differential effects of exports (such as manufacturing workers, services workers, male, female, young, old, skilled, unskilled, urban, and rural).[4] Our results are qualitatively and quantitatively similar to those for India.

Our first question is: What would happen to workers' overall income in Sri Lanka if OECD countries wanted to import more from Sri Lanka? Here, as expected, we find that positive export shocks increase the wage bill significantly for most of the worker types (table 4.3). For example, if there was a US$100 increase in exports per worker, average income would increase by SL Rs 206.

We then look at the impact of export shocks on employment and wages. Here, too, we find that, similar to India, export shocks in Sri Lanka operate primarily through wages rather than employment. As table 4.3 shows, the average wages increase about SL Rs 975 after a US$100 increase in exports per worker. This finding is statistically significant at the 95 percent level (t-statistic is equal to 3.38). The impact of exports on employment is ambiguous because its coefficient is not statistically significant (t-statistic is equal to 0.57).

TABLE 4.3 **Higher Export Demand Raises Wages in Sri Lanka**
Impact of a US$100 increase in exports per worker in Sri Lanka, 2002–13

		Average income		Employment		Wages	
		N	Estimate	N	Estimate	N	Estimate
All	Change	141	206	141	−5,037	141	975
	T-statistic	141	**(2.13)**	141	(−0.57)	141	**(3.38)**
Manufacturing	Change	140	372	141	588	135	837
	T-statistic	140	(0.68)	141	(0.44)	135	−1.51
Services	Change	141	840	141	5,675	141	1,703
	T-statistic	141	**(3.80)**	141	(1.80)	141	**(4.10)**
Male	Change	141	300	141	−6,546	141	1,097
	T-statistic	141	**(2.11)**	141	**(−2.39)**	141	**(4.03)**
Female	Change	141	145	141	1,765	141	795
	T-statistic	141	(1.78)	141	(0.59)	141	(1.80)
Low skilled	Change	141	−69	141	−6,709	141	−152
	T-statistic	141	(−0.98)	141	(−1.30)	141	(−0.53)
High skilled	Change	141	698	141	3,311	141	2,320
	T-statistic	141	**(3.53)**	141	(1.22)	141	**(4.47)**
Young	Change	141	299	141	−5,175	141	1,010
	T-statistic	141	(1.55)	141	**(−2.13)**	141	**(2.64)**
Old	Change	141	181	141	8,130	141	824
	T-statistic	141	(1.58)	141	(1.15)	141	**(2.36)**
Rural	Change	141	289	141	11,561	141	1,156
	T-statistic	141	**(2.82)**	141	(0.73)	141	**(3.24)**
Urban	Change	122	218	141	−3,005	117	1,405
	T-statistic	122	(0.37)	141	(−1.19)	117	−0.85

Note: The table shows the predicted change in total wage income divided by the working-age population in Sri Lanka rupees, number of employed people, and wages in rupees after a $100 increase in exports per worker. T-statistics with significance at the 95 percent level are presented in bold. N represents the number of observations for each regression.

FIGURE 4.7 High-Skilled Workers in Sri Lanka Benefit the Most

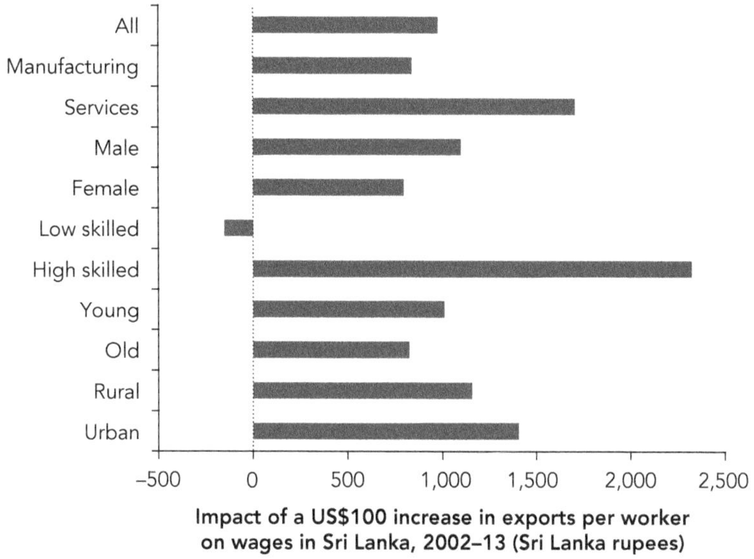

Impact of a US$100 increase in exports per worker
on wages in Sri Lanka, 2002–13 (Sri Lanka rupees)

Source: Calculations are based on regressions.

Which workers benefit most? The largest impact of exports on wage changes is for high-skilled workers, as was the case for India (figure 4.7). Unlike in India, however, we find that both rural and urban workers are affected by the export shocks. In addition, positive export shocks increase the standard deviation of wages, hence the income gap among workers becomes wider (figure 4.8). But we did not find any statistically significant impact of export shocks on formality of workers, unlike in India, although this is probably a result of the data limitations in Sri Lanka.[5] (Detailed results for the regressions on wage bill, employment, and wages are presented in annex 4A, tables 4A.11, 4A.12, and 4A.13; and those on informality and wage inequality are presented in tables 4A.14 and 4A.15.)

Preliminary findings for Bangladesh seem similar to India and Sri Lanka, showing that a positive trade shock affects localized labor markets through higher wages and reductions in informality, and the effects vary among different groups of workers. On the one hand, males, high-skilled, and urban workers seem to experience the largest wage increases. The results for Bangladesh, however, seem greater in magnitude, since a US$100 increase in exports per worker would raise the average annual wage by approximately US$20, while the effect on India and Sri Lanka would be of US$12.7 and US$10.2, respectively. On the other hand, females and younger workers seem to benefit the most regarding informality reductions. Pakistan lacks the sufficient data required for our methodology. Because the results are consistent for Sri Lanka and India, however, we believe it is safe to take policy lessons for all South Asian countries from our findings. Although they face different challenges, labor markets in Bangladesh and

FIGURE 4.8 **Export Shocks in Sri Lanka Increase Wage Inequality**

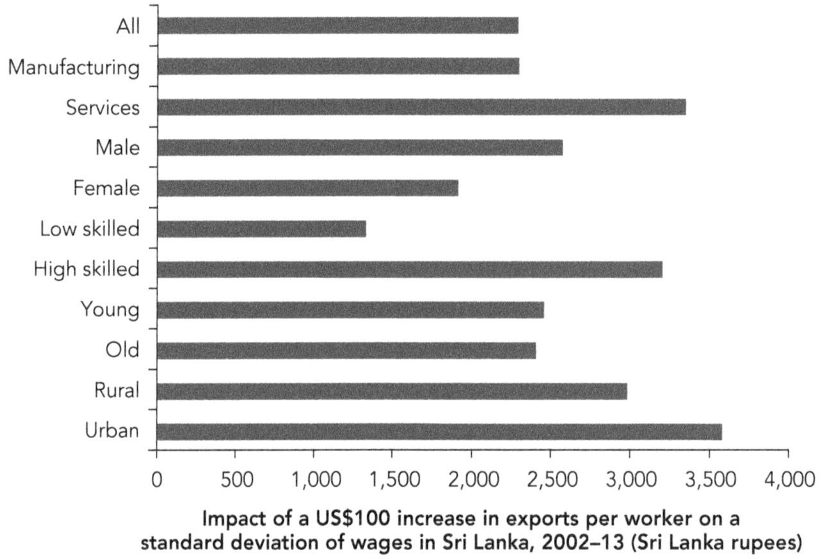

Impact of a US$100 increase in exports per worker on a
standard deviation of wages in Sri Lanka, 2002–13 (Sri Lanka rupees)

Source: Calculations are based on regressions.

Pakistan are more similar to those in India and Sri Lanka than those in other countries (such as Brazil, the United States, and Vietnam), where similar studies have been conducted.

Conclusion

Rising trade is associated with economic growth, but rising trade can come at a cost. Recent studies have shown that rising imports can lower wages and employment, but few studies have focused on the potential effects of exports. Our results, particularly from India and Sri Lanka, suggest that rising exports increase labor demand.

In countries with large informal sectors, workers who are technically employed switch to the formal sector when exports increase. For the lowest-wage workers (who are quite abundant in developing countries), the shift results in a decrease in informality and an increase in wages. For more-skilled and relatively scarce workers (who are much less likely to be found in the informal sector), the increase in demand results in much larger wage gains. In this sense, the results in this chapter illustrate the potential benefits from pursuing an export-led growth strategy: rising formal sector employment and rising wages.

Annex 4A. Detailed Regression Results

TABLE 4A.1 **Total Wage Income of the Working-Age Population in India, 1999–2011**

			1999–2011			1999–2007	
		N	All merchandise exports	Manufacturing exports	N	All merchandise exports	Manufacturing exports
All	Change	440	178	92	440	69	66
	T-statistic	440	**–2.35)**	(1.89)	440	(1.32)	(1.58)
Manufacturing	Change	312	589	597	317	446	434
	T-statistic	312	**(3.02)**	**(3.45)**	317	**(2.32)**	**(2.37)**
Services	Change	437	484	440	437	218	205
	T-statistic	437	**(2.01)**	**(2.71)**	437	(1.29)	(1.48)
Male	Change	440	318	149	440	162	138
	T-statistic	440	**(2.54)**	(1.86)	440	**(1.96)**	**(2.09)**
Female	Change	424	96	86	428	6	18
	T-statistic	424	**(2.62)**	**(3.53)**	428	(0.21)	(0.76)
Below primary	Change	435	20	–7	432	–15	7
	T-statistic	435	(0.47)	(–0.24)	432	(–0.43)	(0.25)
Primary	Change	423	169	106	417	168	151
	T-statistic	423	**(2.23)**	**(2.11)**	417	**(3.06)**	**(3.41)**
Secondary	Change	437	62	31	437	85	60
	T-statistic	437	(0.95)	(0.72)	437	(1.63)	–1.43
Tertiary	Change	373	1,817	1,129	372	784	622
	T-statistic	373	**(5.04)**	**(4.82)**	372	**(4.20)**	**(4.14)**
Young	Change	438	137	129	438	109	100
	T-statistic	438	**(2.10)**	**(3.05)**	438	**(2.21)**	**(2.54)**
Old	Change	438	349	159	438	90	89
	T-statistic	438	**(3.21)**	**(2.27)**	438	(1.15)	(1.42)
Rural	Change	432	–18	–46	432	–48	–40
	T-statistic	432	(–0.31)	(–1.19)	432	(–1.18)	(–1.23)
Urban	Change	401	700	416	401	436	263
	T-statistic	401	**(5.00)**	**(4.53)**	401	**(4.60)**	**–(3.46)**

Note: The table shows the predicted change in the wage bill per person in rupees after a $100 increase in exports per worker. T-statistics with significance at the 95 percent level are presented in bold. N represents the number of observations in each regression.

TABLE 4A.2. Employment in India, 1999–2011

| | | 1999–2011 | | | 1999–2007 | | |
		N	All merchandise exports	Manufacturing exports	N	All merchandise exports	Manufacturing exports
All	Change	440	−488,379	−171,319	440	(772,785)	−840,531
	T-statistic	440	(−0.61)	(−0.32)	440	(−1.02)	(−1.37)
Manufacturing	Change	312	627	580	317	−1,389	−1,491
	T-statistic	312	(0.38)	(0.39)	317	**(−2.86)**	**(−3.18)**
Services	Change	437	−24	−72	437	314	342
	T-statistic	437	(−0.10)	(−0.42)	437	(0.36)	−0.48
Male	Change	440	−17,411	43,912	440	−197,840	−407,123
	T-statistic	440	(−0.05)	−0.2	440	(−0.78)	**(−1.96)**
Female	Change	424	−314,795	−42,109	428	−500,727	−324,023
	T-statistic	424	(−0.49)	(−0.10)	428	(−0.74)	(−0.59)
Below primary	Change	435	−645,117	−263,535	432	−1,334,800	−434,593
	T-statistic	435	(−1.02)	(−0.62)	432	(−1.90)	(−0.76)
Primary	Change	423	−9,539	−27,829	417	−214,011	−140,463
	T-statistic	423	(−0.07)	(−0.29)	417	(−1.36)	(−1.10)
Secondary	Change	437	−557,460	−422,945	437	−450,264	−558,543
	T-statistic	437	**(−2.15)**	**(−2.43)**	437	**(−1.94)**	**(−2.96)**
Tertiary	Change	373	84,258	29,724	372	−42,214	−66,252
	T-statistic	373	(1.25)	(0.66)	372	(−0.81)	(−1.57)
Young	Change	438	387,575	557,224	438	4,264	−242,724
	T-statistic	438	(0.68)	(1.45)	438	−0.01	(−0.63)
Old	Change	438	−721,271	−605,166	438	−675,108	−517,341
	T-statistic	438	(−1.88)	**(−2.36)**	438	(−1.76)	(−1.67)
Rural	Change	432	−550,512	−136,453	432	−411,716	−496,514
	T-statistic	432	(−0.81)	(−0.30)	432	(−0.63)	(−0.93)
Urban	Change	401	164,257	150,340	401	−36,196	1,578
	T-statistic	401	(0.87)	(1.17)	401	(−0.21)	(0.01)

Note: The table shows the predicted change in total employment after a $100 increase in exports per worker. T-statistics with significance at the 95 percent level are presented in bold. N represents the number of observations in each regression.

TABLE 4A.3 **Wages in India, 1999–2011**

			1999–2011			1999–2007	
		N	All merchandise exports	Manufacturing exports	N	All merchandise exports	Manufacturing exports
All	Change	430	572	462	430	652	433
	T-statistic	430	**(1.97)**	**(2.36)**	430	**(3.02)**	**(2.47)**
Manufacturing	Change	185	551	517	187	515	544
	T-statistic	185	(1.76)	(1.82)	187	(1.91)	**(2.10)**
Services	Change	412	543	655	412	714	232
	T-statistic	412	(1.51)	**(2.71)**	412	**(2.90)**	(1.17)
Male	Change	428	655	521	428	815	491
	T-statistic	428	**(2.26)**	**(2.67)**	428	**(3.82)**	**(2.86)**
Female	Change	324	361	336	324	107	144
	T-statistic	324	(1.41)	**(1.98)**	324	(0.41)	(0.68)
Below primary	Change	399	−100	−77	398	−11	9
	T-statistic	399	(−0.74)	(−0.85)	398	(−0.06)	(0.06)
Primary	Change	228	144	213	227	318	261
	T-statistic	228	(0.80)	(1.80)	227	**(2.54)**	**(2.59)**
Secondary	Change	385	−131	−73	385	211	37
	T-statistic	385	(−0.42)	(−0.35)	385	(1.24)	(0.27)
Tertiary	Change	240	2,180	1,983	239	2,076	1,727
	T-statistic	240	**(3.20)**	**(3.78)**	239	**(3.67)**	**(3.46)**
Young	Change	421	319	398	421	823	559
	T-statistic	421	(1.54)	**(2.84)**	421	**(5.06)**	**(4.27)**
Old	Change	419	1,103	794	419	574	379
	T-statistic	419	**(2.46)**	**(2.64)**	419	**(2.14)**	(1.75)
Rural	Change	414	−365	−325	414	−27	−183
	T-statistic	414	(−1.46)	(−1.94)	414	(−0.18)	(−1.55)
Urban	Change	355	546	809	355	365	245
	T-statistic	355	(1.49)	**(2.59)**	355	(1.20)	(0.86)

Note: The table shows the predicted change in the average wage in rupees after a $100 increase in exports per worker. T-statistics with significance at the 95 percent level are presented in bold. N represents the number of observations in each regression.

TABLE 4A.4 **Informality in India, 1999–2011**

			1999–2011			1999–2007	
		N	All merchandise exports	Manufacturing exports	N	All merchandise exports	Manufacturing exports
All	Change	429	−826,599	−777,630	427	−180,569	−55,099
	T-statistic	429	**(−2.26)**	**(−3.21)**	427	(−0.56)	(−0.21)
Manufacturing	Change	165	−65,321	−21,907	172	38,324	36,504
	T-statistic	165	(−1.11)	(−0.42)	172	−0.67	(0.66)
Services	Change	408	−254,964	−364,029	404	−168,931	78,487
	T-statistic	408	(−1.44)	**(−3.07)**	404	(−1.14)	(0.65)
Male	Change	427	−539,326	−592,515	426	−186,743	−13,767
	T-statistic	427	(−1.84)	**(−3.05)**	426	(−0.72)	(−0.07)
Female	Change	306	−211,984	−134,554	315	−31,000	−76,732
	T-statistic	306	(−1.83)	(−1.79)	315	(−0.33)	(−1.01)
Below primary	Change	397	−607,551	−417,418	394	−114,412	−196,089
	T-statistic	397	**(−3.48)**	**(−3.62)**	394	(−0.71)	(−1.48)
Primary	Change	227	−203,675	−138,872	223	−95,862	−36,835
	T-statistic	227	**(−4.36)**	**(−4.68)**	223	**(−2.21)**	(−1.06)
Secondary	Change	376	−198,184	−254,272	379	−147,685	−71,590
	T-statistic	376	(−1.48)	**(−2.87)**	379	(−1.24)	(−0.74)
Tertiary	Change	70	4,087	941	98	3,232	−330
	T-statistic	70	(0.42)	−0.11	98	(0.20)	(−0.02)
Young	Change	417	−387,437	−454,308	419	−186,473	−98,001
	T-statistic	417	(−1.68)	**(−2.98)**	419	(−0.90)	(−0.59)
Old	Change	418	−426,861	−332,106	416	−21,513	32,525
	T-statistic	418	**(−2.53)**	**(−2.98)**	416	(−0.14)	−0.27
Rural	Change	409	−320,821	−236,294	410	41,270	48,714
	T-statistic	409	(−1.29)	(−1.42)	410	(0.19)	(0.28)
Urban	Change	341	−236,176	−217,939	336	132,367	159,019
	T-statistic	341	**(−2.25)**	**(−2.42)**	336	(1.12)	(1.41)

Note: The table shows the predicted change in informality after a $100 increase in exports per worker. T-statistics with significance at the 95 percent level are presented in bold. N represents the number of observations in each regression.

TABLE 4A.5 **Standard Deviation of Wages in India, 1999–2011**

			1999–2011			1999–2007	
		N	All merchandise exports	Manufacturing exports	N	All merchandise exports	Manufacturing exports
All	Change	430	1,313	941	430	2,632	1,700
	T-statistic	430	**(2.07)**	**(2.21)**	430	**(3.85)**	**(3.08)**
Manufacturing	Change	185	1,312	1,341	185	2,480	2,347
	T-statistic	185	**(2.42)**	**(2.72)**	185	**(2.06)**	**(2.03)**
Services	Change	412	903	889	412	1,521	1,275
	T-statistic	412	(1.42)	**(2.07)**	412	**(2.46)**	**(2.53)**
Male	Change	428	1,462	1,004	428	2,790	1,860
	T-statistic	428	**(2.09)**	**(2.14)**	428	**(3.74)**	**(3.08)**
Female	Change	322	804	865	324	688	179
	T-statistic	322	**(2.11)**	**(3.45)**	324	**(1.97)**	(0.64)
Below primary	Change	397	10	47	394	99	152
	T-statistic	397	(0.06)	(0.46)	394	(1.08)	(2.03)
Primary	Change	227	225	359	225	416	125
	T-statistic	227	(0.84)	**(2.05)**	225	**(2.02)**	(0.76)
Secondary	Change	385	270	37	385	1,267	221
	T-statistic	385	(0.33)	(0.07)	385	**(5.66)**	–(1.30)
Tertiary	Change	240	3,298	2,422	239	4,080	3,784
	T-statistic	240	**(4.41)**	**(4.30)**	239	**(2.23)**	**(2.35)**
Young	Change	421	574	717	421	1,737	1,107
	T-statistic	421	(1.82)	**(3.38)**	421	**(7.71)**	**(6.23)**
Old	Change	419	1,881	1,307	419	3,372	2,296
	T-statistic	419	**(2.38)**	**(2.47)**	419	**(3.05)**	**(2.56)**
Rural	Change	414	45	–170	414	233	–44
	T-statistic	414	(0.13)	(–0.75)	414	(1.08)	(–0.25)
Urban	Change	355	1,280	1,292	355	1,954	1,800
	T-statistic	355	**(2,00)**	**(2.37)**	355	**(3.01)**	**(2.97)**

Note: The table shows the predicted change in the standard deviation of wages in rupees after a $100 increase in exports per worker. T-statistics with significance at the 95 percent level are presented in bold. N represents the number of observations in each regression.

TABLE 4A.6 **Wages in India (Industry Regressions), 1999–2011**

| | | | 1999–2011 | | | 1999–2007 | |
		N	All merchandise exports	Tradable dummy	N	All merchandise exports	Tradable dummy
All	Change	279	177	−21,018	283	47	−9,848
	T-statistic	279	**(3.15)**	**(−3.18)**	283	(1.37)	**(−2.34)**
Manufacturing	Change	126	23	−16,726	127	14	1,754
	T-statistic	126	(1.35)	**(−2.13)**	127	(0.69)	(0.23)
Services	Change	132	−7,174	12,331	135	−2,566	−1,005
	T-statistic	132	(−0.71)	(0.17)	135	(−0.23)	(−0.02)
Male	Change	278	194	−19,808	283	50	−10,486
	T-statistic	278	**(3.33)**	**(−2.88)**	283	(1.35)	**(−2.30)**
Female	Change	208	−95	−10,975	206	402	−16,787
	T-statistic	208	(−0.79)	(−1.37)	206	(2.57)	(−2.39)
Below primary	Change	211	−59	−1,786	204	−31	−4,246
	T-statistic	211	(−1.08)	(−0.47)	204	(−0.47)	(−1.44)
Primary	Change	198	−32	−1,008	188	−5	340
	T-statistic	198	(−0.91)	(−0.30)	188	(−0.24)	(0.16)
Secondary	Change	267	23	−11,630	267	54	−7,817
	T-statistic	267	(0.83)	**(−3.69)**	267	**(3.07)**	**(−3.64)**
Tertiary	Change	243	230	−22,953	249	142	−6,592
	T-statistic	243	**(3.18)**	**(−2.59)**	249	**(2.32)**	(−0.83)
Young	Change	267	182	−22,429	275	18	−9,220
	T-statistic	267	**(3.96)**	**(−4.00)**	275	(0.57)	**(−2.35)**
Old	Change	270	221	−17,488	266	88	−8,570
	T-statistic	270	**(3.45)**	**(−2.26)**	266	(1.31)	(−1.01)
Rural	Change	244	37	−12,268	249	8	−14,713
	T-statistic	244	−1.07	**(−2.89)**	249	(0.18)	**(−2.55)**
Urban	Change	273	189	−19,657	276	81	−7,186
	T-statistic	273	**(3.25)**	**(−2.85)**	276	(1.75)	(−1.26)

Note: The table shows the predicted change in wages in rupees after a $100 increase in exports per worker. T-statistics with significance at the 95 percent level are presented in bold. In this regression, the unit of observation is an industry rather than a district. N represents the number of observations in each regression.

TABLE 4A.7 **Employment in India (Industry Regressions), 1999–2011**

			1999–2011			1999–2007	
		N	All merchandise exports	Tradable dummy	N	All merchandise exports	Tradable dummy
All	Change	210	−24,680	1,713,607	222	74,053	1,324,193
	T-statistic	210	(−0.53)	(1.11)	222	(1.09)	(0.91)
Manufacturing	Change	97	−1,175	597,827	109	1,668	−1,111,139
	T-statistic	97	(−0.65)	(0.71)	109	(0.44)	(−1.46)
Services	Change	95	1,786,645	−7,535	95	1,605,807	−4,482
	T-statistic	95	−0.79	(−0.02)	95	(0.76)	(−0.03)
Male	Change	200	−14,976	297,329	214	69,452	311,620
	T-statistic	200	(−0.39)	(0.25)	214	(1.27)	(0.28)
Female	Change	108	−54,788	3,165,583	107	7,433	2,007,295
	T-statistic	108	(−1.84)	**(2.98)**	107	(0.71)	**(1.97)**
Below primary	Change	158	−5,442	966,648	141	53,912	2,692,807
	T-statistic	158	(−0.52)	(0.48)	141	**(2.86)**	(1.33)
Primary	Change	123	−2,668	724,808	126	−5,461	185,921
	T-statistic	123	(−1.12)	(1.95)	126	(−1.27)	−0.51
Secondary	Change	179	−3,055	113,890	192	17,687	275,502
	T-statistic	179	(−0.75)	(0.35)	192	(1.93)	(0.78)
Tertiary	Change	44	17,476	40,427	49	−1,553	26,015
	T-statistic	44	**(2.35)**	**(2.41)**	49	(−0.66)	(0.98)
Young	Change	186	−9,902	1,079,517	207	33,666	831,066
	T-statistic	186	(−1.06)	−0.95	207	(2.00)	(0.91)
Old	Change	172	−25,169	1,496,364	167	−33,019	1,758,662
	T-statistic	172	(−0.73)	−1.74	167	(−0.87)	**(2.18)**
Rural	Change	164	−26,013	1,008,391	173	318,061	−329,884
	T-statistic	164	(−0.42)	−0.44	173	**(2.05)**	(−0.12)
Urban	Change	190	−4,582	342,425	195	560	728,310
	T-statistic	190	(−1.03)	−1.24	195	(0.06)	**(2.58)**

Note: The table shows the predicted change in employment after a $100 increase in exports per worker. T-statistics with significance at the 95 percent level are presented in bold. In this regression, the unit of observation is an industry rather than a district. N represents the number of observations in each regression.

TABLE 4A.8 **Standard Deviation of Wages in India (Industry Regressions), 1999–2011**

| | | 1999–2011 | | | 1999–2007 | | |
		N	All merchandise exports	Tradable dummy	N	All merchandise exports	Tradable dummy
All	Change	279	39	–5,175	283	43	–25,961
	T-statistic	279	(1.95)	**(–2.11)**	283	(0.59)	**(–2.80)**
Manufacturing	Change	126	2	950	127	19	11,466
	T-statistic	126	(0.17)	(0.16)	127	–0.44	–0.72
Services	Change	132	733	–7,774	135	9,034	–45,715
	T-statistic	132	(0.22)	(–0.32)	135	(0.35)	(–0.46)
Male	Change	278	41	–3,957	283	41	–26,271
	T-statistic	278	(1.95)	(–1.50)	283	(0.48)	**(–2.45)**
Female	Change	208	–23	–6,626	206	–21	–1,435
	T-statistic	208	(–0.64)	**(–2.86)**	206	(–0.40)	(–0.62)
Below primary	Change	211	7	–596	204	1	–1,097
	T-statistic	211	(0.77)	(–0.83)	204	(0.10)	(–1.64)
Primary	Change	198	11	–1,144	188	9	–471
	T-statistic	198	(1.17)	(–1.23)	188	(1.14)	(–0.65)
Secondary	Change	267	8	–2,904	267	21	–2,124
	T-statistic	267	(1.13)	**(–3.29)**	267	**(4.25)**	**(–3.40)**
Tertiary	Change	243	43	–6,694	249	82	–36,130
	T-statistic	243	(1.28)	(–1.54)	249	(0.82)	**(–2.73)**
Young	Change	267	52	–6,128	275	19	–2,072
	T-statistic	267	**(3.24)**	**(–3.05)**	275	(1.60)	(–1.40)
Old	Change	270	31	–2,062	266	69	–54,685
	T-statistic	270	(1.55)	(–0.83)	266	(0.60)	**(–3.69)**
Rural	Change	244	16	–3,289	249	2	–2,483
	T-statistic	244	(1.92)	**(–3.10)**	249	(0.26)	**(–3.15)**
Urban	Change	273	43	–5,829	276	67	–33,204
	T-statistic	273	**(2.22)**	**(–2.46)**	276	(0.75)	**(–3.02)**

Note: The table shows the predicted change in the standard deviation of wages in rupees after a $100 increase in exports per worker. T-statistics with significance at the 95 percent level are presented in bold. In this regression, the unit of observation is an industry rather than a district. N represents the number of observations in each regression.

TABLE 4A.9 **Trade Exposure and Wages in India, 1999–2011**
Percent

State	Wage change	Export change	Contribution of trade
Andhra Pradesh	60.5	319.3	5.6
Assam	63.1	147.6	1.2
Bihar	81.3	255.1	1.4
Chandigarh	62.3	457.7	5.1
Chhattisgarh	39.9	421.5	9.4
Delhi	33.9	394.6	6.8
Gujarat	37.0	420.5	10.5
Haryana	93.3	429.4	3.2
Himachal Pradesh	10.6	188.8	0.7
Jammu and Kashmir	14.1	179.1	1.1
Jharkhand	49.3	376.3	16.6
Karnataka	70.1	264.8	5.2
Kerala	61.2	260.8	5.5
Madhya Pradesh	66.8	234.2	3.5
Maharashtra	69.3	342.2	7.1
Manipur	52.5	134.5	0.8
Meghalaya	57.3	76.4	0.3
Mizoram	78.1	93.1	0.3
Orissa	52.6	235.3	4.3
Pondicherry	88.4	616.3	16.8
Punjab	26.5	225.9	4.1
Rajasthan	22.1	179.0	2.2
Sikkim	81.9	120.8	0.5
Tamil Nadu	55.3	201.4	5.6
Tripura	11.3	147.0	0.6
Uttar Pradesh	30.9	181.9	2.3
West Bengal	23.8	536.8	10.3

TABLE 4A.10 **Trade Exposure and Informality in India, 1999–2011**
Percent

State	Informality change	Export change	Contribution of trade
Andhra Pradesh	−8.9	319.3	−3.2
Assam	8.0	147.6	−0.8
Bihar	−2.5	255.1	−0.4
Chandigarh	43.4	457.7	−39.1
Chhattisgarh	−8.5	421.5	−3.5
Delhi	−21.3	394.6	−101.2
Gujarat	−27.8	420.5	−5.1
Haryana	813.8	429.4	−22.8
Himachal Pradesh	−2.0	188.8	−1.3
Jammu and Kashmir	17.3	179.1	−2.1
Jharkhand	9.7	376.3	−11.5
Karnataka	−21.0	264.8	−6.9
Kerala	−5.8	260.8	−3.3
Madhya Pradesh	−7.4	234.2	−1.8
Maharashtra	−21.8	342.2	−42.6
Manipur	14.5	134.5	−1.4
Meghalaya	−7.8	76.4	−0.3
Mizoram	−38.3	93.1	−0.6
Orissa	−10.5	235.3	−1.5
Pondicherry	−36.2	616.3	−8.2
Punjab	−6.7	225.9	−5.3
Rajasthan	18.2	179.0	−2.4
Sikkim	−22.6	120.8	−1.0
Tamil Nadu	−2.2	201.4	−4.2
Tripura	9.1	147.0	−0.3
Uttar Pradesh	14.3	181.9	−2.2
West Bengal	0.2	536.8	−6.8

TABLE 4A.11 **Total Wage Income of the Working-Age Population in Sri Lanka, 2002–13**

		N	All merchandise exports	Manufacturing exports
All	Change	141	206	290
	T-statistic	141	**(2.13)**	**(2.45)**
Manufacturing	Change	140	372	687
	T-statistic	140	−0.68	(1.53)
Services	Change	141	840	1,085
	T-statistic	141	**(3.80)**	**(5.14)**
Male	Change	141	300	359
	T-statistic	141	**(2.11)**	**(2.32)**
Female	Change	141	145	254
	T-statistic	141	(1.78)	**(2.41)**
Low skilled	Change	141	−69	−44
	T-statistic	141	(−0.98)	(−0.56)
High skilled	Change	141	698	917
	T-statistic	141	**(3.53)**	**(4.42)**
Young	Change	141	299	408
	T-statistic	141	(1.55)	**(2.03)**
Old	Change	141	181	263
	T-statistic	141	−(1.58)	(1.88)
Rural	Change	141	289	411
	T-statistic	141	**(2.82)**	**(3.56)**
Urban	Change	122	218	259
	T-statistic	122	(0.37)	(0.41)

Note: The table shows the predicted change in the wage bill per person after a $100 increase in exports per worker. T-statistics with significance at the 95 percent level are presented in bold. N represents the number of observations in each regression.

TABLE 4A.12 **Employment in Sri Lanka, 2002–13**

		N	All merchandise exports	Manufacturing exports
All	Change	141	–5,037	–5,949
	T-statistic	141	(–0.57)	(–0.61)
Manufacturing	Change	141	588	51
	T-statistic	141	(0.44)	(0.04)
Services	Change	141	5,675	6,974
	T-statistic	141	(1.80)	**(2.23)**
Male	Change	141	–6,546	–7,919
	T-statistic	141	**(–2.39)**	**(–2.98)**
Female	Change	141	1,765	2,151
	T-statistic	141	(0.59)	(0.63)
Low skilled	Change	141	–6,709	–7,111
	T-statistic	141	(–1.30)	(–1.30)
High skilled	Change	141	3,311	3,439
	T-statistic	141	(1.22)	(1.20)
Young	Change	141	–5,175	–4,579
	T-statistic	141	**(–2.13)**	**(–2.06)**
Old	Change	141	8,130	6,335
	T-statistic	141	(1.15)	(0.89)
Rural	Change	141	11,561	14,747
	T-statistic	141	(0.73)	(0.75)
Urban	Change	141	–3,005	–3,676
	T-statistic	141	(–1.19)	(–1.22)

Note: The table shows the predicted change in total employment after a $100 increase in exports per worker. T-statistics with significance at the 95 percent level are presented in bold. N represents the number of observations in each regression.

TABLE 4A.13 **Wages in Sri Lanka, 2002–13**

		N	All merchandise exports	Manufacturing exports
All	Change	141	975	1,205
	T-statistic	141	**(3.38)**	**(4.33)**
Manufacturing	Change	135	837	1,117
	T-statistic	135	(1.51)	**(1.97)**
Services	Change	141	1,703	1,993
	T-statistic	141	**(4.10)**	**(4.57)**
Male	Change	141	1,097	1,262
	T-statistic	141	**(4.03)**	**(4.62)**
Female	Change	141	795	1,201
	T-statistic	141	(1.80)	**(2.96)**
Low skilled	Change	141	–152	–54
	T-statistic	141	(–0.53)	(–0.19)
High skilled	Change	141	2,320	2,658
	T-statistic	141	**(4.47)**	**(4.53)**
Young	Change	141	1,010	1,171
	T-statistic	141	**(2.64)**	**(2.92)**
Old	Change	141	824	1,146
	T-statistic	141	**(2.36)**	**(3.97)**
Rural	Change	141	1,156	1,466
	T-statistic	141	**(3.24)**	**(4.44)**
Urban	Change	117	1,405	1,482
	T-statistic	117	(0.85)	(0.81)

Note: The table shows the predicted change in the average wage in Sri Lanka rupees after a $100 increase in exports per worker. T-statistics with significance at the 95 percent level are presented in bold. N represents the number of observations in each regression.

TABLE 4A.14 Informality in Sri Lanka, 2002–13

		N	All merchandise exports	Manufacturing exports
All	Change	87	16,657	7,899
	T-statistic	87	(0.66)	(0.33)
Manufacturing	Change	82	397	−1,107
	T-statistic	82	(0.06)	(−0.19)
Services	Change	87	−2,317	−3,983
	T-statistic	87	(−0.28)	(−0.47)
Male	Change	87	4,279	1,537
	T-statistic	87	(0.21)	(0.08)
Female	Change	87	9,732	5,847
	T-statistic	87	(0.97)	(0.58)
Low skilled	Change	87	20,185	17,924
	T-statistic	87	(0.89)	(0.89)
High skilled	Change	87	2,405	1,041
	T-statistic	87	(0.36)	(0.17)
Young	Change	87	3,228	1,528
	T-statistic	87	(0.28)	(0.15)
Old	Change	87	13,883	7,376
	T-statistic	87	(0.83)	(0.47)
Rural	Change	87	18,475	9,694
	T-statistic	87	(0.83)	(0.43)
Urban	Change	69	7,141	8,278
	T-statistic	69	(0.76)	(0.87)

Note: The table shows the predicted change in informality after a $100 increase in exports per worker. T-statistics with significance at the 95 percent level are presented in bold. N represents the number of observations in each regression.

TABLE 4A.15 **Standard Deviation of Wages in Sri Lanka, 2002–13**

		N	All merchandise exports	Manufacturing exports
All	Change	141	2,292	2,604
	T-statistic	141	**(3.68)**	**(4.22)**
Manufacturing	Change	135	2,300	2,741
	T-statistic	135	(1.89)	**(2.09)**
Services	Change	141	3,349	3,811
	T-statistic	141	**(4.48)**	**(5.00)**
Male	Change	141	2,575	2,832
	T-statistic	141	**(3.79)**	**(4.15)**
Female	Change	141	1,915	2,364
	T-statistic	141	**(3.69)**	**(4.61)**
Low skilled	Change	141	1,336	1,538
	T-statistic	141	**(2.90)**	**(3.30)**
High skilled	Change	141	3,203	3,759
	T-statistic	141	**(3.25)**	**(3.74)**
Young	Change	141	2,456	2,760
	T-statistic	141	**(5.77)**	**(6.19)**
Old	Change	141	2,405	2,748
	T-statistic	141	**(2.98)**	**(3.44)**
Rural	Change	141	2,985	3,528
	T-statistic	141	**(4.73)**	**(5.86)**
Urban	Change	117	3,579	3,816
	T-statistic	117	(1.67)	(1.58)

Note: The table shows the predicted change in the standard deviation of wages in Sri Lanka rupees after a $100 increase in exports per worker. T-statistics with significance at the 95 percent level are presented in bold. N represents the number of observations in each regression.

Notes

1. This alternative methodology requires minor changes in the regression equations and is explained thoroughly in chapter 3.

2. In some developing countries with deficient social security systems, such as those that lack unemployment insurance, workers have very low reservation wages and have to find some employment to survive. This might result in almost full employment.

3. In this regard, we estimated the changes in the dependent and independent variables between 2002–03, 2003–04, 2004–07, 2007–08, 2008–11, 2011–12, and 2012–13. Even though data before 2002 and after 2013 from the Annual Labour Force Surveys might be available, it was necessary to restrict the time span to those years with the same industrial classification system, that is, ISIC Rev 3, to make our trade measure comparable across years. Likewise, because we had annual trade data, using higher-frequency labor surveys like the Quarterly Labour Force Surveys was not possible.

4. See chapter 3 for details on the minor modifications made to the main regression equation.

5. Beginning in 2007 revisions to the Sri Lanka Labour Force Survey were made that provided additional information on informal employment. Despite our efforts to estimate regressions on informality for the period 2007–13, the lack of enough observations made it difficult to find statistically significant results.

References

Autor, David H., David Dorn, and Gordon Hanson. 2013. "The China Syndrome: Local Labor Market Effects of Import Competition in the United States." *American Economic Review* 103 (6): 2121–68.

———. 2016. "The China Shock: Learning from Labor-Market Adjustment to Large Changes in Trade." *Annual Review of Economics* 8: 205–40.

Autor, David H., David Dorn, Gordon Hanson, and Jae Song. 2014. "Trade Adjustment: Worker Level Evidence." *Quarterly Journal of Economics* 129 (4): 1799–1860.

Bartik, Timothy J. 1991. "Who Benefits from State and Local Economic Development Policies?" Upjohn Institute for Employment Research, Kalamazoo, MI.

Cooper, Russell W., and John C. Haltiwanger. 2006. "On the Nature of Capital Adjustment Costs." *The Review of Economic Studies* 73 (3): 611–33.

Hasan, Rana, Devashish Mitra, and K. V. Ramaswamy. 2007. "Trade Reforms, Labor Regulations, and Labor-Demand Elasticities: Empirical Evidence from India." *Review of Economics and Statistics* 89 (3): 466–81.

Hasan, Rana, Devashish Mitra, Priya Ranjan, and Reshad N. Ahsan. 2012. "Trade Liberalization and Unemployment: Theory and Evidence from India." *Journal of Development Economics* 97 (2): 269–80.

Hasan, Rana, Devashish Mitra, and Beyza Ural. 2007. "Trade Liberalization, Labor-Market Institutions, and Poverty Reduction: Evidence from Indian States." *Indian Policy Forum* 3 (1): 71–122.

Kovak, Brian. 2013. "Regional Effects of Trade Reform: What Is the Correct Measure of Liberalization?" *American Economic Review* 103 (5): 1960–76.

Melitz, M. J. 2003. "The Impact of Trade on Intra-Industry Reallocations and Aggregate Industry Productivity." *Econometrica* 71: 1695–1725

Pierce, Justin R., and Peter K. Schott. 2016. "The Surprisingly Swift Decline of U.S. Manufacturing Employment." *American Economic Review* 106 (7): 1632–62.

Rodrik, Dani. 1997. *Has Globalization Gone Too Far?* Washington, DC: Institute for International Economics.

Topalova, Petia. 2010. "Factor Immobility and Regional Impacts of Trade Liberalization: Evidence on Poverty from India." *American Economic Journal: Applied Economics* 2 (4): 1–41.

World Bank. 2018. "South Asia Economic Focus, Spring 2018: Jobless Growth?" Internal report, World Bank, Washington, DC. https://openknowledge.worldbank.org/handle/10986/29650 License: CC BY 3.0 IGO.

CHAPTER 5

Spreading the Labor Market Gains from Exports

Key Messages

- If South Asia sharply increases its exports to the levels of competitors like Brazil or China, it could achieve higher wage gains and lower informal employment.

- If South Asia focuses on boosting exports in labor-intensive industries, it could significantly lower informality for groups like rural and less-educated workers.

- If South Asia increases the skills of workers and participation of women and young workers in the labor force, it could make an even bigger dent in informal employment.

- South Asia could spread the labor market gains more widely by focusing on (1) boosting and connecting exports to people (for example, by removing trade barriers and investment in infrastructure); (2) eliminating distortions in production (for example, by more efficient allocation of inputs); and (3) protecting workers (for example, by investing in their education and skills).

Introduction

South Asian economies face what some may perceive as a paradox: very high and impressive growth rates but job growth that is not inclusive. In addition, trade as a fraction of total gross domestic product (GDP) is much lower in South Asia than in other regions, and lately it has been falling. Why is the story in South Asia different from that in other regions—where trade, growth, and jobs typically go hand in hand—and what can be done about it?

By rigorously estimating the potential impact from higher South Asian exports per worker on wages and employment over a 10-year period, this report so far has established that an increase in exports would improve labor market outcomes. Our key finding is that a higher demand for South Asian goods from Organisation for Economic Co-operation and Development countries should go hand in hand with higher wages but not necessarily with more job creation. The benefits will flow mainly to college graduates, urban workers, males, and more experienced workers. South Asian countries would also see less informality, especially for less-skilled workers.

Our findings, however, show that gains from exports benefit mainly groups that are more well-off and may not be inclusive of groups like women and low-skilled workers. This is not surprising: exports usually require more-skilled workers. And when workers are immobile—reflecting barriers to higher productivity at a worker, firm, or locality level—export shocks benefit only those in the sector directly facing the shock. This finding raises the question of how the benefits of exports can be spread more evenly.

In this chapter, we develop three policy options that may help to spread the gains from exports to wider parts of the population (box 5.1). In addition, these policy scenarios also show how increasing export growth can be useful in overcoming the labor

---

BOX 5.1 Analytical Framework

For India, following the approach established in chapters 3 and 4, we calculate the estimates on the basis of regressions that have the difference in the average annual wages between 2011 and 1999 (in real Indian rupees) as the dependent variable and the difference in annual trade volume per worker between 2011 and 1999 (in real U.S. dollars) as the independent variable. For the estimates on informality, the dependent variable is the difference in the share of informal workers between 2011 and 1999, and the independent variable is the difference in the annual trade volume per worker between 2011 and 1999 (in real U.S. dollars).

For Sri Lanka, we also calculate the estimates on the basis of regressions that have the difference in the average annual wages (in real Sri Lanka rupees) as the dependent variable and the difference in annual trade volume per worker (in real U.S. dollars) as the independent variable. Because of the small number of districts in Sri Lanka, however, we pooled time-series data to construct a sufficient number of time-district observations. In particular, we estimated the changes in the dependent and independent variables between 2002–03, 2003–04, 2004–07, 2007–08, 2008–11, 2011–12, and 2012–13. Even though data prior to 2002 and after 2013 from the Annual Labour Force Surveys might be available, we included only those years that use the same industrial classification system, that is, ISIC Rev 3, to guarantee consistency in our estimates across years. Given that we use annual trade data, higher frequency labor surveys like the Quarterly Labour Force Surveys cannot be used. Furthermore, we may still have sample size limitations in some cases. For example, we have few observations in the regressions for urban workers, which may affect the significance of the findings. Sri Lankan Labor Force Surveys started to include information regarding informality in 2007. For all previous years, it is not possible to identify whether any worker is in the informal or formal sector. We estimated the regression on informality for the period 2007–13, even though insufficient sample sizes in the regressions make it difficult to find any conclusive evidence.

market challenges of growing wage gaps and the persistent informality discussed in chapter 2. Our focus is on India and Sri Lanka, but our findings are also applicable to Bangladesh and Pakistan, which face similar challenges in how their export and labor markets function. Specifically, we are trying to understand the following:

- Would labor market outcomes improve—and if so, by how much—if the *scale of exports* rose to the levels of South Asia's main competitors such as Brazil and China?

- Would labor market outcomes improve if countries made efforts to *change the composition of exports* to help disadvantaged groups? In other words, does the source of the export shock (labor-intensive versus capital-intensive industries) influence how widely the gains from exports are shared?[1]

- Would labor market outcomes improve by *changing the composition of the labor force* to help disadvantaged groups? For example, would getting more female workers in export industries help reduce informality?

Option 1: Increasing the Scale of Exports

In the first scenario, we ask, if India's or Sri Lanka's exports per worker rose on average over a 10-year period to three different levels—(1) a benchmark case (US$250 rise, which is the average exports per worker in India); (2) the level of Brazil (US$1,000 increase); and (3) the level of China (US$1,500 increase)—by how much would labor market outcomes improve, in terms of wages and informality? Our results are shown in figure 5.1.

In India, our results show that a US$250 increase in exports per worker increases wages, on average, by Rs 1,430; a US$1,000 increase, by Rs 5,720; and a US$1,500 increase, by Rs 8,580. During the same 10-year span, 2.1 million workers would transition to the formal sector after a US$250 export shock; 8.3 million after a US$1,000 export shock; and 12.4 million after a US$1,500 export shock. In Sri Lanka, a similar pattern is evident for wages. Higher exports per worker increase wages on average between SL Rs 2,000 and SL Rs 14,600, depending on the scale of export growth—that is, the more the better.

Option 2: Changing the Composition of Exports to Help Disadvantaged Groups

Although increasing exports per worker generally improves labor market outcomes, our results imply that the degree to which exports might contribute to enhancing labor market outcomes for disadvantaged groups depends on the source of the export shock in capital- versus labor-intensive industries. In this section we analyze the impact of a US$250 export shock on wages and informality across groups under the following scenarios: (1) "all industries" export shock, which consists of all merchandise exports; (2) manufacturing export shock; (3) capital-intensive export shock; and (4) labor-intensive

FIGURE 5.1 **As Exports Rise, so Do Wages, and Informality Lessens**

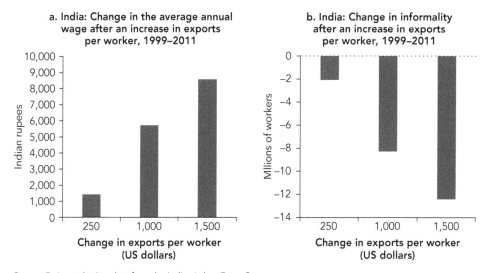

a. India: Change in the average annual wage after an increase in exports per worker, 1999–2011

b. India: Change in informality after an increase in exports per worker, 1999–2011

Source: Estimated using data from the Indian Labor Force Surveys.
Note: Results are shown at the significance level of less than 10 percent.

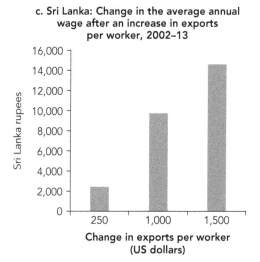

c. Sri Lanka: Change in the average annual wage after an increase in exports per worker, 2002–13

Source: Estimated using data from the Sri Lankan Labor Force Surveys.
Note: Results are shown at the significance level of less than 10 percent.

export shock[2] (table 5.1 and table 5.2). Further results concerning US$1,000 and US$1,500 increases in exports per worker are presented in annex 5A.

Overall, our results show significant differences in the impact of export shocks according to the type of shock. On the one hand, in the case of India, a labor-intensive shock may benefit disadvantaged groups in terms of wages and lower casual work (informality). For example, this type of shock is likely to increase the wages of low-skilled and rural workers, as well as help younger and rural workers to shift to formal jobs. On the other hand, more well-off groups—such as high-skilled and older workers—may benefit the most from a capital-intensive export shock in terms of wage rises. For Sri Lanka,

TABLE 5.1 Effect of Different Types of Export Shocks on Wages across the Population

a. India: Change in the average annual wage after a US$250 increase in exports per worker (Indian rupees, 1999–2011)

Types of affected workers	Type of export shocks			
	All industries	Manufacturing	Capital intensive	Labor intensive
All	1,430	1,156	1,422	
Industry type				
Manufacturing	1,377	1,293	1,338	2,958
Services		1,638		2,554
Capital intensive	1,753	1,450	1,746	
Labor intensive				
Gender				
Male	1,638	1,303	1,616	
Female		841		
Highest education				
Below primary				520
Primary		531		1,092
Secondary				1,518
Tertiary	5,450	4,956	5,318	3,792
Age				
Young		994		
Old	2,757	1,984	2,703	2,212
Location				
Rural		–812		909
Urban		2,022		1,769

Source: Authors' estimates using data from the Indian Labor Force Surveys.
Note: Only results significant at 1 percent, 5 percent, and 10 percent levels are shown in the table.

b. Sri Lanka: Change in the average annual wage after a US$250 increase in exports per worker (Sri Lanka rupees, 2002–13)

Types of affected workers	Type of export shocks			
	All industries	Manufacturing	Capital intensive	Labor intensive
All	2,437	3,013	3,665	
Industry type				
Manufacturing		2,793		
Services	4,258	4,983	6,470	
Capital intensive				
Labor intensive		2,233		6,745
Gender				
Male	2,743	3,155	3,568	5,880
Female	1,986	3,003	3,985	
Highest education				
Low skilled				
High skilled	5,798	6,645	8,670	7,423
Age				
Young	2,525	2,928	3,650	
Old	2,061	2,865	3,138	
Location				
Rural	2,890	3,665	4,460	
Urban				

Source: Authors' estimates using data from the Sri Lankan Labor Force Surveys.
Note: Only results significant at 1 percent, 5 percent, and 10 percent levels are shown in the table.

TABLE 5.2 Effect of Different Types of Export Shocks on Informality across the Population

a. India: Change in informality (workers) after a US$250 increase in exports per worker, 1999–2011

Types of affected workers	Type of export shocks			
	All industries	Manufacturing	Capital intensive	Labor intensive
All	−2,066,497	−1,944,074	−2,057,557	−1,397,686
Industry type				
Manufacturing				−767,936
Services		−910,073		−1,234,618
Capital intensive	−2,164,540	−2,034,212	−2,171,682	−1,238,485
Labor intensive	−405,653	−279,834	−356,730	−372,925
Gender				
Male	−1,348,314	−1,481,288	−1,351,538	
Female	−529,961	−336,384	−526,558	
Highest education				
Below primary	−1,518,878	−1,043,546	−1,465,640	−1,197,402
Primary	−509,189	−347,179	−490,178	−340,252
Secondary		−635,681		−1,116,371
Tertiary				
Age				
Young	−968,591	−1,135,771	−954,835	−1,239,845
Old	−1,067,152	−830,266	−1,059,673	−636,035
Location				
Rural				−918,472
Urban	−590,441	−544,847	−586,187	−767,693

b. India: Change in informality (percentage) after a US$250 increase in exports per worker, 1999–2011

Types of affected workers	Type of export shocks			
	All industries	Manufacturing	Capital intensive	Labor intensive
All	−2.0	−1.9	−2.0	−1.4
Industry-type				
Manufacturing				−6.7
Services		−0.9		−1.3
Capital intensive	−2.2	−2.1	−2.2	−1.3
Labor intensive	−9.6	−6.6	−8.5	−8.8
Gender				
Male	−1.7	−1.9	−1.7	
Female	−2.3	−1.4	−2.2	
Highest education				
Below primary	−2.8	−1.9	−2.7	−2.2
Primary	−5.3	−3.6	−5.1	−3.5
Secondary		−2.2		−3.9
Tertiary				
Age				
Young	−1.6	−1.9	−1.6	−2.1
Old	−2.4	−1.9	−2.4	−1.4
Location				
Rural				−1.3
Urban	−1.9	−1.7	−1.8	−2.4

Source: Authors' estimates using data from the Indian Labor Force Surveys.
Note: Only results significant at 1 percent, 5 percent, and 10 percent levels are shown in the table.

the picture is not as clear as for India. Even though the results also show significant differences in the effects of different types of export shocks, a generalized pattern of the benefits of a particular type of shock on specific groups of workers is not evident.

Skills. In India, generalized and capital-intensive trade shocks are expected to have significant impacts only on high-skilled workers with tertiary education, increasing their average wages by Rs 5,450 and Rs 5,318, respectively. Although a labor-intensive export shock would also have a positive effect on wages for this group of workers, the size of the effect would be considerably smaller. This is not the case for low-skilled workers, given that a labor-intensive shock is likely to envisage the largest boosts in wages for workers with below primary, primary, and secondary education. Meanwhile, concerning informality, substantial reductions are observed in the least-skilled groups under any kind of export shock. The results show a drop in informality of between 1.0 million and 1.5 million workers for those with below primary education, and 0.3 million and 0.5 million for those with primary education, depending on the type of export shock. In Sri Lanka, we find significant effects of an increase in exports per worker on wages only for the most-skilled workers, with a capital-intensive shock accounting for the greatest impact.

Age. We find that wages of more experienced (that is, older) workers will positively respond to any trade shock in India, with the largest increases observed under a generalized or a capital-intensive export shock. Younger workers, however, seem to benefit only from manufacturing export shocks, and the size of the effect is markedly smaller. In the case of informality reductions, capital-intensive export shocks seem to benefit more well-off workers to a greater extent—the older ones—whereas labor-intensive shocks help disadvantaged workers—the younger ones—the most. The results for Sri Lanka show that increases in exports per worker (except labor-intensive shocks) raise the wages of both young and old workers homogeneously.[3]

Gender. In India, a positive export shock would increase wages for male workers much more than for females. For example, a capital-intensive shock would boost males' average wages by Rs 1,616, whereas there is no significant effect on females' wages. The only scenario where women experience an increase in their average wage after a trade shock assumes a manufacturing trade shock; nevertheless, the effect is still substantially smaller than that for men. Even though women experience a higher rate of formalization compared to men, given that they represent a lower share of the workforce in the merchandise export sector, fewer women than men will become more formalized: 0.5 million versus 1.3 million workers.[4] Meanwhile, as in India, almost all types of export shocks in Sri Lanka are likely to benefit male workers more than females. For example, a generalized trade shock would increase men's average wages by SL Rs 2,743 versus SL Rs 1,986 for women.

Location. A manufacturing export shock in India would envisage the highest increases in urban workers' average wages (Rs 2,022); this, however, could negatively affect rural workers. Alternatively, a labor-intensive export shock would benefit both groups of workers in terms of wage rises. Similarly, increasing exports per worker from labor-intensive industries will result in a considerable drop in informality for rural (0.9 million) and urban (0.8 million) workers.

Option 3: Changing the Composition of the Workforce to Help Disadvantaged Groups

Having established the importance of the scale of exports and labor-intensive export shocks in improving labor market outcomes for disadvantaged groups, we now examine what would happen to informality if we change the composition of the labor force to help those groups. We do not analyze the direct impact of the counterfactual change in composition here; instead, our estimations show only the interaction of the counterfactual change in labor composition and the change in trade. We show this interaction by (1) increasing the share of a particular group to the 75th percentile of the labor force participation rates of that group across districts and (2) increasing the share of a particular group to 100 percent of the labor force. The results discussed below are also illustrated in table 5.3, which shows all estimations carried out under the assumption of a $US250 export shock for different types of export shock.

The 75th percentile of the independent variables is created by taking the value of a given variable at the 75th percentile. We then use this value to calculate the impact of a given trade shock. For example, assume that the ratio of women in the labor force changes from 10 to 50 percent across districts. Assume that, at the 75th percentile, 35 percent of the labor force is female and 65 percent is male. We calculate the impact using a weighted average of coefficients for female and male, with weights 0.35 and 0.65, respectively.

Overall, we observe that, on increasing the participation of some disadvantaged groups in the labor force, the biggest reductions in informality come after labor-intensive shocks. For example, increasing the skills of workers and a greater participation of rural and young workers in the labor force yield significantly substantial informality reductions if the export shock comes from labor-intensive industries. Similarly, increasing the share of female workers in the labor force could reduce informality substantially after an all-industry export shock.

Education. We observe reductions in informality for skilled workers on increasing their respective shares in the workforce after a labor-intensive export shock. For example, if we increase the share of skilled workers (those with secondary education) to the 75th percentile of their labor force participation rates across districts, we observe a reduction in informality of about 3.8 million workers after a labor-intensive shock. This reduction in informality rises to 4.9 million workers if we consider increasing the share of skilled workers to 100 percent of the labor force.

Age. Increasing participation of young workers in the labor force could result in significant reductions in informality after a labor-intensive export shock. For example, if we increase the share of young workers either to the 75th percentile of their labor force participation rates across districts or to 100 percent in the labor force, we observe a reduction in informality of between 2.4 million and 2.8 million workers after an increase in labor-intensive exports (table 5.3).

Industry types. The labor-intensive sector exhibits the highest synergies in terms of reduction of informality with other sectors. For example, an increase in the share of

TABLE 5.3 **Change in the Composition of the Labor Force and the Impact on Informality Reduction in India**

a. Simulated change in informality (workers) after a US$250 increase in exports per worker and increasing the share of a particular group to the 75th percentile of the labor force distribution across districts, 1999–2011

Types of affected workers	Type of export shocks			
	All industries	Manufacturing	Capital intensive	Labor intensive
Industry type				
Manufacturing				−2,395,590
Services		−2,105,168		−2,605,958
Capital intensive	−2,173,465	−2,043,600	−2,172,759	−1,734,539
Labor intensive	−2,394,692	−2,148,741	−2,336,100	−2,090,011
Gender				
Male	−1,830,565	−1,887,884	−1,832,601	
Female	−1,930,519	−1,806,992	−1,929,172	
Highest education				
Below primary	−2,737,130	−2,083,431	−2,641,574	−3,361,027
Primary	−3,007,457	−2,323,492	−2,900,994	−3,596,321
Secondary		−2,171,004		−3,837,770
Tertiary				
Age				
Young	−2,003,756	−1,971,068	−1,982,199	−2,433,261
Old	−2,085,805	−1,965,785	−2,064,933	−2,342,260
Location				
Rural				−1,897,343
Urban	−1,420,314	−1,166,794	−1,414,187	−2,143,424

b. Simulated change in informality (workers) after a US$250 increase in exports per worker and increasing the share of a particular group to 100 percent of the labor force, 1999–2011

Types of affected workers	Type of export shocks			
	All industries	Manufacturing	Capital intensive	Labor intensive
Industry type				
Manufacturing				−7,266,290
Services		−2,362,518		−3,917,234
Capital intensive	−2,280,871	−2,143,538	−2,288,397	−1,686,038
Labor intensive	−9,944,772	−6,860,260	−8,745,416	−9,142,427
Gender				
Male	−1,765,983	−1,940,149	−1,770,206	
Female	−2,333,303	−1,481,025	−2,318,320	
Highest education				
Below primary	−2,896,550	−1,990,076	−2,795,024	−3,042,541
Primary	−5,446,258	−3,713,413	−5,242,922	−4,209,027
Secondary		−2,306,787		−4,850,352
Tertiary				
Age				
Young	−1,697,741	−1,990,772	−1,673,628	−2,772,668
Old	−2,492,956	−1,939,570	−2,475,484	−1,890,681
Location				
Rural				−1,803,151
Urban	−1,918,975	−1,770,794	−1,905,149	−2,810,831

Source: Authors' estimates using data from the Indian Labor Force Surveys.
Note: Only results significant at 1 percent, 5 percent, and 10 percent levels are shown in the table.

workers in manufacturing, either to the 75th percentile of their labor force participation rates across districts or to 100 percent of the labor force, is likely to reduce informality by 2.4 million workers and 7.3 million workers, respectively, after only a labor-intensive export shock (table 5.3). Similarly, if we increase the share of workers in services either to the 75th percentile of their labor force participation rates across districts or to 100 percent of the labor force, it would yield significant reductions in informality of about 2.6 million workers and 3.9 million workers, respectively, after a labor-intensive export shock (table 5.3).

Location. Increasing the participation of rural workers could reduce casual work (informality) only after labor-intensive export shocks (table 5.3). After a labor-intensive export shock, we observe an informality reduction of about 1.9 million workers if an increase in the share of rural workers is based on the 75th percentile of their labor force participation rates across districts and 1.8 million workers if the share of rural workers is increased to 100 percent of the labor force.

A higher level of urbanization is also likely to reduce the number of informal workers in the labor force by 2.8 million after a labor-intensive export shock if we increase the share of urban workers to 100 percent in the labor force, and 2.1 million workers if the increase is based on the 75th percentile of their labor force participation rates across districts. This result is significant, given that urbanization is accelerating in the region. Recent studies show that urbanization improves firm productivity and enhances growth in a region (Ellis and Roberts 2016).

Gender. If we increase the share of women in the labor force on the basis of the 75th percentile of their labor force participation rates across districts, we observe a reduction in informality of about 1.9 million workers after an all-industry export shock. This informality reduction rises to 2.3 million workers if we increase the share of female workers to 100 percent of the labor force after an all-industry shock. Unlike for other groups, the increase in participation of women in the labor force does not entail any significant informality reduction after labor-intensive export shocks.

Suggestions for Tackling Obstacles to Higher Exports

The policy options discussed above underline the importance of scale and composition of exports, and the composition of the workforce, in extending the gains of trade to disadvantaged groups. In India, for example, we find that (1) the bigger the export shock the larger the effect on wages and informality, (2) labor-intensive export shocks can reduce informality, and (3) increasing the share of underrepresented groups, like women and young workers, in merchandise exports can improve their labor market outcomes and particularly reduce informality. In contrast, in Sri Lanka, a manufacturing shock seems to have the biggest gains in terms of wages.

The region, however, is grappling with certain issues that restrict the scale and type of exports, and the participation of certain groups in the labor force. These issues include

(1) inadequate infrastructure that restricts the scale of exports and trade barriers; (2) distortions in the allocation of inputs, low female labor force participation (FLFP), and lack of worker mobility; and (3) low skill levels and inadequate safety nets to help workers to adjust to trade shocks. In order to spread the gains from trade as described under the policy options, it is then vital to push for policies that promote exports by (1) boosting and connecting exports to people through freer trade, better connectivity, and better infrastructure; (2) eliminating distortions in production; and (3) protecting workers. We discuss the need for these complementary policies in greater detail in this section.

POLICIES TARGETED TO IMPROVE SCALE AND CONNECTIVITY OF EXPORTS

Improving infrastructure. The state of physical infrastructure could be substantially improved, with many studies pointing out how inadequate quality of infrastructure has resulted in higher transport costs (De 2010). Firms in South Asia, on average, face 25 power outages per month—the highest number of outages faced by any region—accounting for 11 percent of their annual sales. Congested ports further increase the cost of exporting. On average, it takes nearly 11 days for exports from a South Asian firm to clear customs.[5] Documentation processes are time consuming, bribery undermines institutional integrity, and high levels of irregular and underground trade exist in the region (Iqbal and Nawaz 2017). South Asia lags behind East Asia and Pacific economies in deploying technology in customs administration. For example, Electronic Data Interchange is widely adopted in Indonesia, the Philippines, Singapore, and Thailand, but is yet to be implemented in Bhutan, Nepal, and Sri Lanka (Singh 2017).

These infrastructural bottlenecks create an unfavorable environment for greater export activity, thereby restricting the scale and connectivity of exports to people. Given that connectivity is imperative to a trade-boosting environment, the region could increasingly focus policies for building and improving physical infrastructure to ensure greater trade activity and facilitation.[6] Emphasis should be on improving roadway and railway networks to allow greater connectivity within the region. What would better road networks mean for local labor markets? Our results from a correlation exercise show that better road networks go hand in hand with higher exports (0.33) (table 5.4). Furthermore, road networks reduce informality and increase wages through export shocks.[7] Governments could also focus their efforts on ensuring that projects on roadway networks are not delayed by time overruns and budgetary constraints (Banik and Gilbert 2010). Simultaneous investments in institutional and digital infrastructure could further help in promoting trade.

Promotion of freer trade. Today, intraregional trade accounts for just 5 percent of South Asia's total trade, compared to 25 percent for the Association of Southeast Asian Nations (Kathuria 2018). Despite the presence of the South Asian Free Trade Area, trade is suffering because of high tariff barriers and other restrictions on connectivity and

TABLE 5.4 **Roads Pave the Way for Better Labor Market Outcomes, 1999–2011**

	Export change	Informality change	Wage change	Contribution to informality	Contribution to wages	Road intensity	Station intensity
Export change	1	–0.177	0.017	–0.528	0.796	0.331	0.17
Informality change	–0.177	1	–0.478	0.158	–0.185	0.229	–0.177
Wage change	0.017	–0.478	1	0.063	–0.01	0.014	–0.113
Contribution to informality	–0.528	0.158	0.063	1	–0.2	–0.571	–0.674
Contribution to wages	0.796	–0.185	–0.01	–0.2	1	0.163	0.115
Road intensity	0.331	0.229	0.014	–0.571	0.163	1	0.62
Station intensity	0.17	–0.177	–0.113	–0.674	0.115	0.62	1

Note: The table reports correlations. Road intensity is defined as roads per 1,000 square kilometers, and station intensity is defined as stations per 1,000 square kilometers.

mobility of people. Political tension has further hampered free trade within the region. Addressing these challenges requires policies targeted at reducing high tariffs, improving border infrastructure by reforming customs, and improving resource mobility.[8]

POLICIES TARGETED TO CHANGE THE COMPOSITION OF EXPORTS

Efficient input allocation and reducing barriers to mobility. Much of South Asia's resources are locked away in small and low-productivity enterprises, which has greatly contributed to a "misallocation" of resources. For example, a recent study found that the optimal level of employment of firms in India and Sri Lanka is 3.3 times current employment levels, indicating underuse of labor[9] (Lopez-Acevedo, Medvedev, and Palmade 2017). The existence of significant barriers to free movement of resources across internal geographical borders is another major problem.[10]

The removal of policy-induced distortions that limit the efficient allocation of labor, capital, and land could enable more-productive firms to grow.[11] One way to do this is by encouraging firms to diversify their production base, which would require modifying labor regulations that might cause distortions. For example, some labor laws prevent firms from increasing in size because the laws apply only when a firm reaches a certain number of workers and therefore create incentives to keep firms (formally) small. An indication of the problem is that larger-sized firms are mostly present in states without size-based labor regulations (Hasan and others 2012). The economic literature also provides studies showing that certain labor regulations prevent firms from adjusting their workforce quickly to changing economic conditions, which can lead to lower output, employment, investment, and productivity in formal manufacturing (Aghion and others 2008; Ahsan and Pages 2009; Besley and Burgess 2004); lower sensitivity of industrial employment to local demand shocks (Adhvaryu, Chari, and Sharm 2013); or lower employment in the retail sector (Amin 2009).

Transitioning women to manufacturing. South Asia is experiencing lower rates of FLFP, with FLFP rates falling for countries like India and Sri Lanka.[12] Female workers constitute only 18 percent of the workforce in an average formal firm in South Asia—the lowest across regions. This share is only 11 percent in India, where women continue to perform the bulk of unpaid work—and, when they are employed to do paid work, it is disproportionately in the informal sector.

Our results suggest that helping women enter the labor force will enable workers to move out of informal sectors. This transition would entail changes in regulations that discriminate against women in India and Sri Lanka—such as Maharashtra Shops and Establishments and the Factories Act (1948) in India and Employment of Females in Mines Ordinance No. 13 in Sri Lanka. South Asian countries should continue to direct their efforts to provide adequate childcare support—such as India's 2017 amendment to its Maternity Benefit Act (1961), which requires firms that employ 50 or more workers to provide a nursery for children. Countries should promote gender-sensitive infrastructure, provide safe public transportation and public spaces, and offer financial incentives like tax rebates to companies that achieve gender diversity targets (Solotaroff, Joseph, and Kuriakose 2018).

POLICIES TARGETED TO CHANGE THE COMPOSITION OF THE LABOR FORCE

Investing in skills. An inadequately educated workforce poses a major threat for South Asian countries, with 9 percent and 16 percent of formal firms reporting the same in India and Sri Lanka, respectively.[13] Significantly stepping up investment in training could help boost productivity (Dearden, Reed, and Van Reenen 2006).[14] At this point, formal training opportunities in the region are quite low, with only 28 percent of formal firms providing training to their workers.[15] The proportion of firms in India[16] offering formal training is only 36 percent, and in Sri Lanka only 18 percent—compared with China's 79 percent.

South Asian governments can initiate policies that foster greater synergies between the private sector and vocational institutes to improve training—in both the formal and the informal sectors. Within South Asia, a successful example of an integrated training model is the Chittagong Skills Development Centre in Bangladesh, where high-quality training resources are shared by corporate members, facilitating cost-effective access to training for workers (Nayar 2011).

Subsidies and tax benefits can greatly encourage enterprises, especially the larger ones, to invest in job training. A successful example is the Republic of Korea's levy-rebate system, which encourages larger firms to initiate training by setting aside a portion of a payroll tax on employers for a training fund and then providing reimbursement out of the fund if the employers offer training. Smaller firms operating in the same sectors and regions can be encouraged to take up training by forming training consortiums and jointly hiring trainers to overcome cost issues like in the case of Korea (Almeida, Behrman, and Robalino 2012).

Skills training is important for informal enterprises as well. Managerial inputs are extremely vital for increased productivity levels, greater product quality, and production for international markets; and the managers of informal firms are considerably less educated to achieve this (La Porta and Shleifer 2008, 2014). These firms might also face hurdles in accessing finance if banks lend only to skilled entrepreneurs. La Porta and Shleifer (2014) argue that the best way to overcome this problem would be to train better entrepreneurs and a better-skilled labor force to enable transition to formality. This view resonates with our results showing reductions in informality due to export growth—because only efficient, adequately skilled, and formal enterprises export.

Governments could also safeguard the interests of workers by providing suitable trade assistance programs for workers affected by trade. Although comprehensive trade adjustment programs implemented in places such as Australia, the European Union, and the United States are apt, they are too costly for South Asian countries with limited finances and capabilities. However, a context-specific and targeted mechanism— such as the Argentina REPRO (*Programa de Recuperacion Productiva*, Program for the Recovery of Production)—may be more manageable for South Asia (see annex 5B for details on this and other programs).

Conclusion

The bottom line is that our results show the positive side of globalization in South Asia (especially in India and Sri Lanka) that stems from higher exports. Rising wages and a shift from informal to formal employment are exactly the kinds of benefits governments hoped for when they opened up their economies to international trade. However, our results also highlight that the key beneficiaries are mainly the more well-off groups—notably males, more-educated workers, and urban workers. What can be done to ensure that these benefits are more widely spread among the working population? We suggest the following three policy options:

1. **Increasing the scale of exports.** The degree to which exports might contribute to better labor market outcomes in general depends on the scale of export growth. Certainly, increasing exports in South Asian countries to the levels of Brazil and China would help greatly. We find that higher exports per worker in India increase wages on average between Rs 1,000 and Rs 8,000, and reduce informality between 2.1 million and 12.4 million workers, depending on the scale of export growth—that is, the more the better. In Sri Lanka, a similar pattern is evident for wages.

2. **Changing the composition of exports to help disadvantaged groups.** The extent to which the increase in exports would benefit specific groups in society depends on the type of export shock. For example, an increase in labor-intensive (as opposed to

capital-intensive) exports is likely to have a broader impact on the wages of workers across all educational backgrounds, even those in rural areas. Added to this impact is the bigger reduction in informality—particularly for rural workers and those with secondary education or below.

3. **Changing the composition of the workforce to help disadvantaged groups**. Increasing the participation of disadvantaged groups in the working-age population could also entail reductions in informal work. For example, we find that increasing the skills of workers and increasing the participation of rural and young workers in the labor force to the 75th percentile of their labor force participation rates across districts yield significantly substantial informality reductions if the export shock comes from labor-intensive industries. Similarly, increasing the share of women workers in the labor force to the 75th percentile of their labor force participation rates across districts could reduce informality substantially after an all-industry export shock.

However, making these gains of trade more inclusive requires complementary policies that could potentially address certain issues that restrict the scale and source of exports, and participation of certain groups in the labor force in the region. Some of these policies could focus on (1) boosting and connecting exports to people (for example, by investing in infrastructure and better connectivity and freer trade); (2) eliminating distortions in production (for example, by eliminating distortions in capital/labor inputs, increasing participation of women in merchandise exports, and increasing worker mobility); and (3) protecting workers (for example, by investing in education and skills).

Given that connectivity is imperative to ensure a trade-boosting environment, the region could increasingly target policies at improving the quality of infrastructure. Our results from a correlation exercise show that better road networks go hand in hand with higher exports, and road networks reduce informality and increase wages through export shocks. In this regard, efforts can be directed to ensure that roadway network projects are not delayed by time overruns and budgetary constraints. Simultaneous investments in institutional and digital infrastructure could also promote trade. To boost trade, governments in the region could also promote freer trade by taking actions to reduce high tariffs, improve border infrastructure by reforming customs, and improve resource mobility.

Removing policy distortions that limit the flexibility of labor, capital, and land markets could enable more productive firms to grow. Specifically, efforts could be undertaken to ensure that labor regulations support formal job growth and are effectively implemented for all firms. Greater participation of women in export-oriented industries could also improve labor market outcomes. This would entail changes in the regulations that may discriminate against women in India and Sri Lanka—such as Maharashtra Shops and Establishments and the Factories Act (1948) in India and Employment of Females in Mines Ordinance No. 13 in Sri Lanka—as well as investments in gender-sensitive infrastructure in the workplace (Solotaroff, Joseph, and Kuriakose 2018).

Economic and social obstacles that prevent women from joining the workforce would have to be reduced. Some of these obstacles may already be found in the education system because poor education of women acts as barrier to successful job entry and high-quality jobs.

The region could also make progress in improving skills of workers to prepare the workforce to handle the complexities of globalized production systems. To achieve this progress, greater partnerships between the private sector and vocational institutes could be promoted to improve training—in both the formal and the informal sectors. Other policies like subsidies and tax benefits can greatly encourage enterprises, especially the larger ones, to invest in job training (Almeida, Behrman, and Robalino 2012). Governments could also safeguard the interests of workers by providing suitable trade assistance programs for workers affected by trade.

Annex 5A. The Impact of Different Types of Export Shocks on Specific Groups in India and Sri Lanka

FIGURE 5A.1 Effect of Export Shocks on Different Skill Levels, India and Sri Lanka

a. India: Change in the average annual wage after an increase in exports per worker, by educational attainment and type of trade exposure, 1999–2011

b. India: Change in informality after an increase in exports per worker, by educational attainment and type of trade exposure, 1999–2011

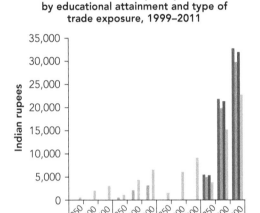
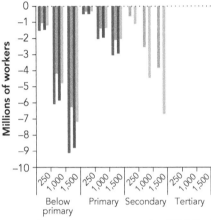

Source: Estimated using data from the Indian Labor Force Surveys.
Note: Results are shown at the significance level of less than 10 percent.

c. Sri Lanka: Change in the average annual wage after an increase in exports per worker, 2002–13

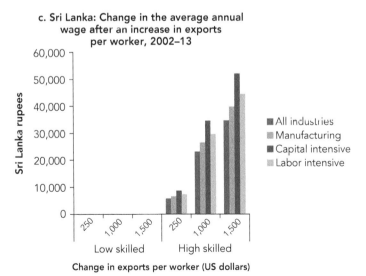

Source: Estimated using data from the Sri Lankan Labor Force Surveys.
Note: Results are shown at the significance level of less than 10 percent.

FIGURE 5A.2 **Effect of Export Shocks on Older and Younger Workers, India and Sri Lanka**

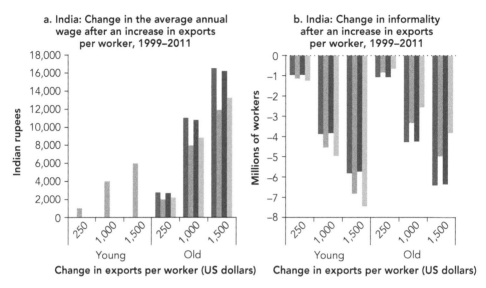

Source: Estimated using data from the Indian Labor Force Surveys.
Note: Results are shown at the significance level of less than 10 percent.

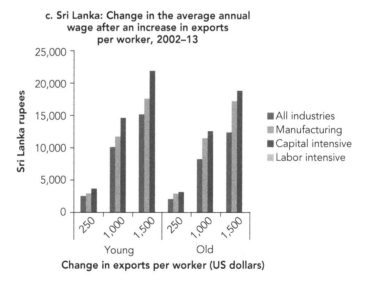

Source: Estimated using data from the Sri Lankan Labor Force Surveys.
Note: Results are shown at the significance level of less than 10 percent.

FIGURE 5A.3 **Effect of Export Shocks on Male and Female Workers, India and Sri Lanka**

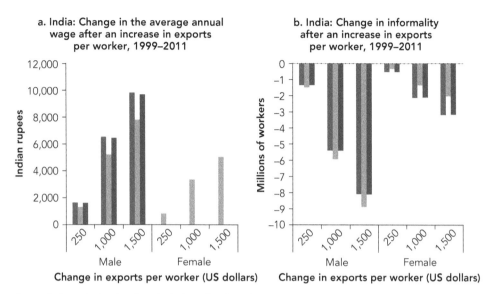

a. India: Change in the average annual wage after an increase in exports per worker, 1999–2011

b. India: Change in informality after an increase in exports per worker, 1999–2011

Source: Estimated using data from the Indian Labor Force Surveys.
Note: Results are shown at the significance level of less than 10 percent.

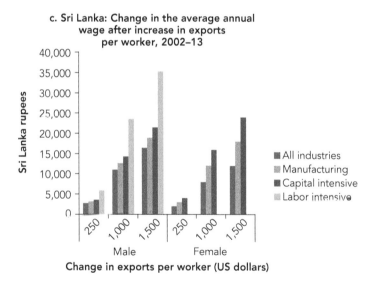

c. Sri Lanka: Change in the average annual wage after increase in exports per worker, 2002–13

Source: Estimated using data from the Sri Lankan Labor Force Surveys.
Note: Results are shown at the significance level of less than 10 percent.

FIGURE 5A.4 **Effect of Export Shocks on Urban and Rural Workers, India and Sri Lanka**

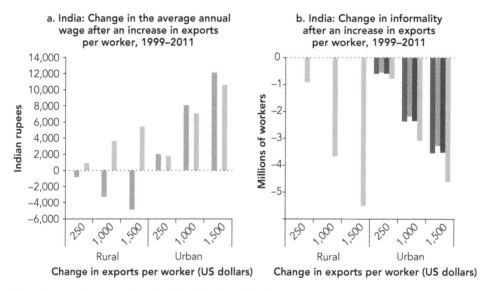

Source: Estimated using data from the Indian Labor Force Surveys.
Note: Results are shown at the significance level of less than 10 percent.

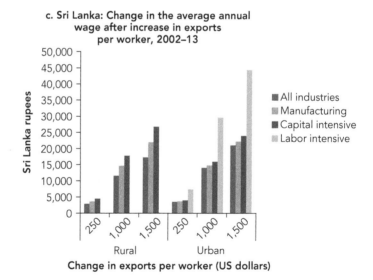

Source: Estimated using data from the Sri Lankan Labor Force Surveys.
Note: Results are shown at the significance level of less than 10 percent, except for urban workers.

Annex 5B. Examples of Trade Adjustment Assistance Programs

DEVELOPED COUNTRIES

U.S. Trade Adjustment Assistance Program (US TAA). This federal program, founded in 1962, assists workers affected by trade to reduce labor adjustment costs by providing resources to help them acquire new skills for reemployment. It is jointly administered by the U.S. Department of Labor, U.S. Department of Agriculture, and U.S. Department of Commerce. The program is aimed at eliminating skills mismatches, and it provides services such as job search assistance, training, wage subsidies, health insurance for the unemployed, and reallocation allowances. This program has undergone several revisions over the decades, and its reviews are mixed. Program evaluations suggest that, despite the boost in employment levels, the US TAA did not raise earnings of program recipients (Decker and Corson 1995; Marcal 2001; Reynolds and Palatucci 2008).

Compensation Payments in European Union Agriculture (CAP). CAP was introduced in the 1960s to protect European Union farmers from foreign competition. The program set high import tariffs, granted export refunds, set quotas on select products, and fixed prices (Porto and Hoekman 2010, chapter 24). Swinnen and Van Herck (2010) conclude that the program resulted in increased farm incomes, but that the increase was mostly due to integrating rural areas into factor markets. Over the long run, CAP has not been effective in protecting employment in the agricultural sector. Farmers appear to have been compensated for losses due to the removal of subsidized prices rather than for losses from foreign competition.

Austrian Steel Foundation. This program was designed and implemented in 1987 to assist workers transitioning from the steel sector to other sectors after the privatization of the Austrian steel industry and subsequent massive layoffs. The program supported workers by providing vocational orientation, assistance in small-business start-up, training, formal education, and aid in conducting job searches (OECD 2005). The results have been positive, prompting the foundation to expand the program to include a larger array of recipients following the financial crisis. An impact evaluation by Winter-Ebmer (2001) concluded that trainees had higher chances of finding gainful employment five years into the program, compared to those in the control group. The estimated total benefits of the program were about US$75 million to US$93 million (in 1998 prices).

DEVELOPING COUNTRIES

Brazil Labor Market Reforms of 1986. These reforms, which started just before Brazil's trade liberalization in 1992, established unemployment insurance, employment subsidies, and other active labor market policies. Both the unemployment insurance and employment subsidy programs targeted workers in formal firms and in formal jobs. In an evaluation, Cunningham (2000) found that the program was not effective in increasing the wages of workers who had collected the insurance, but there was a positive correlation between unemployment insurance and the likelihood of being self-employed. The evaluation of the training and job assistance programs suggested that recipients were 3–4 percent more likely to be employed six months and a year into the program (World Bank 2002). Those who participated in the job search program were slightly more likely to be employed (2 to 3 percentage points) and more likely to be in a formal sector job than those who did not participate in any of the programs (World Bank 2002).

Mexico PROCAMPO. PROCAMPO (*Programa de Apoyos Directos al Campo*, or Farmers Direct Support Program), established in the early 1990s, is by far the largest agricultural program in Mexico. It is aimed at compensating crop producers who expected price declines upon entering the North American Free Trade Agreement. The program entails cash transfers fixed on a per-hectare basis. Recipients were determined by the hectares of their crop production for one of nine crops (maize, beans, wheat, cotton, soybeans, sorghum, rice, barley, and safflower) in one of the three agricultural cycles preceding August 1993 (Cord and Wodon 2001). The program gained massive coverage in 1997—about 90 percent of the country's cultivated area. In their evaluation of *ejido*[17] (which represented 75 percent of Mexican farmers), Cord and Wodon (2001) found that the program reduced poverty in the region and that one peso of the cash transfer resulted in an increase of two pesos in household income.

Mexico PROBECAT. PROBECAT (*Programa de Becas de Capacitacion para Desempleados*, or Scholarship Program for the Training of Unemployed Workers) was created in 1984 to provide skills training to unemployed workers—registered in the State Employment Services Offices—in urban areas hit by the 1982 economic crisis. The program encompassed training in three modules: (1) school-based training, (2) in-service training, and (3) training for the self-employed. The government not only paid stipends to those in in-service training but also obliged employers to hire at least 70 percent of the trainees. The program started out with 50,000 people and expanded to 550,000 over the 1996–98 period (Wodon and Minowa 2001). Despite the success in numbers, program evaluators have found mixed results. Revenga, Riboud, and Tan (1994) report that the program helped recipients attain higher wages and find employment faster than those in the control group. But other evaluators, who accounted for self-selection into the program, report that the program did not have a statistically significant impact on employment or wages (Ravallion and Wodon 1998).

Argentina REPRO. REPRO (*Programa de Recuperacion Productiva*, or Program for the Recovery of Production) was established in Argentina in 2002 to assist workers who were affected by massive layoffs after the country's 2001 economic and financial crisis. It supported firms located in areas that were heavily affected by the crisis. Firms with a sound balance sheet prior to the crisis could apply for the financing scheme for one fiscal year to disburse monthly compensations of up to US$150 to each worker. Participating firms were obliged to keep workers, although they could deduct compensation from the worker's salary and forgo social security. An evaluation by Trucco and Tussie (2012) found that the program prevented 145,235 layoffs at an average cost of US$951 per job to taxpayers.

Notes

1. In this chapter, we also consider the effects of different types of trade shocks, such as capital- and labor-intensive trade shocks. To define capital-intensive and labor-intensive industries, we computed a capital-to-labor ratio by industry at the 3-digit level National Industrial Classification (NIC) 2008 using data from the Indian Labor Force Survey and the Annual Survey of Industries factory data for 2014. Labor-intensive sectors were defined as all those industries corresponding to the 33rd percentile of this measure; capital-intensive are all other industries.

2. It is well established that firms in South Asia often use a high proportion of capital. India uses more capital-intensive techniques of production in manufacturing than countries at similar levels of development (and similar factor endowments), including China. Most authors attribute this in part to stringent labor regulations that impose costs on labor use, driving firms to substitute capital for labor (Hasan and others 2012). Also, this high capital intensity is out of line with India's revealed comparative advantage estimates and relative prices (Dougherty, Herd, and Chalaux 2009).

3. The average wages of both the young and the elderly seem to respond to the same extent to higher exports per capita, except those stemming from labor-intensive industries.

4. A possible explanation of this pattern is that male workers constitute a larger share in the capital-intensive manufacturing industries. Still, the effect of a trade shock on formalization is larger for women in terms of rates of 2.3 percent for women compared to 1.7 percent for men.

5. Data from the World Bank Enterprise Surveys (see http://www.enterprisesurveys.org/0).

6. The government of India, for example, has created special economic zones and coastal employment zones, and has launched large transport infrastructure projects (including Bharatmala for roads and Sagarmala for ports and industrial corridors) that are helping to improve logistics and ease of trading and will definitely promote exports. The pace of the construction of physical infrastructure has been substantially improved, resulting in huge improvements in port dwell time and customs release time for exports. The government is also increasingly adopting technology to reduce manual intervention. Initiatives such as IceGate and e-Sanchit have been introduced to make the transactions faster and without human intervention (Ministry of Commerce and Industry, India, http://commerce.gov.in).

7. Road intensity is negatively correlated with the contribution of trade to an increase in informality (−0.57), and positively correlated with the contribution of trade to an increase in wages (0.16).

8. The government of India, for example, is focused on improving road/rail connectivity with neighboring countries such as Bangladesh and Nepal by initiating several steps: (1) integrated check posts are being developed and land customs stations are being upgraded to improve intraregional trade; and (2) customs procedures are being simplified to ease trade

(Ministry of Commerce and Industry, India, http://commerce.gov.in). Geographical mobility of the workforce within national borders and beyond increases economic efficiency; however, cultural and social barriers may prevent people from being "perfectly" mobile.

9. Most large firms in South Asia do not operate close to optimum efficiency levels given the prevailing factor prices, costing themselves lost profits and bringing down aggregate productivity (Lopez-Acevedo, Medvedev, and Palmade 2017).

10. Lopez-Acevedo, Medvedev, and Palmade (2017) found impediments to the efficient allocation of resources between districts to be stronger than distortions within districts for all South Asian countries in markets for goods, and in India in markets for labor and capital as well. In India, for example, the highest levels of labor movement occur within the same district, whereas the flow of migrant laborers across state lines is a trickle (data from the 2001 Census of India; see http://www.censusindia.gov.in/2011-common/census_data_2001.html).

11. Policy actions should differ so they can target within and between types of misallocations. For example, a reduction in the cost of migration between areas will likely affect misallocation (of capital and labor) across places. Other policies such as a relaxation of the strict zoning policies in Indian cities like Mumbai are expected to improve the efficiency of factor allocation in those areas where these regulations are the most binding.

12. India's FLFP rate fell sharply from just over 37 percent in 2005 to 27 percent in 2017. A similar trend is seen in Sri Lanka, where despite steady economic growth the FLFP rate has declined to 35 percent in 2017 from 41 percent in 2010.

13. The World Bank Enterprise Survey was conducted across countries in different years. Data reported for Sri Lanka are for 2011, data for India are for 2014, data for Pakistan are for 2013, and data for Bangladesh are for 2013.

14. The returns can be large—international evidence shows that a 1 percent increase in training is associated with 0.6 percent increase in value added per hour (Dearden, Reed, and Van Reenen 2006).

15. Data from the World Bank Enterprise Surveys (see http://www.enterprisesurveys.org/). An estimated 42 percent of formal firms in Latin America and the Caribbean, 37 percent of formal firms in Europe and Central Asia, and 32 percent of formal firms in East Asia and Pacific report offering formal training for permanent, full-time workers.

16. In India, training opportunities are lower in labor-intensive sectors than in capital-intensive sectors (Nayar 2011).

17. *Ejido* is communal holding farm land in which community members individually farm designated parcels.

References

Adhvaryu, Achyuta, Amalavoyal Chari, and Siddharth Sharm. 2013. "Firing Costs and Flexibility: Evidence from Firms' Labor Adjustments to Shocks in India." *Review of Economics and Statistics* 95 (3): 725–40.

Aghion Philippe, Robin Burgess, Stephen Redding, and Fabrizio Zilibotti. 2008. "The Unequal Effects of Liberalization: Evidence from Dismantling the License Raj in India." *American Economic Review* 94 (4): 1397–1412.

Ahsan, Ahmad, and Carmen Pages. 2009. "Are All Labor Regulations Equal? Evidence from Indian Manufacturing." *Journal of Comparative Economics* 37: 62–75.

Almeida, Rita, Jere Behrman, and David Robalino. 2012. *The Right Skills for the Job? Rethinking Training Policies for Workers.* Human Development Perspectives. Washington, DC: World Bank.

Amin, Mohammad. 2009. "Labor Regulation and Employment in India's Retail Stores." *Journal of Comparative Economics* 37 (1): 47–61.

Banik, Nilanjan, and John Gilbert. 2010. "Regional Integration and Trade Costs in South Asia." In *Trade Facilitation and Regional Cooperation in Asia,* edited by Douglas H. Brooks and Susan F. Stone, 123–55. Edward Elgar Publishing.

Besley, Timothy, and Robin Burgess. 2004. "Can Labor Regulation Hinder Economic Performance? Evidence from India." *Quarterly Journal of Economics* 119 (1): 91–134.

Cord, Louise, and Quentin Wodon. 2001. "Do Mexico's Agricultural Programs Alleviate Poverty? Evidence from the Ejido Sector." World Bank, Washington, DC.

Cunningham, W. V. 2000. "Unemployment Insurance in Brazil: Unemployment Duration, Wages, and Sectoral Choice." Working Paper, World Bank, Washington, DC.

De, Prabir. 2010. "Governance, Institutions, and Regional Infrastructure in Asia." ADBI Working Paper No. 183, Asian Development Bank Institute, Tokyo.

Dearden, Lorraine, Howard Reed, and John Van Reenen. 2006. "The Impact of Training on Productivity and Wages: Evidence from British Panel Data." *Oxford Bulletin of Economics and Statistics* 68 (4): 397–421.

Decker, Paul T., and Walter Corson. 1995. "International Trade and Worker Displacement: Evaluation of the Trade Adjustment Assistance Program." *Industrial and Labor Relations Review* 48 (4): 758–74.

Dougherty, Sean, Richard Herd, and Thomas Chalaux. 2009. "What Is Holding Back Productivity Growth in India? Recent Microevidence." *OECD Journal of Economic Studies* 2009 (1): 1–22.

Ellis, Peter, and Mark Roberts. 2016. *Leveraging Urbanization in South Asia: Managing Spatial Transformation for Prosperity and Livability.* Washington, DC: World Bank.

Hasan, Rana, and Karl Robert L. Jandoc. 2012. "Labor Regulations and the Firm Size Distribution in Indian Manufacturing." Working Paper No. 2012-3, Program on Indian Economic Policies, School of International and Public Affairs, Columbia University, New York.

Hasan, Rana, Devashish Mitra, Priya Ranjan, and Reshad N. Ahsan. 2012. "Trade Liberalization and Unemployment: Theory and Evidence from India." *Journal of Development Economics* 97 (2): 269–80.

Iqbal, Nasir, and Saima Nawaz. 2017. "Pakistan's Bilateral Trade under MFN and SAFTA: Do Institutional and Non-Institutional Arrangements Matter?" *The Pakistan Development Review* 56 (1): 59–78.

Kathuria, Sanjay. 2018. *A Glass Half Full: The Promise of Regional Trade in South Asia.* South Asia Development Forum. Washington, DC: World Bank.

La Porta, Rafael, and Andrei Shleifer. 2008. "The Unofficial Economy and Economic Development." NBER Working Paper w14520. National Bureau of Economic Research, Cambridge, MA. https://ssrn.com/abstract=1672174.

———. 2014. "Informality and Development." *Journal of Economic Perspectives* 28 (3): 109–26.

Lopez-Acevedo, Gladys, Denis Medvedev, and Vincent Palmade. 2017. *South Asia's Turn: Policies to Boost Competitiveness and Create the Next Export Powerhouse.* South Asia Development Matters. Washington, DC: World Bank.

Marcal, Leah H. 2001. "Does Trade Adjustment Assistance Help Trade-Displaced Workers?" *Contemporary Economic Policy* 19 (1): 59–72.

Nayar, Reema. 2011. *More and Better Jobs in South Asia.* Washington, DC: World Bank.

OECD (Organisation for Economic Co-operation and Development). 2005. *OECD Employment Outlook.* Paris: OECD.

Porto, Guido, and Bernard M. Hoekman, eds. 2010. *Trade Adjustment Costs in Developing Countries: Impacts, Determinants and Policy Responses.* Washington, DC: World Bank.

Ravallion, Martin, and Q. Wodon. 1998. "Evaluating a Targeted Social Program When Placement Is Decentralized." Policy Research Working Paper 1945, World Bank, Washington, DC.

Revenga, A., M. Riboud, and H. Tan. 1994. "The Impact of Mexico's Retraining Program on Employment and Wages." *World Bank Economic Review* 8 (2): 247–77.

Reynolds, Kara M., and John S. Palatucci. 2008. "Does Trade Adjustment Assistance Make a Difference?" Working Paper No 2008-12, American University, Washington, DC. http://nw08 .american.edu/~reynolds/TAA.pdf.

Singh, Harsha Vardhana. 2017. "Trade Policy Reform in India since 1991." Brookings India Working Paper, The Brookings Institution, Washington, DC, March.

Solotaroff, Jennifer L., George Joseph, and Anne Kuriakose. 2018. *Getting to Work: Unlocking Women's Potential in Sri Lanka's Labor Force.* Directions in Development—Countries and Regions. Washington, DC: World Bank.

Swinnen, Johan F. M., and Kristine Van Herck. 2010. "Compensation Payments in EU Agriculture." In *Trade Adjustment Costs in Developing Countries: Impacts, Determinants and Policy Responses*, edited by Guido Porto and Bernard M. Hoekman, 361–81. Washington, DC: World Bank.

Trucco, Pablo, and Diana Tussie. 2012. "Learning from Past Battles in Argentina? The Role of REPRO in the Prevention of Crisis-Induced Layoffs." GTA Analytical Paper No.7, Center for Policy Research, Washington, DC.

Winter-Ebmer, Rudolf, 2001. "Evaluating an Innovative Redundancy-Retraining Project: The Austrian Steel Foundation." IZA Discussion Papers 277, Institute for the Study of Labor, Bonn.

Wodon, Quentin, and Mari Minowa. 2001. "Training for the Urban Unemployed: A Reevaluation of Mexico's Training Program, Probecat." MPRA Paper 12310, University Library of Munich, Germany. https://ideas.repec.org/p/pra/mprapa/12310.html.

World Bank. 2002. "Brazil Jobs Report." World Bank, Washington, DC.

Literature Review: Trade and Local Labor Markets

How Trade Affects Labor Market Outcomes

The effects of "globalization" on wages depend critically on how globalization is defined. Given the worldwide trend toward more international trade and investment, the question of how trade affects workers has been prominent among both policy makers and academics.

Although many different models could be used to generate predictions about the link between globalization and labor market outcomes, most studies begin by at least mentioning the Heckscher–Ohlin–Samuelson (HOS) framework. This restrictive neoclassical model predicts that labor-abundant countries will produce and export labor-intensive goods, and capital-abundant countries will produce and export capital-intensive goods. The rise of the developing countries, which are largely considered to be labor abundant, has been largely driven by exports of labor-intensive goods like apparel and assembly.

The HOS framework also includes implications for wages and employment. The prediction for wages comes mainly from the Stolper–Samuelson theorem, which argues that an increase in the price of labor-intensive goods, such as would occur in developing countries that begin to export their labor-intensive goods to the world, would increase the wages of workers and reduce the earnings of capital. The opposite would then occur in the developed countries, which would buy cheaper labor-intensive goods from developing countries. As the price of labor-intensive goods falls, so do the wages of workers in the developed countries. Although models that seem to dominate current trade studies are based on the Melitz (2003) idea that industries are made up of a variety of larger and smaller firms, other studies have shown that the Stolper-Samuelson predictions still hold.

The HOS framework also has implications for employment that are not always appreciated. The first is that the HOS framework assumes full employment, which means that all workers who want to work have a job. The second is that trade liberalization causes production, and therefore workers, to shift from the import-competing industries to the exported industries. The model assumes that workers move costlessly and between industries. As such, trade policies would not affect aggregate employment levels, but they can cause changes in the sectors in which workers work. Unemployment, to the extent that it is a symptom of business cycles, would not be affected by changes in trade policy.

WAGE LEVELS AND INEQUALITY

Not surprisingly, the wave of trade liberalization that swept through developing countries in the 1990s was followed by a wave of academic studies that wanted to evaluate the link between globalization and wages, including wage inequality. Although South Asia's ratio of trade to gross domestic product (GDP) increased more rapidly after about 1990 (chapter 1, figure 1.2), the rate of poverty reduction (as measured by millions of poor) declined in the mid-2000s (chapter 1, figure 1.1).

One possible reason for the lag in poverty reduction is that trade liberalization usually begins with a reduction in protection from imports. Over time, rising imports cause a reallocation of production from the import-competing sectors to the export sectors. In the short run, however, the increase in competition leads some firms to contract or close. When the firms contract or close, they have to lay off workers. When the workers are laid off, they have to look for work. Often the factories that are expanding are in different parts of the country, and it may be difficult for workers to learn about and find these new jobs. This process may take time, and during the adjustment process one might observe various results. As a result, inequality following liberalization may rise at first as workers lose their jobs because of import competition but then fall in the longer run as workers move to the exporting sectors and wages increase. A heuristic review of the literature suggests this might be the case.

The first step of the reforms of the late 1980s and early 1990s was usually drastic tariff reductions, often paired with a significant reduction in nontariff trade barriers. In Colombia, the nontariff barriers declined from 72.2 percent in 1986 to 1.1 percent in 1992. In Mexico, the share of manufacturing production subject to import licenses dropped from 92.0 percent in 1985 to 23.2 percent in 1988. In India, the share of manufacturing imports covered by nontariff barriers declined from 80 percent in 1990 to 17 percent in 1999 (Mishra and Kumar 2005).

Economists were quick to analyze the short-run wage effects, but less work has been done on the longer-term effects. Hundreds of studies have examined trade liberalization in developing countries, and, by definition, most of them focus on the effects of falling barriers to imports. Goldberg and Pavcnik (2007) suggest that trade liberalization may increase poverty and inequality and lower wages and employment, especially in the short run—a story corroborated by studies from Latin America, which suggest that wage inequality rose, rather than fell, immediately following trade liberalization (Wood 1997). However, over the longer run, there is growing evidence that wage inequality is reduced as occurred in Mexico (box A.1).

BOX A.1 Mexico: Trade Liberalization and Wage Inequality

Initial wage inequality. When Mexico joined the General Agreement on Tariffs and Trade (GATT) in 1986, it was arguably among the less-skilled economies of the signatories. By entering GATT, it reduced tariffs in the most protected sectors, which were sectors that intensively used less-skilled workers. The unskilled sector took the hardest hit in terms of wages and employment. The relative price of skill-intensive goods rose, pulling up with it the relative wages of skilled workers (Robertson 2004). These developments were in part explained by a decline in industrial production and labor demand (Revenga 1997). Also, there was substantial heterogeneity across firms in rent sharing. Firms with a higher proportion of skilled workers showed stronger rent sharing than those with a higher fraction of unskilled workers (Revenga 1997, 42), which may have resulted in lower wages for unskilled workers.

Subsequent greater wage equality. Then, in 1994, Mexico further liberalized trade by joining the North American Free Trade Agreement (NAFTA) with the United States and Canada. NAFTA members reduced tariffs and fostered deeper North American integration by harmonizing standards, facilitating capital flows, and reducing nontariff barriers (Robertson 2004, 388). Tariff reductions in Mexico due to NAFTA were bigger in more skill-intensive sectors, suggesting the end of the increase in skill premiums. After NAFTA, Robertson (2004) found that the relative price of skill-abundant goods fell and so did the relative wages of skilled workers, thereby reversing the rise in wage inequality.

The popular idea that liberalization increases wage inequality (Goldberg and Pavcnik 2007) is based on the short-term effects and not the longer-term effects that show that wage inequality in Mexico—along with much of Latin America and the Caribbean and most of East Asia and Pacific—ultimately fell dramatically after trade liberalization (see Wood 1997 for a description of East Asian wage inequality and Rodriguez-Castelan et al. 2016 for a description of Latin American wage inequality in the 2000s).

In addition, it is important to consider other dimensions of trade beyond reducing tariffs of final (often import-competing) goods. We know that reducing tariffs on inputs used in manufacturing can lower production costs and encourage domestic manufacturing to expand. Concurrent with their trade reforms, several developing countries experienced increased trade in intermediate inputs, and others saw a significant increase in foreign direct investment. All of these factors helped to boost trade in developing countries in the 1980s and 1990s (Goldberg and Pavcnik 2007) (box A.2).

In India, the lowering of trade barriers in the 1990s coincided with substantial changes in poverty and income inequality at the subnational level. A paper close to our study (Topalova 2010) focuses on the variation in timing and degree of liberalization across industries to examine whether a causal link exists between liberalization and changes in poverty and inequality in India. It does this by estimating the link between poverty and inequality at the district level and district-specific trade shocks. It finds that trade liberalization led to an increase in poverty rates and a wider poverty gap in rural districts where industries more exposed to liberalization were concentrated. A rural district experiencing the average level of tariff reduction saw a 2 percent increase in poverty incidence as compared to a rural district that experienced no change in tariff reduction (Topalova 2010, 2).

> ### BOX A.2 Indonesia: Reducing Poverty by Reducing Tariffs on Inputs
>
> In Indonesia, trade liberalization from 1993 to 2000 coincided with reduced poverty, particularly in districts with greater industry exposure to input tariff reductions. Amiti and Davis (2011) used highly detailed census data on Indonesian manufacturing for the period 1991–2000 and found that a fall in output tariffs lowers wages at import-competing firms while it boosts wages at exporting firms. This result is consistent with rising prices of exports and falling prices of imports, which is the mechanism driving the Heckscher–Ohlin–Samuelson model.
>
> Using district-level data, Kis-Katos and Sparrow (2015) suggest that falling poverty in Indonesia was due to the increased employment of low- and medium-skilled workers in response to a reduction in import tariffs on intermediate goods (rather than a reduction in import tariffs on final outputs). Kis-Katos and Sparrow (2015) conclude that better access to imported inputs seems to have driven poverty reduction in Indonesia.

This finding would be puzzling in the context of traditional trade theory, particularly the Heckscher–Ohlin and Stolper–Samuelson models, where factors are mobile both geographically and across industries. In the case of India, however, evidence from the study suggests that mobility of factors is extremely limited. The geographical dimension of inequality is explained by absence of reallocation, where migration is remarkably low with no evidence of an upward trend in the postreform period (Topalova 2010).

The short-run increase in wage inequality that followed trade liberalization inspired many economists to look for other explanations (Harrison, McLaren, and McMillan 2010, 3). One alternative explanation suggests that changes in technology (such as greater use of computers) could increase the demand for skilled workers. Other possible factors include the weakening of labor market institutions such as unions, the declining real value of minimum wages, differential access to schooling, and immigration (Harrison, McLaren, and McMillan 2010). Not surprisingly, these studies find various levels of support for these alternative explanations, but rarely are these alternative explanations compared directly to trade. It is therefore possible that trade may be having significant effects that vary over time, depending on the speed of adjustment in employment.

EMPLOYMENT AND INFORMALITY

How about employment levels and changes in informality? Given that the neoclassical trade models assume full employment, they do not predict large effects of trade policy on employment levels. But this perception differs from popular ones that often posit strong links between trade policy and employment. Empirically, however, the link between trade policy reform and aggregate unemployment does not seem to be strong (Cirera, Willenbockel, and Lakshman 2014). Wacziarg and Wallack (2004) evaluate the link between trade liberalization in 25 middle-income countries and find that trade reforms have little to no effect on aggregate worker reallocation.

When trade policy is linked to job reallocation, the strongest results are for changes in tariffs protecting import-competing sectors. For Brazil, Menezes-Filho and Muendler (2011) find that tariff cuts induced job loss from the import-competing sectors, with workers moving into unemployment or out of the labor force. Instead, falling tariffs on inputs into manufacturing increased employment, but it was not necessarily the same workers moving from the import-competing industries to the expanding exporting industries.

Firms can also respond to import competition in ways other than by adjusting labor. A labor demand model developed by Currie and Harrison (1997) allows for imperfect competition, and endogenous technological change shows that firms can respond to trade reforms by cutting profit margins and raising productivity. When the authors apply this model to Morocco, they find that firms display a range of responses. The 21 percent decline in tariff protection experienced by firms in the most affected sectors—textiles, beverages, and apparel—was associated with a 3.5 percent decline in employment. Among exporting firms, a 24 percent decline in tariff protection was associated with nearly a 6 percent decline in employment (Currie and Harrison 1997). At the same time, however, a significant fraction of manufacturing firms did not adjust wages or employment in response to tariff reductions and the elimination of quotas. Unlike private firms, government-owned firms actually increased employment in response to tariff reductions, mostly by hiring low-paid temporary workers. As a result, wages fell. Productivity in these firms also increased as quota coverage fell. Government firms thus experienced a less-painful mode of adjustment, wherein excess profits absorbed trade shocks, leaving the labor force unaffected (Currie and Harrison 1997).

Informality plays a very important role in developing country employment. When workers do not have income support, such as unemployment insurance or government income assistance, working is necessary for survival. As a result, informal work is common and plays the role that unemployment insurance might play in developed countries. Workers in developing countries therefore move between the formal and informal sectors when labor demand changes. In a given city with both formal and informal workers, an increase in demand in the export sector could cause workers to move from working in the informal sector to working in the formal sector. Such a move could increase their wages, because wages are often higher in the formal sector, but may not show up as a change in aggregate (city-wide) employment. This result would be especially prevalent for less-educated workers because they tend to have less-formal attachment to the labor force and are the most vulnerable.

The informal labor force is defined using different variables in different countries, but usually informality is defined as being outside of formal government oversight. For example, firms that do not register with Mexico's social security agency have been identified as informal. In general, informal workers are not covered by social insurance, minimum wages, or other legal protections. Both firms and workers can be considered informal, and formal firms (such as those that pay taxes and register with the government) may employ workers "off the books" who are considered informal.

Thus, informality is an important dimension of the labor market outcomes that are considered in this report. To date, there are relatively few studies that consider the link between changes in trade policy and informality. Goldberg and Pavcnik (2007) describe some of the exceptions. They show that the evidence is mixed. Labor markets that are characterized by effective regulation, and thus are considered "inflexible," tend to have more firms that favor informal employment. But labor markets that are more flexible tend to have less informal employment after trade liberalization.

Location, Location, Location: Why Local Labor Markets Matter

How do these various labor market impacts play out at the local level? One of the several intriguing results from Topalova (2010) is that the effects of tariff reductions were highly localized. In other words, geographic regions that produced goods with falling protection experienced the largest (adverse) labor market outcomes. Localized labor market effects have been demonstrated by labor economists for decades. Topel (1986) is one of the first studies to demonstrate the importance of studying local labor markets. Using data from the United States, Topel (1986) shows that workers face adjustment costs when local conditions change, but not all workers face the same costs. Topel (1986) shows that workers with less education were more tied to the local labor market than workers with more education. The main implication of this result was that adverse local labor demand shocks hit the least-educated and lowest-paid workers hardest. Topalova (2010) applies this idea to India but also identifies falling barriers to imports as a specific kind of labor market shock.

Topalova was not the first to bring together trade policy and labor market adjustment costs. Davidson, Matusz, and Nelson (2007) build on several of their previous papers that explicitly incorporate adjustment costs into trade models in order to evaluate the net welfare effects of trade liberalization. Many subsequent studies recognize and incorporate adjustment costs into trade models, but few explicitly distinguish between firm-level and worker-level adjustment costs. Before discussing these papers in detail, it is first important to describe the different types of adjustment costs.

UNDERSTANDING LABOR MARKET ADJUSTMENT COSTS

Labor markets, like all markets, have both a demand side and a supply side. The demand side consists of those who demand (hire) labor: firms. The supply side consists of those who supply labor: workers. Labor market adjustment costs are important on both sides of the labor market. On the one hand, training, searching, hiring, and firing are costly for firms. Several papers, such as Hamermesh (1993) and Galeazzi and Hamermesh (1993) estimate firm-level adjustment costs and compile existing estimates using labor demand models. For example, Shapiro (1986) and Burgess and Dolado (1989) find significant firm-level adjustment costs in the United Kingdom and the United States. Firm-level adjustment cost estimates from developing countries are relatively rare. Robertson and Dutkowsky (2002) find that firm-level adjustment costs are an order of magnitude smaller in Mexico than in the United States.[1] It seems likely that de facto firm-level adjustment costs in developing countries may be quite low.

On the other hand, on the supply side of the labor market, workers face their own costs of adjustment. It is costly for workers to change jobs, industries, and geographic location. These costs include, but are not limited to, moving costs, loss of relationships and particular skills (Neal 1995), preference for amenities, and perhaps the psychic costs of changing (especially losing) jobs. Economists have long recognized that worker-level adjustment costs have significant implications for labor markets. For example, the "job lock" literature[2] identifies job characteristics, such as health insurance, that would reduce job mobility by increasing the cost to workers from moving. Empirical estimates suggest "job lock" may reduce mobility by 20 to 40 percent. Although a few authors such as Monheit and Cooper (1994) and Berger, Black, and Scott (2004) question the magnitude of the effect, most[3] agree that these adjustment costs reduce voluntary worker turnover. In other words, workers may be quite slow to move from one job to another, even when new opportunities arise in other areas of the country.

The ability to estimate worker-level adjustment costs took a major step forward in 2010 when Artuç, Chaudhuri, and McLaren (2010) developed a model to estimate worker-level adjustment costs. A key aspect of their model was that the earnings possibility in a given destination (the "option value") plays an important role in migration decisions. The idea of the option value found empirical support in Kennan and Walker's (2011) study of individuals' migration decisions in the United States. It shows that interstate migration decisions are influenced to a substantial degree by income prospects in the destination state. In other words, decisions are made to maximize the expected present value of lifetime income (Kennan and Walker 2011, 246). This finding seems to suggest that a starting point in analyzing the spread of local labor market shocks across the rest of the economy is to identify industry expansions or contractions elsewhere in the economy. Labor mobility barriers become a valid starting point for analyzing localized labor market impacts of trade shocks when tangible job opportunities exist elsewhere in the economy.

Artuç, Chaudhuri, and McLaren (2010) apply their model to the United States and find that worker-level adjustment costs are quite large—perhaps as much as eight times annual earnings. Workers, it seems, are not very responsive to wage changes in other industries in the sense that the evolving wage differences between industries have very small effects on worker movement between industries. Therefore, when trying to estimate the effects of trade policy, tariff liberalization, or, in our case, exports, it is important to focus on local labor market effects.

The authors also find adjustment costs to be high in Turkey; and Hollweg et al. (2014) find that adjustment costs to workers in several developing countries are high, on the basis of data on net employment flows and wages. Their sample, however, does not contain any

South Asian economy. Together, these results suggest that the adjustment costs that workers face may be one of the more important factors affecting movement between sectors in developing countries.

RECENT STUDIES ON DEVELOPED AND DEVELOPING LOCAL LABOR MARKETS

So far, most of the work on trade effects in local labor markets has focused on trade shocks to developed countries, and it finds that trade effects of import competition are localized and large. But the few recent studies on developing countries (such as Brazil, India, Morocco, Sri Lanka, and Vietnam) show mixed results (either positive, negative, or neutral), suggesting that the effects are not well understood.

Local markets in Europe. Several recent studies focus on the effect of China's export growth on local labor markets in developed countries. Dauth, Findeisen, and Suedekum (2013) focus on Germany and show that employment grew in regions specializing in export-oriented industries as trade between Germany and China and Eastern Europe rose over the 1988–2008 period. Import-competing regions, however, experienced substantial job losses in manufacturing and in other sectors. People seem also to resist changing occupations, as Traiberman (2016) shows using Danish administrative data—with older and less-educated workers especially resistant to changing occupations.

Local markets in the United States. Focusing on rising competition from China in the United States, Autor, Dorn, and Hanson (2013) find reduced wages and employment in those labor markets producing goods that competed with China, with little change in the populations in the regions that were hurt. Nearly a decade of import competition was not enough to get people to move to a new location. Caliendo, Dvorkin, and Parro (2015) complement these results by finding that Chinese competition reduced U.S. manufacturing employment by about 800,000 jobs and that these job losses were concentrated in particular regions. Harrison, McLaren, and McMillan (2010) and McLaren (2016) echo these findings and reiterate that workers tend not to move to new jobs because of domestic barriers— whether geographic, occupational, or institutional.

As for increased competition from Mexico following the North American Free Trade Agreement (NAFTA), Hakobyan and McLaren (2010) find that workers in vulnerable industries suffered large absolute declines in real wages, whereas college-educated workers were mainly unharmed. They also find that reductions in the local average tariff were associated with substantial decreases in the locality's blue collar wages (even for workers in the service sector). The blue collar workers, particularly those workers who never finished high school, were hurt by the agreement. At the same time, college-educated workers were mainly unharmed. Thus, as the result of the agreement, blue collar workers in highly affected industries experienced substantially lower wage growth than workers in other industries (Hakobyan and McLaren 2010).

Further, trade expansion had a negative impact on female employment relative to male employment in states with greater exports to Mexico. Hakobyan and McLaren (2016) study the differential impact of tariff reductions on men's and women's wage growth and labor force participation decisions over the 1990s by exploiting the exogenous nature of the NAFTA shock. Using U.S. Census data from 1990 and 2000, they estimate the simultaneous differential impact of a trade shock within dimensions of location, gender, marital status, industry of employment, and education (Hakobyan and McLaren 2016, 4). Results suggest that declining blue collar wage growth as a result of NAFTA tariff reductions was much larger for women than men, and much larger for married women than single. One possible explanation suggested was the fact that married female workers adjust to a trade shock by leaving the labor market (Hakobyan and McLaren 2016, 36).

Offshoring, or the transfer of production activities from one country to another, is another way that trade with developing countries can affect labor markets in developed countries. Artuç and McLaren (2014) conduct simulations for occupations and sectors abroad (offshorable) that illustrate how a sharp drop in wages could be followed by recovery within a decade, thereby leading to a modest welfare loss for offshorable workers in the affected industry. Simulations of offshore shocks further show a welfare gain for workers in nonoffshorable industries. The simulations also show modest reduction in the welfare of less-educated workers in other industries, because of increased labor supply released by the offshoring sector, with a corresponding gain for college-educated workers in those other industries (Artuç and McLaren 2014, 292). Artuç and McLaren (2014) also show that trade shock–induced labor-switching costs are significant and similar in magnitude both for sectoral and occupational switching. Trade shock simulations using this model showed temporary sharp drops in wages in import-competing sectors, followed by recovery within a decade. In terms of labor welfare, this resulted in a modest loss for workers in the affected industry regardless of occupation or educational status.

Local markets in Brazil. Empirical evidence confirms a painful adjustment for workers in import-competing industries after trade liberalization in the 1990s—with the impact of tariff changes in regional earnings 20 years after liberalization three times the effect after 10 years. The reasons why are many.

Search frictions. One study shows a very slow transition to services, as well as rising unemployment and exit from the labor force (Menezes-Filho and Muendler 2011). Using Brazilian longitudinal data, it finds that workers separated from a job because of import competition tend to take years to find work in a new industry, and often spend long intervals in the informal sector. Another study shows that regional wage differentials caused by the local effects of the 1991 trade liberalization were not eliminated or even narrowed 20 years later (in fact, they widened) (Dix-Carneiro and Kovak 2017). The novelty of the paper is that it empirically investigates the mechanisms responsible for these effects. The authors find that the negative effects of liberalization are amplified by imperfect interregional labor mobility and dynamics in labor demand, driven by slow capital adjustments and agglomeration economics.

Human capital barriers. In analyzing intersectoral reallocation of labor in response to trade reform in Brazil, Cosar (2013) uses a general equilibrium model with overlapping generations and human capital that is uniquely tied to a sector (sector-specific human capital). The choice of modeling is based on evidence that labor reallocation is very sluggish. Moreover, the costs of losing a job (also called displacement) are higher the older the age of the worker. Simulation results showed that labor market adjustment in response to a reallocation shock can take a very long time because of labor market frictions and the sector-specific nature of human capital. Uniqueness of human capital at the sector level was found to pose a much bigger barrier to labor mobility than search frictions.

Occupational barriers. A third study suggests that trade liberalization in Brazil is associated with additional barriers to labor mobility, including long transition times, high cost of mobility, and imperfectly transferable worker experience (Dix-Carneiro 2010). It analyzes trade-induced transitional dynamics in the Brazilian labor market by estimating a structural dynamic equilibrium model featuring a multisector economy with overlapping generations, heterogeneous workers, endogenous accumulation of sector-specific worker experience, and costly switching of sectors. The results show a median cost of mobility that ranges from 1.4 to 2.7 times annual average wages (Dix-Carneiro 2010, 3). Furthermore, results show that the experience of workers is imperfectly transferable across sectors.

Geographical barriers. A study of the effect and magnitude of migration costs on labor mobility in Brazil finds substantial costs associated with labor migration across geography (Morten and Oliveira 2016). A spatial equilibrium model of 18 million intermunicipality migrations in Brazil over 1980–2000 shows that mobility is determined not only by idiosyncratic tastes but also by moving costs—which, measured as a proportion of mean wages, were found to be considerable. The average observed migration cost between two municipalities is equal to 0.8 to 1.2 times the annual wage, controlling for distance between origin and destination (Morten and Oliveira 2016, 38). The observed costly migration implies that (i) population elasticity of migration to wage shocks depends on the ease of accessing other labor markets, and (ii) costly migration leads to highly concentrated distributional effects of regional shocks. Simulations from the model show that the incidence of the same wage shock is 30 times higher in the case of costly migration than it is in the costless migration.

Local markets in Vietnam. Not all studies of developing countries find sluggish adjustment. In a study analyzing the labor market impacts of Vietnam's free trade agreement with the United States, McCaig and Pavcnik (2014) find significant reallocation of labor from informal household businesses to employers in the formal enterprise sector. Greater reallocation appeared in industries that experienced larger declines in U.S. tariffs on Vietnamese exports because of the United States–Vietnam Bilateral Trade Agreement. The reallocation was larger for workers in more internationally integrated provinces and among younger workers (McCaig and Pavcnik 2014, 1). Results of this study also suggest that expanded export opportunities increased employment in the enterprise sector in manufacturing by 15 percent (McCaig and Pavcnik 2014, 3). At the same time, the aggregate share of household business declined in Vietnam during the early 2000s. Within the context of trade theory, the results indicate that removal of export market distortions, which harm the profitability of more-productive firms, induces a movement of labor away from less-productive employers in the small business sector toward the more-productive formal enterprise sector. In turn, this leads to sizable gains in aggregate productivity (McCaig and Pavcnik 2014).

Notes

1. Kaplan, Sadka, and Silva-Mendez (2007) suggest that one reason for this is that the higher legally imposed firing costs may not often be enforced.
2. Gruber and Madrian (2002) provide a thorough review of this literature.
3. Examples include Adams (2004), Gilleskie and Lutz (2002), Madrian (1994), and Sanz-de-Galdeano (2006).

References

Adams, Scott. J. 2004. "Employer-Provided Health Insurance and Job Change." *Contemporary Economic Policy* 22: 357–69.

Amiti, Mary, and Donald R. Davis. 2011. "Trade, Firms and Wages: Theory and Evidence." *Review of Economic Studies* 79 (1): 1–36.

Artuç, Erhan, Shubham Chaudhuri, and John McLaren. 2010. "Trade Shocks and Labor Adjustment: A Structural Empirical Approach" *The American Economic Review* 100 (3): 1008–45.

Artuç, Erhan, and John McLaren. 2014. "Trade Policy and Wage Inequality: A Structural Analysis with Occupational and Sectoral Mobility." *Journal of International Economics* 97 (2): 278–94.

Autor, David H., David Dorn, and Gordon Hanson. 2013. "The China Syndrome: Local Labor Market Effects of Import Competition in the United States." *The American Economic Review* 103 (6): 2121–68.

Berger, Mark C., Dan A. Black, and Frank A. Scott. 2004. "Is There Job Lock? Evidence from the Pre-HIPAA Era." *Southern Economic Journal* 70 (4): 953–76.

Burgess, Simon M., and Juan J. Dolado. 1989. "Intertemporal Rules with Variable Speed of Adjustment: An Application to U.K. Manufacturing Employment." *Economic Journal* 99 (396): 347–65.

Caliendo, Lorenzo, Maximilano Dvorkin, and Fernando Parro. 2015. "The Impact of Trade on Labor Market Dynamics." NBER Working Paper 21149, National Bureau of Economic Research, Cambridge, MA.

Cirera, X., D. Willenbockel, and R. W. Lakshman. 2014. "Evidence on the Impact of Tariff Reductions on Employment in Developing Countries: A Systematic Review." *Journal of Economic Surveys* 28 (3): 449 71.

Cosar, A. Kerem. 2013. "Adjusting to Trade Liberalization: Reallocation and Labor Market Policies." Booth School of Business, University of Chicago. http://economics.yale.edu/sites/default/files/files/Workshops-Seminars/International-Trade/cosar-101103.pdf.

Currie, Janet, and Ann Harrison. 1997. "Sharing the Costs: The Impact of Trade Reform on Capital and Labor in Morocco." *Journal of Labor Economics* 15 (S3): S44–S71.

Dauth, Wolfgang, Sebastian Findeisen, and Jens Suedekum. 2013. "The Rise of the East and the Far East: German Labor Markets and Trade Integration." *Journal of the European Economic Association* 12 (6): 1643–75.

Davidson, Carl, Steven Matusz, and Douglas Nelson. 2007. "Can Compensation Save Free Trade?" *Journal of International Economics* 71 (1): 167–86.

Dix-Carneiro, Rafael. 2010. "Trade Liberalization and Labor Market Dynamics." Job Market Paper, Princeton University, Princeton, NJ

Dix-Carneiro, Rafael, and Brian K. Kovak 2017. "Trade Liberalization and Regional Dynamics." *American Economic Review* 107 (10): 2908–46.

Galeazzi, Giorgio, and Daniel Hamermesh, eds. 1993. *Dynamic Labor Demand and Adjustment Costs*. International Library of Critical Writings in Economics series. Edward Elgar Publishing.

Gilleskie, Donna B., and Byron F. Lutz. 2002. "The Impact of Employer-Provided Health Insurance on Dynamic Employment Transitions." *Journal of Human Resources* 37 (1): 129–62.

Goldberg, Pinelopi Koujianou, and Nina Pavcnik. 2007. "Distributional Effects of Globalization in Developing Countries." *Journal of Economic Literature* 45 (1): 39–82.

Gruber, Jonathan, and Brigitte C. Madrian. 2002. "Health Insurance, Labor Supply, and Job Mobility: A Critical Review of the Literature." NBER Working Paper 8817, National Bureau of Economic Research, Cambridge, MA.

Hakobyan, Shushanik, and John McLaren. 2010. "Looking for Local Labor Market Effects of NAFTA." NBER Working Paper 16535, National Bureau of Economic Research, Cambridge, MA.

———. 2016. "Looking for Local Labor Market Effects of NAFTA." *Review of Economics and Statistics* 98 (4): 728–41.

Hamermesh, Daniel. 1993. *Labor Demand*. Princeton, NJ: Princeton University Press.

Harrison, Ann, John McLaren, and Margaret McMillan. 2010. "Recent Findings on Trade and Inequality." NBER Working Paper 16425, National Bureau of Economic Research, Cambridge, MA.

Hollweg, Claire H., Daniel Lederman, Diego Rojas, and Elizabeth Ruppert Bulmer. 2014. *Sticky Feet: How Labor Market Frictions Shape the Impact of International Trade on Jobs and Wages*. Washington, DC: World Bank.

Kaplan, David S., Joyce Sadka, and Jorge Luis Silva-Mendez. 2007. "Litigation and Settlement: New Evidence from Labor Courts in Mexico." Policy Research Working Paper 4434, World Bank, Washington, DC.

Kennan, John, and James R. Walker. 2011 "The Effect of Expected Income on Individual Migration Decisions." *Econometrica* 79 (1): 211–51.

Kis-Katos, Krisztina, and Robert Sparrow. 2015. "Poverty, Labor Markets and Trade Liberalization in Indonesia." *Journal of Development Economics* 117: 94–106.

Madrian, Brigitte C. 1994. "Employment-Based Health Insurance and Job Mobility: Is There Evidence of Job-Lock?" *Quarterly Journal of Economics* 109 (1): 27–54.

McCaig, Brian, and Nina Pavcnik. 2014. "Export Markets and Labor Allocation in a Low-Income Country." NBER Working Paper 20455, National Bureau of Economic Research, Cambridge, MA.

McLaren, John. 2016. "Globalization and Labor Market Dynamics." University of Virginia. http://www.people.virginia.edu/~jem6x/globalization%20and%20labor%20market%20dynamics%20mclaren%20081516%20draft.pdf.

Melitz, M. J. 2003. "The Impact of Trade on Intra-Industry Reallocations and Aggregate Industry Productivity." *Econometrica* 71: 1695–1725.

Menezes-Filho, Naercio A., and Marc-Andreas Muendler. 2011. "Labor Reallocation in Response to Trade Reform." NBER Working Paper 17372, National Bureau of Economic Research, Cambridge, MA.

Mishra, Prachi, and Utsav Kumar. 2005. "Trade Liberalization and Wage Inequality: Evidence from India." IMF Working Paper 05/20, International Monetary Fund, Washington, DC.

Monheit, Alan, and Phillip Cooper. 1994. "Health Insurance and Job Mobility: Theory and Evidence." *Industrial and Labor Relations Review* 48 (1): 68–85.

Morten, Melanie, and Jaqueline Oliveira. 2016. "Paving the Way to Development: Costly Migration and Labor Market Integration." NBER Working Paper 22158, National Bureau of Economic Research, Cambridge, MA.

Neal, Derek. 1995. "Industry-Specific Human Capital: Evidence from Displaced Workers." *Journal of Labor Economics* 13 (4): 653–77.

Revenga, Ana. 1997. "Employment and Wage Effects of Trade Liberalization: The Case of Mexican Manufacturing." *Journal of Labor Economics* 15 (S3): S20–S43.

Robertson, Raymond. 2004. "Relative Prices and Wage Inequality: Evidence from Mexico." *Journal of International Economics* 64: 387–409.

Robertson, R., and D. H. Dutkowsky. 2002. "Labor Adjustment Costs in a Destination Country: The Case of Mexico." *Journal of Development Economics* 67 (1): 29–54.

Rodriguez-Castelan, Carlos, Luis F. Lopez-Calva, Nora Lustig, and Daniel Valderrama. 2016. "Understanding the Dynamics of Labor Income Inequality in Latin America." Policy Research Working Paper 7795, World Bank, Washington, DC.

Sanz-De-Galdeano, Anna. 2006. "Job-Lock and Public Policy: Clinton's Second Mandate." *Industrial and Labor Relations Review* 59 (3): 430–37.

Shapiro, Matthew D. 1986. "The Dynamic Demand for Capital and Labor." *The Quarterly Journal of Economics* 101 (3): 513–42.

Topalova, Petia. 2010. "Factor Immobility and Regional Impacts of Trade Liberalization: Evidence on Poverty from India." *American Economic Journal: Applied Economics* 2 (4): 1–41.

Topel, Robert. 1986. "Local Labor Markets" *Journal of Political Economy* 94 (3, pt. 2): S111–S143.

Traiberman, Sharon. 2016. "Occupations and Import Competition: Evidence from Danish Matched Employee-Employer Data." Job Market Paper, Princeton University, Princeton, NJ.

Wacziarg, R., and J. S. Wallack. 2004. "Trade Liberalization and Intersectoral Labor Movements." *Journal of International Economics* 64 (2): 411–39.

Wood, Adrian. 1997. "Openness and Wage Inequality in Developing Countries: The Latin American Challenge to East Asian Conventional Wisdom." *World Bank Economic Review* 11 (1): 33–57.

Entangled Workers and Shared Prosperity in South Asian Labor Markets: Construction of Databases

General

This research aims at better understanding the impacts of trade shocks on workers' well-being. In particular, we are trying to understand how and if workers or certain groups of workers can adjust to trade shocks, for example, by moving geographically or by switching occupations. Moreover, our research strives to highlight the distributional consequences of such shocks on different groups, that is, whether international trade affects certain groups of workers disproportionately. For our empirical analysis, we consider trade flows at the industry level and labor market outcomes at the worker level in South Asia. We use sets of microdata for three countries in South Asia: Bangladesh, India, and Sri Lanka. In particular, we construct country-specific databases using household/labor force surveys for several years between 1992 and 2015 and combine these data with another dataset on international trade flows. All household/labor force surveys provide information on individuals' employment status, earnings, and other socioeconomic variables such as gender, education, religion, and others. For Pakistan, we use data from the International Labour Organization and the United Nations (UN) Comtrade database.[1]

In order to link these labor market data to international trade, we use annual, bilateral trade data from Comtrade on the 4-digit commodity level in value terms for the years 1990–2015 (HSO 1988/92). We calculate total export/import values by commodity for several country groups (for example, the total of all Indian exports, or the sum of all imports by Organisation for Economic Co-operation and Development countries). We subsequently match the commodity-level trade values with industries according to the ISIC Rev.3.1 classification (UN International Standard Industrial Classification of All Economic Activities, Rev.3). We use the impact of the financial and economic crisis of 2007–08 on trade values as an exogenous trade shock and compare labor market and socioeconomic outcomes before and after this shock.

Comparing household/labor force surveys over such a long time span poses some challenges. Questionnaires, industry structures, and geographical entities usually change over time. Hence, several variables are not comparable over time and needed to be harmonized. We describe in detail below how we have constructed the databases for each of the three countries.

Bangladesh

For Bangladesh, we use the labor force survey (LFS) provided by Bangladesh Bureau of Statistics, which is designed to measure the levels and trends of employment, unemployment, and underemployment by groups on the basis of socioeconomic characteristics. This household-based sample survey provides data at the national, rural, and urban levels with further stratification possible. Units of analysis are individuals and households.

Although the LFS had been conducted in eight rounds from 1980 to 2000, the 2002–03 survey (9th round) was done with the National Child Labor Survey and is not strictly comparable to the other sources because of the short period of collection. After that round, the LFS returned to its original design. To avoid any inconsistency issues, we adopt only the years post-2002. The analysis in this report is based on the LFS for 2005 (10th round), 2010 (11th round), 2013 (12th round), and the first round of the Quarterly Labor Force Survey introduced in 2015–16.

As with India and Sri Lanka, we select the following variables for our analysis: sex, age, occupational status, earnings, educational attainment level, marital status, an informality indicator, religion, ethnicity, and employment. The LFS collects information on primary and secondary occupations. However, within this study we examine only individuals' primary occupation.

The survey questionnaire and reported variables have witnessed dramatic changes within the period 2006–15 that hinder effective cross-temporal analysis. To ensure compatibility over time, we reaggregate the "marital status" variable from 5 to 4 categories, "relationship to household head" variable from 9 to 6 categories, and the "education" variable from 19 to 6 categories. The "informality" variable is created from multiple categories of the "principle activity status" variable. The number and description of categories change over time, but efforts were made to ensure that the coverage includes self-employed, contributing family members, and day laborers across years.

Efforts were made to develop a taxonomy for translating geographic and industrial classifications over time into a singular nomenclature. A concordance was developed for the Bangladesh Standard Industrial Classification (BSIC). The structure of the BSIC 2001 is similar to the ISIC Rev.3. The structure of BSIC 2009 corresponds to ISIC Rev.4 with an additional division, 6 new groups, and 93 new classes to better correspond to Bangladeshi requirements. A concordance was developed to link BSIC 2001 with BSIC

2009 and ISIC Rev.3.1 for further merging with the HSO–1988/92 trade classification that the UN Comtrade data correspond to. Table B.1 provides an overview of the dataset for Bangladesh.

TABLE B.1 **Overview of the Dataset for Bangladesh**

Survey year	Frequency	Percent	Cumulative
2005	187,324	17.91	17.91
2010	199,274	19.05	36.96
2013	156,987	15.01	51.97
2015	502,394	48.03	100
Total	1,045,979	100	

Variables

Variable name	Variable label
countrycode	Country code
year	Year of the survey (starting in year)
HH_id	Household unique identification number (primary key)
person_id	Person unique identification number (secondary key)
HH_size	Household size
division	Division/Bibhag
district	District/Zila
upazila	Union Council/Upazila
psu	Primary sampling units/Census block number
HH_wt	Household weight
urban	Urban
sex	Sex (male = 1, female = 2)
male	Dummy for male individuals
age	Age in years
religion	Religion
kinship	Relation to household head
marital_status	Marital status
school_status	Current attendance in educational institution (1–2)
edu_not_lit	Educational level: not literate
education	General level of education (1–6)
edu_below_prim	Educational level: Below primary (including not literate)
edu_prim	Educational level: Primary
edu_second	Educational level: Secondary
edu_tertiary	Educational level: Tertiary
voc_train	Type of vocational training received (1–8)
in_laborforce	Person is in the labor force
emp	Whether employed on any day in past week (no = 0, yes = 1)
unempl	Whether unemployed on all 7 days (yes = 1, no = 2)
princ_act_ind	Weekly principal activity industry
princ_act_occ	Weekly principal activity occupation
princ_act_status	Weekly principal activity status (1–99)
wage_total	Total weekly wage from principal job
informal_worker	Whether person is in informal employment (proxy)
isic3_code	ISIC rev.3

India

A primary input of this analysis for the case of India is the *Employment and Unemployment* section from the National Sample Survey (NSS), which includes data on various indicators of the labor force at national and state levels with the unit of analysis being individuals. Although the NSS is conducted annually, our particular section of interest is, in principal, only conducted once every five years. Despite the quinquennial survey design for the *Employment and Unemployment* section in the NSS, the application is more frequent and we make use of the surveys conducted in 1999 (55th round), 2004 (61st round), 2007 (64th round), 2009 (66th round), and 2011 (68th round). To conduct our analysis, we select the following variables: sex, age, wages, occupational status, earnings, educational attainment level, school status, daily activities, activity intensity, marital status, an informality indicator, activity status, caste, religion, employment status, and a vocational training indicator.

State and district borders have changed several times between 1999 and 2011. Because geographical mobility of labor is of high interest, we harmonize districts and states according to the broadest grid. All districts are harmonized over time according to the status of 1993. However, in an effort to match the current division of the states, new states that came into being after 2000 (Chhattisgarh, Jharkhand, and Uttarakhand) were recreated in the 1999 dataset. We define a new variable "geography" on the basis of the state and district codes that uniquely identify a district between 1999 and 2011. The industry codes are all harmonized according to ISIC Rev.3.1, which has previously been matched to commodity trade data.

Several labor market variables also require harmonization. The NSS questionnaires collect individuals' education data in the form of a 1–13 ranking system, slightly differing across the rounds. We harmonize this information across the years into four exhaustive categories: (a) below primary education, (b) primary education, (c) secondary education, and (d) tertiary education. We also include an additional illiterate category that is not mutually exclusive to the prior four categories. Additionally, with respect to technical education, the raw data are categorized into a ranking system with a range of 1–12. We harmonize this by creating one binary variable highlighting whether or not an individual has a technical degree. Similarly, the social group of the household was initially formatted into four categories (1–3 or 9). This information has been harmonized across the years into social group dummies with three categories: (a) social group—scheduled tribe, (b) social group—scheduled caste, and (c) social group—others. Information about eight different categories of religion is provided in the NSS (1–7 or 9). We create a religion dummy variable over these eight categories: (a) Hinduism, (b) Islam, (c) Christianity, (d) Sikhism, (e) Jainism, (f) Buddhism, (g) Zoroastrianism, and (h) Others.

Concerning the employment status, we harmonize the data to have seven distinct categories: (a) own-account worker, (b) employer, (c) unpaid family worker, (d) regular salaried/wage employee, (e) casual wage worker, (f) unemployed, and

(g) inactive. Additionally, we also use these data to generate two other separate dummies: (a) whether the individual is part of the labor force, and (b) whether the person is in informal employment (proxy). We define informal employment on the following grounds: person is an own-account worker, is an unpaid family worker, or worked as a casual wage labor in public works or in other types of work. Furthermore, we create several activity intensity variables from the raw data depicting intensity of activities per week.

Finally, some modifications were necessary to harmonize monetary units over time. Nominal total wages (remuneration in cash and in-kind from all activities) are provided in current Indian rupees. We also create a new variable with wages converted into real terms using the Indian consumer price index.

Our final dataset for India therefore consists of microdata in the form of observations of individuals over five years (repeated cross-sectional data) that were obtained through a combination of NSS and Comtrade data. Table B.2 provides a brief overview of the dataset for India.

TABLE B.2 **Overview of the Dataset for India**

Survey year	Frequency	Percent	Cumulative
1999	595,529	22.19	22.19
2004	599,163	22.33	44.52
2007	572,254	21.32	65.84
2009	459,784	17.13	82.97
2011	456,999	17.03	100
Total	**2,683,729**	**100**	

Variables

Variable name	Variable label
Geography	Parent district code in year 1993
Year	Year of the survey (starting in year)
HH_id	Household unique identification number (primary key)
Person_id	Person unique identification number (secondary key)
Sex	Sex (male–1, female–2)
Male	Dummy for male individuals
Industry	Weekly activity industry (principal activity industry, if missing)
Princ_act_status	Person's usual principal activity status (11–99)
activity_status_weekly	Current weekly activity status (11–98)
activity_status_daily1	1 activity_status_daily
activity_status_daily2	2 activity_status_daily
activity_status_daily3	3 activity_status_daily
activity_status_daily4	4 activity_status_daily
activity_status_daily5	5 activity_status_daily

(Table continues on next page)

TABLE B.2 **Overview of the Dataset for India** (continued)
Variables

Variable name	Variable label
daily_act_ind1	1 daily_act_ind
daily_act_ind2	2 daily_act_ind
daily_act_ind3	3 daily_act_ind
daily_act_ind4	4 daily_act_ind
daily_act_ind5	5 daily_act_ind
wage_total1	1 wage_total
wage_total2	2 wage_total
wage_total3	3 wage_total
wage_total4	4 wage_total
wage_total5	5 wage_total
HH_size	Household size
HH_type	Type of household: (1, 2, 3, 4, 8, or 9; 4 for rural areas only) – employment status
HH_wt	Weight to attach at specific subround level
activity_intensity1	1 activity_intensity
activity_intensity2	2 activity_intensity
activity_intensity3	3 activity_intensity
activity_intensity4	4 activity_intensity
activity_intensity5	5 activity_intensity
activity_intensity_perc1	1 activity_intensity_perc
activity_intensity_perc2	2 activity_intensity_perc
activity_intensity_perc3	3 activity_intensity_perc
activity_intensity_perc4	4 activity_intensity_perc
activity_intensity_perc5	5 activity_intensity_perc
Age	Age in years
bank_account	Whether any household member held a recurring deposit account (yes = 1, no = 2, don't know = 9)
edu_below_prim	Educational level: Below primary (incl. not literate)
edu_not_lit	Educational level: Not literate
edu_prim	Educational level: Primary
edu_second	Educational level: Secondary
edu_technical	Person has a technical degree = 1 or not = 0
edu_tertiary	Educational level: Tertiary
Education	General level of education (1–13)
education_technical	Technical level of education (specialization) (1–12)
informal_worker	Person is in the labor force
Kinship	Whether person is in informal employment (proxy)
marital_status	Relation to head of household (1–9)
new_district_code	Marital status (not = 1, married = 2, widowed = 3, separated = 4)
new_district_name	District name (1993–2011)
new_state_code	
new_state_name	State name (1993–2011)
occupation_princ1	1 occupation_princ
occupation_princ2	2 occupation_princ
occupation_princ3	3 occupation_princ
occupation_princ4	4 occupation_princ
occupation_princ5	5 occupation_princ

TABLE B.2 **Overview of the Dataset for India** *(continued)*

Variables

Variable name	Variable label
princ_act_occ1	1 princ_act_occ
princ_act_occ2	2 princ_act_occ
princ_act_occ3	3 princ_act_occ
princ_act_occ4	4 princ_act_occ
princ_act_occ5	5 princ_act_occ
Religion	Religion of the household: (1–7, or 9)
school_status	Current attendance in educational institution (1–43)
soc_caste	Social group: Scheduled caste
soc_group	Social group of the household (1–3, or 9)
soc_others	Social group: Others
soc_tribe	Social group: Scheduled tribe
status_casual	Employment status: Casual wage worker
status_employee	Employment status: Regular salaried/wage employee
status_employer	Employment status: Employer
status_inactive	Employment status: Inactive
status_ownaccount	Employment status: Own-account worker
status_unemployed	Employment status: Unemployed
status_unpaid_fw	Employment status: Unpaid family worker
subsid_act_occ1	1 subsid_act_occ
subsid_act_occ2	2 subsid_act_occ
subsid_act_occ3	3 subsid_act_occ
subsid_act_occ4	4 subsid_act_occ
subsid_act_occ5	5 subsid_act_occ
Unempl	Whether unemployed on all 7 days (yes = 1, no = 2)
voc_train	Whether person received any type of vocational training (1–7)
isic3_code	4-digit ISIC code = Master variable
trade1998	Indian global commodity exports (USD 000)
trade1999	Indian global commodity exports (USD 000)
Trade2000	Indian global commodity exports (USD 000)
Trade2001	Indian global commodity exports (USD 000)
Trade2002	Indian global commodity exports (USD 000)
Trade2003	Indian global commodity exports (USD 000)
Trade2004	Indian global commodity exports (USD 000)
Trade2005	Indian global commodity exports (USD 000)
Trade2006	Indian global commodity exports (USD 000)
Trade2007	Indian global commodity exports (USD 000)
Trade2008	Indian global commodity exports (USD 000)
Trade2009	Indian global commodity exports (USD 000)
Trade2010	Indian global commodity exports (USD 000)
Trade2011	Indian global commodity exports (USD 000)
Trade2012	Indian global commodity exports (USD 000)
oecdtotal1998	OECD global imports (USD 000)
oecdtotal1999	OECD global imports (USD 000)
oecdtotal2000	OECD global imports (USD 000)
oecdtotal2001	OECD global imports (USD 000)

(Table continues on next page)

TABLE B.2 **Overview of the Dataset for India** *(continued)*

Variables

Variable name	Variable label
oecdtotal2002	OECD global imports (USD 000)
oecdtotal2003	OECD global imports (USD 000)
oecdtotal2004	OECD global imports (USD 000)
oecdtotal2005	OECD global imports (USD 000)
oecdtotal2006	OECD global imports (USD 000)
oecdtotal2007	OECD global imports (USD 000)
oecdtotal2008	OECD global imports (USD 000)
oecdtotal2009	OECD global imports (USD 000)
oecdtotal2010	OECD global imports (USD 000)
oecdtotal2011	OECD global imports (USD 000)
oecdtotal2012	OECD global imports (USD 000)
oecdindia1998	OECD imports from India (USD 000)
oecdindia1999	OECD imports from India (USD 000)
oecdindia2000	OECD imports from India (USD 000)
oecdindia2001	OECD imports from India (USD 000)
oecdindia2002	OECD imports from India (USD 000)
oecdindia2003	OECD imports from India (USD 000)
oecdindia2004	OECD imports from India (USD 000)
oecdindia2005	OECD imports from India (USD 000)
oecdindia2006	OECD imports from India (USD 000)
oecdindia2007	OECD imports from India (USD 000)
oecdindia2008	OECD imports from India (USD 000)
oecdindia2009	OECD imports from India (USD 000)
oecdindia2010	OECD imports from India (USD 000)
oecdindia2011	OECD imports from India (USD 000)
oecdindia2012	OECD imports from India (USD 000)
services2000	Indian global services exports (USD 000)
services2001	Indian global services exports (USD 000)
services2002	Indian global services exports (USD 000)
services2003	Indian global services exports (USD 000)
services2004	Indian global services exports (USD 000)
services2005	Indian global services exports (USD 000)
services2006	Indian global services exports (USD 000)
services2007	Indian global services exports (USD 000)
services2008	Indian global services exports (USD 000)
services2009	Indian global services exports (USD 000)
services2010	Indian global services exports (USD 000)
services2011	Indian global services exports (USD 000)
services2012	Indian global services exports (USD 000)
geo2	Geography (integer value)
isic3_code_name	Description
isic3_code_2dig	2-digit ISIC codes
isic3_code_2dig_name	Description

Sri Lanka

For Sri Lanka, we make use of the Labor Force Survey (LFS) provided by the National Department of Census and Statistics. We employ the survey data from 1992 to 2015 with the exception of some missing years.[2] The LFS contains labor market and socio-economic information and is designed to measure the levels and trends of employment, unemployment, and the labor force in Sri Lanka. The LFS has been conducted quarterly by the Sample Survey division originating in the first quarter of 1990, enabling high-frequency time periods in our analysis. The unit of analysis is individuals. The lower bound of the working-age population considered in the LFS is age 10 from 1992 to 2012 and age 15 for surveys from 2013 onward. For the purpose of this report, we analyze individuals age 15 and up.

Note that 2005 has been intentionally omitted from the analysis because data collection was halted that year in response to the devastating effects of the tsunami. As for geographic coverage of the survey, conflict-affected provinces, namely Northern and Eastern provinces, have had limited coverage. The Northern province is excluded from our sampling design up until 2004, and for the years 2007 and 2008. The Eastern province was excluded until 2003 and for the year 2007.

As in the case of India, we select the following variables for our analysis: sex, age, occupational status, earnings, educational attainment level, marital status, an informality indicator, religion, ethnicity, and employment. The LFS collects information on primary and secondary occupations. However, for the purpose of this study we examine only an individual's primary occupation.

Survey datasets were harmonized to accommodate significant revisions made to the LFS questionnaires in 1996, 2006, and 2013. For example, the codification of the educational attainment variable changed from 8 categories to 18 categories in 1996. Hence, categories for the educational attainment variables from 1996 through 2013 were aggregated to reflect the 8 categories in the previous years (see table B.3). Sectoral classifications also changed from two categories (urban and rural) to three categories (urban, rural, and estate) from 1996 onward. In later years, rural and estate categories were merged into one rural category. The consumer price index for Sri Lanka was used to deflate all wage values in national currency with a base period of 2010.

Our analysis on informality was carried out for years only after 2006, because LFS questions on informal sector employment were added in 2006. The Sri Lankan Department of Census and Statistics characterizes informality through instructional practices and employment conditions. A formal institution, by and large, is governed by three principles: it is registered in the Employment Provident Fund or in the Department of Inland Revenue; it keeps formal accounts; and it has 10 or more employees. Any institution that fails to meet any of these three criteria is considered to be in the informal sector.

The Sri Lankan LFS categorizes status in employment as the following: employee, employer, own-account worker, and unpaid family worker. Information on informal

TABLE B.3 **Recodification of Education Variables**

Labor Force Survey 2005–06			Labor Force Survey 2009–10		
Education categories	Old code	New code	Education categories	Old code	New code
No education	0	0	No education	1	0
No class has been passed	1	0	Technical/ vocational education	10	0
Technical education (technical/ vocational, etc.)	10	0	Others	11	0
Others	11	0			
Classes I–V	2	1	Classes I–V	2	1
Classes VI–VII	3	2	Classes VI–VIII	3	2
Class IX	4	3	Classes IX–X	4	3
Secondary or equivalent	5	3	Secondary School Certificate (SSC) or equivalent	5	3
Intermediate or equivalent	6	4	Higher Secondary Certificate Examination (HSC) or equivalent	6	4
Graduate or equivalent	7	5	Bachelor degree or equivalent	7	5
Postgraduate or equivalent	8	6	Master's degree or equivalent	8	6
Medical/ engineering	9	6	Medical/ engineering degree	9	6

institutions is collected through information of employers and own-account workers. As for paid employees, those who work for an employer that does not contribute to a pension scheme or Provident fund on their behalf, or workers who are not entitled to paid leave or leave encashment, are considered to be working informally. Unpaid family workers are without exception considered to be in the informal sector. Informality, for the purpose of this report, encompasses employers and own-account workers who operate informal institutions as well as paid employees and unpaid family workers who work under informal conditions.

Labor Force Survey 2013			Quarterly Labor Force Survey 2015–16		
Education categories	Old code	New code	Education categories	Old code	New code
Preschool	0	0	No class passed	0	0
Don't know	98	0	Madrasha	99	0
No class passed	99	0			
Class I	1	1	Class 1	1	1
Class II	2	1	Class 2	2	1
Class III	3	1	Class 3	3	1
Class IV	4	1	Class 4	4	1
Class V	5	1	PSC	5	1
Class VI	6	2	Class 6	6	2
Class VII	7	2	Class 7	7	2
Class VIII	8	2	JSC	8	2
Class IX	9	3	Class 9	9	3
Class X	10	3	Secondary School Certificate (SSC) or equivalent	10	3
Class XI	11	4	Higher Secondary Certificate Examination (HSC) or equivalent	11	4
Class XII	12	4			
Diploma	13	5	Diploma	12	5
Graduate	14	5	Bachelor degree	13	5
Master's degree	15	6	Master's degree	14	6
PhD	16	6	PhD	15	6

Industry classifications have changed over time. Because documentation of industry classification in earlier years, namely 1992 through 2001, is unclear, our analysis using industry classification starts from 2002 onward. From 2002 to 2012, the LFS uses Sri Lanka Standard Industry Classification Rev.3.1, which matches ISIC Rev.3. Data from 2013 to 2015 use SLIC Rev.4, which has 5 digits and is identical to ISIC Rev.4 at the 4-digit level. All classifications were recoded to match ISIC Rev.3.1 classification, a key step to merging results with Comtrade data for our study.

Table B.4 provides a brief overview of the dataset for Sri Lanka.

TABLE B.4 **Overview of the Dataset for Sri Lanka**

Survey year	Frequency	Percent	Cumulative
1992	91,624	7.94	7.94
1994	34,996	3.03	10.97
1995	34,148	2.96	13.93
1996	68,462	5.93	19.86
1998	60,239	5.22	25.08
1999	59,469	5.15	30.24
2000	58,588	5.08	35.31
2001	44,601	3.86	39.18
2002	58,675	5.08	44.26
2003	66,868	5.79	50.05
2004	93,237	8.08	58.13
2007	68,193	5.91	64.04
2008	73,459	6.37	70.41
2011	56,172	4.87	75.28
2012	62,298	5.4	80.67
2013	58,869	5.1	85.77
2014	81,376	7.05	92.83
2015	82,800	7.17	100
Total	**1,154,074**	**100**	

Survey month	Frequency	Percent	Cumulative
1	132,584	11.49	11.49
2	95,874	8.31	19.8
3	51,231	4.44	24.23
4	133,731	11.59	35.82
5	96,454	8.36	44.18
6	57,881	5.02	49.2
7	141,930	12.3	61.49
8	105,283	9.12	70.62
9	57,963	5.02	75.64
10	134,090	11.62	87.26
11	96,824	8.39	95.65
12	50,229	4.35	100
Total	**1,154,074**	**100**	

TABLE B.4 **Overview of the Dataset for Sri Lanka** *(continued)*

Variables

Variable name	Variable label
district	District
Sector[a]	Sector; Urban = 1, Rural = 2, Estate = 3
strata	Strata
psu	Primary sampling units/Census block number
year	Survey year
month	Survey month
hhsize	Household size
HH_id	Household unique identification number (primary key)
person_id	Person unique identification number (secondary key)
geography	Geography (Province + District)
urban	Urban
HH_wt	Household weight
male	Male
sex	Sex
age	Age
education	Educational attainment
religion	Religion
ethnic	Ethnicity
marital_status	Marital status
kinship	Relation to household head
formal[a]	Whether person works in formal job
employed_weekly	Currently employed [time frame: last week]
employed_yearly	Usually employed [time frame: past 12 months]
laborforce_weekly	Currently in labor force [time frame: last week]
laborforce_yearly	Usually in labor force [time frame: past 12 months]
not_laborforce_weekly	Currently not in labor force [time frame: last week]
not_laborforce_yearly	Usually not in labor force [time frame: past 12 months]
unemployed_weekly	Currently unemployed [time frame: last week]
unemployed_yearly	Usually unemployed [time frame: past 12 months]
wage_total_principal	Wage/salary last month from main job with or without in-kind payments
weekly_princ_industry	Nature of the main work: Industry
weekly_princ_occupation	Nature of the main work: Occupation [time frame: last week]
weekly_princ_sector	Nature of the main work: Sector [time frame: last week]
weekly_princ_status	Nature of the main work: Status [time frame: last week]
occupation_type	Occupation type
primary	Whether person is an employee in the main occupation

a. This variable is inconsistent throughout the years.

Notes

1. For more information, see https://comtrade.un.org.

2. The analysis of Sri Lanka covers all years except 1993, 1997, 2005, 2006, 2009, and 2010.

Developed Economies

IMPORTS			
Economy	What happened and when	What was implemented	What happened to workers and firms
United States	1. North American Free Trade Agreement (NAFTA) (1993) 2. China import competition (1991–2007)	1. Elimination of tariffs. The average tariff was only 4.8 percent in 1982; tariffs declined on average by 0.6 percentage points to 4.2 percent between 1982 and 1992. Also, many nontariff barriers to bilateral trade among Canada, Mexico, and the United States were eliminated. 2. The value of annual U.S. imports from China increased by 1,156 percent, with much less increase in U.S. exports to China.	1. An average of 37,000 jobs were lost per year between 1982 and 1999 because of increased Mexican trade. Blue collar workers in vulnerable industries suffered large absolute declines in real wages as a result of the agreement. NAFTA tariff reductions were associated with substantial reduction of average wages for married blue collar women in the United States, which could partially be explained by selective nonparticipation in the labor market on their part as they adjusted to industry shrinking because of the trade shock. Declining domestic employment of U.S. multinationals between 1982 and 1999 was primarily due to (i) falling prices of investment goods such as computers, which substitute for labor; and (ii) overall skill-biased technological change, which played an important role in the evolution of

IMPORTS			
Economy	What happened and when	What was implemented	What happened to workers and firms
United States (*continued*)			the U.S. wage structure in that decade. These two factors accounted for 16.02 percent of the decline in manufacturing employment.
			2. Chinese import competition explains 25 percent of U.S. manufacturing job losses in 1990–2007. The U.S. economy faced severe adverse effects on local labor markets because of the rapidly increasing Chinese import penetration. Regions strongly prone to Chinese import competition experienced severe negative impacts on their labor markets, such as lower manufacturing employment, rising unemployment, or lower labor force participation.
			This import shock negatively affected U.S. local labor markets through manufacturing as well as nonmanufacturing employment and wages. Reduction in both employment and wage levels led to a steep drop in the average earnings of households. In turn, these changes prompted increased transfer payments through federal and state programs, indicating an important policy of adjustment mechanism to trade-induced job losses. Rising Chinese import competition over 1999–2011 cost 2 million to 2.4 million U.S. jobs.

IMPORTS			
Economy	What happened and when	What was implemented	What happened to workers and firms
Denmark	The government of Denmark built and estimated a model of occupational choice, reflecting growing interest in measuring the dynamic and distributional impact of trade shocks.	Denmark built and estimated a model of occupational choice. In each period, workers choose their occupation, weighing their menu of wages against the costs of switching occupations and the inability to transfer skills across jobs. In the model, trade shocks reduce the demand for labor in some occupations while increasing it in others, inducing workers to engage in costly readjustment.	The costs of occupational switching are large. These costs vary substantially with worker demographics— as much as several years' income for some workers. Low-productivity, uneducated. and older workers face particularly high barriers to occupational mobility. Also, intrasectoral moving costs are three times larger than intersectoral moving costs. This reflects the fact that, when workers switch sectors, they usually switch into the same occupation within that sector. Moreover, returns to occupational-specific tenure can be large and are just as important to workers' life-cycle profile as general labor market experience. Effects of foreign trade price changes largely depend on one's initial position at the onset of the change. This is for two reasons. First, adjustment can be slow with some occupations taking up to 10 years to fully adjust their skill prices to long-run equilibrium. Second, certain occupations are more or less substitutable with foreign competition. For example, machinists in manufacturing can lose up to US$5,000 in terms of the net present value of lifetime income, whereas workers in other closely related occupations can actually gain. These affects also vary with one's age and skill level.

IMPORTS			
Economy	What happened and when	What was implemented	What happened to workers and firms
Canada	Canada–U.S. Free Trade Agreement (CUSFTA) (1987)	CUSFTA called for the removal of all tariffs between the two countries over a 10-year period ending in January 1999. Although most tariffs were to be eliminated over a 10-year period, tariffs on some products were eliminated immediately and others were eliminated over the first five years.	CUSFTA tariff reductions lowered employment predominantly among less-skilled workers. It did not affect the earnings of either skilled or less-skilled workers in the manufacturing industry. The employment effects were due to the fact that relatively less-skill-intensive industries were more highly protected than high-skill-intensive industries prior to CUSFTA. Canadian tariff reductions did not affect the earnings of either nonproduction (skilled) or production workers (less skilled). However, Canadian tariff reductions lowered employment among production workers but had little or no effect on nonproduction employment. This result is also consistent with the observation that skilled voters in Canada supported the agreement, whereas less-skilled voters opposed it.
Germany	1. The "rise of China," 1988–2008 2. The rise of German exports to Eastern Europe, 1988–2008 3. The decline in the power of labor unions (mid-1990s) 4. 2003–05 labor market reforms 5. 2008–09 recession	1. Import competition increased, particularly in such sectors as textiles, toys, and office and computer equipment. Market opportunities for German exporters rose substantially, most notably in sectors such as automobiles, specialized machinery, electronics, and medical equipment. 2. The rise of German exports to Eastern Europe outpaced export growth to China. Many Eastern European countries adopted concrete steps of trade integration early on, for example in 1995. Several of them (including	1. Chinese import exposure did not seem to cause major job losses. Because the "rise of China" mainly diverted imports from other countries, it had only negligible job displacement effects. German regions that specialized in import-competing sectors saw a decline in manufacturing employment attributable to the impact of trade. Yet this negative impact was, on average, more than offset by a positive causal effect of export exposure. The export-oriented regions built up manufacturing employment as a result of the new market opportunities.

IMPORTS			
Economy	What happened and when	What was implemented	What happened to workers and firms
Germany *(continued)*		the Czech Republic, Hungary, and Poland) joined the World Trade Organization, which increased German export and import volumes. 3. Between 1996 and 2008, union coverage shrank from 70 percent to 55 percent in the western part of the country and from 57 percent to 40 percent in the east. 4. The reforms may loosely be grouped into those reducing reservation wages (and therefore reducing wages), those increasing the efficiency of the job search process (and therefore increasing wages), and those allowing employers more flexibility (probably reducing wages). The reforms helped reduce unemployment by acting as a brake on rising unemployment in the recession, and therefore also acting as a brake on employment losses. 5. Despite the recession, employment barely fell and unemployment hardly rose.	Changes in trade exposure in industries where imports from China grew the most (textiles, for example) had negligible labor market effects. The reason seems to be that Germany already tended to import those labor-intensive goods in the 1980s, and China subsequently became the world's dominant supplier. When the Chinese rise gained momentum, this then mainly led to a diversion of German import flows from other countries (such as Italy or Greece), but it has not caused major job displacements in Germany. 2. The rise of Eastern Europe had much stronger effects on German local labor markets. It caused substantial job losses, but even stronger job gains in certain regions. The rise of the East retained some 442,000 full-time equivalent jobs in Germany over the period 1988–2008 that would not have existed without this trade integration. Export-oriented regions saw significant total employment gains and reductions in unemployment. Germany initially tended to export goods where the subsequent Eastern European rise was particularly strong. Hence, there were substantial displacement effects from rising Eastern European import penetration across German regions. Yet, in the aggregate, those employment losses were more than offset by the creation of new manufacturing jobs stemming from rising German exports to that area. This strongly contrasts with the U.S. experience, where rising

IMPORTS			
Economy	What happened and when	What was implemented	What happened to workers and firms
Germany (*continued*)			import penetration from China fueled a large overall trade deficit and hurt domestic workers on balance.
			3. Between 1996 and 2008, union coverage shrank from 70 percent to 55 percent in the western part of the country and from 57 percent to 40 percent in the east. Wage drift (payment of wages above the collectively bargained rate) also declined in the 2000s. Wage growth stagnated from 2001 until 2008.
			4. Results for Germany differ from those for the United States. Trade liberalization with China was likely to bring welfare gains for the United States, for example, through gains in productivity or consumption diversity. Yet, in the short to medium term, the U.S. economy faced severe adverse effects on local labor markets, even though the rise of China created both import penetration and new export opportunities. The situation of Germany seemed quite different, at least on average: the overall labor market consequences were largely positive, even in the medium term. This finding may be explained by the fact that overall trade between Germany and China was much more balanced than U.S.–China trade. Furthermore, focusing only on China gives an incomplete picture in the case of Germany. The rise of Eastern Europe had a much stronger impact on German local labor markets than the rise of China, possibly reflecting the fact that the Eastern European markets were geographically much closer.

Developing Economies

IMPORTS			
Economy	What happened and when	What was implemented	What happened to workers and firms
Mexico	1. General Agreement on Tariffs and Trade (1986) 2. Growth in foreign direct investment flows (between 1983 and 1989) 3. North American Free Trade Agreement (NAFTA) (1994) 4. Mexico's 1994 peso crisis	1. Reduced tariffs to 12.5 percent in the most-protected and less-skilled sectors. Prior to the reforms tariff levels were high, averaging 23.5 percent. 2. A major destination for foreign direct investment was the creation of maquiladoras. By 2000, maquiladoras accounted for 35 percent of Mexico's imports from the United States, and for 48 percent of its exports to the United States. 3. Reduced tariffs in skill-intensive sectors. 4. The peso lost half of its original value, overshadowing the average tariff changes from NAFTA.	1. The unskilled sector took the hardest hit in terms of wage and employment. The relative price of skill-intensive goods rose, pulling up with it the relative wages of skilled workers. There was also substantial heterogeneity across firms in rent sharing. Firms with a higher proportion of skilled workers showed stronger rent sharing than those with a higher fraction of unskilled workers, which may have resulted in lower wages for the unskilled. 2. Between 1983 and 1990, employment in maquiladoras increased from 150,867 workers to 460,293 workers, as the share of maquiladora workers in national manufacturing employment expanded from 4.90 percent to 18.96 percent.

IMPORTS			
Economy	**What happened and when**	**What was implemented**	**What happened to workers and firms**
Mexico *(continued)*			3. The relative price of skill-abundant goods fell and so did the relative wages of skilled workers (in manufacturing and other sectors). These trends reversed the rise in wage inequality and benefitted less-skilled workers by trading with more-skilled countries.
			4. Although wages increased in absolute terms in the aftermath of the peso crisis, the wages of white collar workers employed in high-productivity plants increased by more, thus contributing to an increase in wage inequality.
Morocco	Balance-of-payment crisis (1983)	Reduced the maximum tariffs from 165 percent to 45 percent over a six-year period.	A significant fraction of manufacturing employment at firm level did not adjust either wages or employment in response to trade reform. A labor demand model that allows for imperfect competition and endogenous technological change demonstrated that many firms, including those that failed to adjust employment, responded to the reforms by cutting profit margins and raising productivity. This represented a less-painful mode of adjustment where firms with excess profits could absorb trade shocks, leaving the labor force unaffected.
			Firms in Morocco started hiring more temporary workers (who are not entitled to benefits) in the period following the trade reform.

IMPORTS			
Economy	What happened and when	What was implemented	What happened to workers and firms
India	1. The "License Raj" system was established by India's Industries Development and Regulation Act of 1951 2. Balance-of-payment crisis (1991) 3. Indian trade reforms, initiated in 1991. Steps to liberalize industries were implemented fully in 1991. The first industrial reform, applied by Rajiv Gandhi in 1985, dismantled the "License Raj" in a small number of industries by exempting them from licensing requirements for capacity expansion.	1. A very restrictive industrial regime was implemented. Firms were required to obtain an official license from the central government to operate. The license allowed the firm to operate, and also specified the firm's allowed amount of output during the specific period of the license. The government enforced this license by controlling the quantity of raw materials (like fuel and coal) assigned to each firm. 2. In sectors with unskilled workers, tariffs were reduced in a phased manner from a high of 117 percent to 73 percent. 3. Tighter labor regulations were implemented—through restrictions on layoffs, for example. Hiring and firing laws were quite rigid until the amendment of the Industrial Disputes Act in 2001. Areas with flexible labor laws and more reallocation likely enjoyed higher growth, and thus in aggregate did relatively better because of liberalization. As predicted by trade theory, the market-share reallocations were important in increasing India's productivity growth, but only in the years immediately following the start of the major trade reforms.	1. This industrial regime was part of the economic program aimed at the development of the domestic market and industrialization. The regime favored state-owned companies and small private firms. In 1990, the average manufacturing Indian firm was more than 10 times smaller than the average manufacturing firm in the United States. Beyond costs imposed by not effectively exploiting scale, firms had limited incentives to invest. To the extent that scale matters for innovation, this likely affected firms' innovation activities. Trade reforms increased labor demand elasticities by a greater degree in states with more labor market flexibility. 2. Tariff reductions in the Indian case were relatively larger in sectors with a higher proportion of unskilled workers. These sectors experienced an increase in relative wages, and unskilled workers experienced an increase in incomes relative to skilled workers. Thus, the 1991 trade liberalization led to decreased wage inequality in India and a substantial increase in trade flows. 3. Indian states with inflexible labor laws, where reallocation of labor across sectors may have been impeded, are precisely the areas where the adverse impact of trade opening on poverty was felt the most. In contrast, in states with flexible labor laws, movements of capital and labor across sectors and the overall faster growth of manufacturing eased the shock of the relative price change.

IMPORTS			
Economy	What happened and when	What was implemented	What happened to workers and firms
India (continued)			4. Industry-level data disaggregated by states show a positive impact of trade liberalization on the absolute value of labor demand elasticities in the Indian manufacturing sector. The magnitudes of these elasticities were negatively correlated to protection levels that varied across industries and over time. 5. These elasticities were larger for Indian states with more flexible labor regulations. Such states were also more affected by trade reforms. 6. Trade reforms led to a reduction in the share of labor in total output. Value added may be the result of a loss of labor bargaining power, again brought about by an increase in labor demand elasticities.
Indonesia	1. Trade regime in the mid-1980s 2. Reforms of fiscal policy, tax reforms, and financial deregulation in the early 1990s 3. Trade liberalization in 1991–2000 4. Uruguay round (1994) 5. World Trade Organization membership (1995), which involved giving various commitments to liberalize trade over a 10-year period 6. Monetary crisis, in part a result of the International Monetary Fund conditionality package, starting in 1999	1. Reduction in tariff lines and nontariff barriers 2. Tariffs were rationalized and reduced across the board, and some nontariff barriers were removed, especially in import licensing and import monopolies. 3. From 1991 to 2000, average output tariffs fell from 21 percent to 8 percent, and average input tariffs fell from 14 percent to 6 percent. 4. Indonesia committed to substantially lowering its remaining tariff barriers across all tradable goods over the following 10 years. The tariff reductions were concentrated in the hitherto most-protected sectors and resulted in an overall convergence of sectoral protection levels.	1. Analysis suggests that reducing input tariffs produced a large, positive, within-firm effect on the wage skill premium for importers, whereas changes in output tariffs had an insignificant effect. 3. Cuts in output tariffs reduced wages at firms oriented exclusively to the domestic market but raised wages at firms that export a sufficient share of their output. Cuts in input tariffs raised wages at firms that imported inputs while having an insignificant effect on wages of workers at firms that failed to import. 4. Average import tariff lines decreased from about 17.2 percent in 1993 to 6.6 percent in 2002. During the same period, poverty rates also declined, although it is a priori unclear to what extent this decrease can be attributed to trade liberalization.

IMPORTS			
Economy	What happened and when	What was implemented	What happened to workers and firms
Indonesia (continued)		5. Tariff reductions were not gradual. 6. Substantial wave of tariff reductions occurred.	5. Output tariffs in Indonesia fell from an average of 22 percent in 1991 to 8 percent in 2000, and over this same period input tariffs fell from an average of 14 percent to 6 percent. There was also large variation in both input and output tariffs across industries, with output tariffs higher than 100 percent in some industries, for example on motor vehicles. 6. Indonesian families coped with the 1998 crisis by increasing their within-household production.
Sri Lanka	1. The South Asian Association for Regional Cooperation (SAARC) Preferential Trading Agreement (SAPTA) (1995) a. The Indo–Sri Lanka Free Trade agreement (IS–FTA) signed in 1998 and implemented since 2000 b. This was soon followed by the Pakistan–Sri Lanka Free Trade Agreement (PS–FTA) in 2002 2. The Bay of Bengal Initiative for Multi-Sectoral Technical and Economic Cooperation (BIMST-EC) agreement and the Indian Ocean Rim Association for Regional Cooperation (IOR-ARC)	The success of the trade agreements in improving trade was limited. Reasons for the low levels of utilization of concessions included the narrow range of products covered by agreements, narrow levels of preferential margins given, and weak capacity of the suppliers to make use of preferred access. Other impediments included rules of origin criteria, nontariff barriers, and non-trade-related conditions.	With the expansion of exports, employment in Sri Lanka shifted away from agriculture toward industries and services. By 2006, there were 2 million industrial jobs, double the 1 million jobs in the early 1990s. Most of these jobs were created in the light manufacturing sector. Most new jobs went to young females who were mainly internal migrants living away from home. Real wages improved between 1996 and 2000, the period when export performance was good. But wages declined in the 2000–06 period. The global economic downturn that started in 2008 resulted in job losses and a slight increase in unemployment. But, the effect of job losses on unemployment was marginal, as much of the redundant labor was absorbed by the informal sector agriculture and wholesale and retail sectors.

IMPORTS			
Economy	What happened and when	What was implemented	What happened to workers and firms
Vietnam	Vietnam Bilateral Trade Agreement (BTA) (2001)	Tariff cuts significantly impacted the volume and structure of Vietnamese exports to the United States and worldwide. The BTA immediate reduced U.S. tariffs on Vietnamese exports by an average of 21.1 percent, which substantially lowered Vietnam's cost of exporting. This resulted in a substantial positive shock to Vietnam's trade. Between 2001 and 2004 Vietnamese exports to the United States grew from 7.1 to 19.0 percent of total exports and exports to the United States grew from 3.6 to 10.4 percent of Vietnam's GDP. Tariff cuts varied widely across industries. Industries within manufacturing experienced the largest average tariff cut of 30.3 percentage points, with the average tariff falling from 33.8 to 3.4 percent. The implementation of the BTA led to a significant surge in exports. This break is especially pronounced for manufactured exports, which experienced substantially larger BTA tariff cuts than primary sector exports. The share of Vietnamese exports going to the United States grew rapidly from 5.1 percent in 2000 to 19.0 percent in 2004 and this increase was primarily driven by manufacturing, where U.S. exports accounted for 26.1 percent of Vietnamese exports by 2004.	The aggregate share of workers in household businesses declined in Vietnam during the early 2000s. (In Vietnam, about 85 percent of workers economy-wide and 66 percent in manufacturing were employed in household businesses at the onset of the BTA.) Approximately half of this decline could be attributed to the reallocation of labor from household businesses to employers in the enterprise sector within industries. The within-industry component was particularly pronounced in manufacturing. Importantly, workers in industries that experienced larger declines in tariffs on Vietnamese exports to the United States observed a greater decrease in household business employment during the early 2000s. At the same time, individuals living in more internationally integrated provinces and younger workers were more likely to reallocate from household businesses toward employers in the enterprise sector in response to lower export costs. This heterogeneity is consistent with lower adjustment costs to trade shocks among the young and with lower geographic trade costs.

IMPORTS			
Economy	What happened and when	What was implemented	What happened to workers and firms
Brazil	1. Large-scale trade liberalization between 1988 and 1991	1. The far-reaching trade reform in 1990 involved both the removal of nontariff barriers (import penetration steadily increased) and the adoption of a new tariff structure. All nontariff barriers were abolished by presidential decree and a tariff schedule with lower levels and less cross-sectoral dispersion; the new schedule was completely implemented by 1993. Although product tariffs ranged between 21 (metallic products) and 63 percent (apparel and textiles) in 1990, they had dropped to between 9 percent (chemicals) and 34 percent (transport equipment) in 1997. In 1990, product tariffs were about 45 percent above intermediate-input tariffs in value-added terms. By 1997 the reduced cross-sector dispersion of tariffs resulted in a smaller rate of effective protection of about 20 percent on average. The reforms reduced average tariff levels. Additional reforms partly coincided with trade liberalization. Privatization efforts for public utilities began in the early 1990s and accelerated in the mid-1990s, and Brazil simultaneously removed capital-account restrictions.	1. Individual worker trajectories in the labor market after trade liberalization in the 1990s showed significant worker displacement. There was a very slow transition to services, as well as rising unemployment and exit from the labor force. Brazil's trade liberalization triggered worker displacements, particularly from more-protected industries. However, neither exporting firms nor comparative-advantage industries absorbed trade-displaced workers for several years. In fact, exporters hired significantly fewer workers than the average employer after trade liberalization.

IMPORTS			
Economy	What happened and when	What was implemented	What happened to workers and firms
Bangladesh	Trade liberalization measures initiated by Bangladesh during the early 1980s	Trade liberalization measures initiated by Bangladesh during the early 1980s marked the shift out of the import-substituting industrialization strategy of 1970s to an export-led industrialization strategy. The growth of exports was also positive for almost all years since the early 1990s. The rapid growth of exports along with various trade liberalization measures also stimulated imports, especially imports of industrial raw materials and capital machinery. Import and export growth rates more or less followed a similar path.	In Bangladesh, trade liberalization led to creation of new jobs in domestically owned industries. Moreover, jobs were created in various multinational or foreign firms, which invested in Bangladesh as a consequence of liberalization of regulations relating to foreign investment. For example, majority shares of most of the cellular phone companies in Bangladesh are owned by foreign firms and these firms have created new job opportunities for educated youths.
Pakistan	1. Two major trade shocks can be identified in the recent history of Pakistan: (i) the trade liberalization policies introduced by the government in the 1990s; and (ii) the global financial crisis in 2008, which also resulted in a big collapse in trading activity across the world. The first one can be considered a "shock" because the government switched from import-substitution to export-promotion policies. However, the implementation of these trade liberalization policies was gradual in nature.	1. Trade liberalization mostly included reductions in tariffs and nontariff barriers.	1. The import-substitution policies helped the protected industries to grow faster than nonprotected industries. Especially in electrical goods, machinery products, and rubber products, there was double-digit growth in employment and wages for unskilled (production) workers. The skilled (nonproduction) workers in these protected industries also experienced growth in employment and wages, although less than the unskilled workers. 2. Despite such high growth in these protected industries, there was not much change in the aggregate labor market. Only a small fraction of the workforce was employed in these sectors. Conversely, under the export-promotion policy begun in the late 1980s, the exporting sectors grew much faster than nonexporting sectors. Skilled workers experienced higher growth in employment and wages than unskilled workers in these growing sectors.